# ITALIAN AMERICANS

## A Retrospective
## on the
## Twentieth Century

edited by

Paola Alessandra Sensi-Isolani
&
Anthony Julian Tamburri

American Italian Historical Association

American Italian Historical Association. Conference (32nd : 1999 : San Francisco, Calif.)
    Italian Americans : a retrospective on the twentieth century / edited by Paola Alessandra Sensi-Isolani & Anthony Julian Tamburri.
        p.   cm.   (AIHA ; 32)
    ISBN 0-934675-49-X (alk. paper) -- ISBN 0-934675-50-3
    1. Italian Americans--Social conditions--20th century--Congresses. 2. Italian Americans--Politics and government--20th century--Congresses. 3. Italian Americans--Economic conditions--20th century--Congresses. 4. Italian American arts--Congresses. 5. United States--Ethnic relations--Congresses. I. Sensi Isolani, Paola A. II. Tamburri, Anthony Julian. III. Title. IV. AIHA (Series) ; 32.
E184.I8 A524 1999
305.851'073—dc21                                2001034115

COVER DESIGN by *Cynthia Borcena-Jones,* a freelance graphic designer from the San Francisco Bay area, who specializes in designing for publication, identity systems, and collateral materials.

AIHA
Chicago Heights, IL


ISBN:   9-934675-49-X (soft)
            9-934675-50-3 (hard)
ISSN:   0743-474X

# ITALIAN AMERICANS
## A Retrospective on the Twentieth Century

edited by

Paola Alessandra Sensi-Isolani
Anthony Julian Tamburri

# INTRODUCTION

This selection of essays presented at the 32<sup>nd</sup> Annual Conference of the American Italian Historical Association held in San Francisco, November 11–13, 1999, brings together the work of 13 scholars from diverse academic fields, and from three continents, Europe, the United States, and Australia. The volume is divided into four sections, covering different aspects of the Italian immigrant experience: the social and political world, contact with other ethnic groups, the world of work, and socio-cultural transformation. With the exception of one paper, all of them focus on the United States. As a testimony to the growing presence in our organization of Italian scholars, and of the editors' strong belief that a basic knowledge of Italian is essential for any student of Italian emigration, each paper is preceded by a summary in Italian.

The first section covers Italian Americans in the social and political worlds. It spans the 19<sup>th</sup> and 20<sup>th</sup> centuries, beginning with Magliari's essay on G. B. DeBernardi, who forms part of the tradition of Italian immigrant radicalism, and concluding with Michaud's study of the political assimilation of Italian American voters in the 1950s. Born near Turin, DeBernardi, part of the radical Italian immigrant tradition that fought for greater social justice for farmers and workers of all kinds, arrived in the United States in 1858, eventually settling in Missouri where he founded the last authentic producer movement in the United States. Belmonte's essay provides an overview of the role of Italian Americans in the two World Wars, pointing out that they served in disproportionately high numbers and suffered a high percentage of casualties compared to their proportion of the US population. Stefano Luconi's essay examines the timing and mechanics of the desertion of Italian American voters from the Democratic Party in the aftermath of the outbreak of World War

II. Michaud's paper concludes this section with a study of the political assimilation of Italians in the U.S. as the 1920s stereotype of the Italian radical immigrant was replaced in the 1950s, by the anti-communist Italian American voter, mobilized to export American principles to Italy.

At no time in their history, were immigrants isolated in exclusively Italian ethnic ghettoes. The second section explores this theme with three papers, which cover different aspects of the contact between Italian immigrants and other ethnic groups. Wallace's paper focuses on the educator Angelo Patri, who from the early 1900s worked in the New York Public School system to help the children of European immigrants maintain their language and heritage while becoming part of a multi-ethnic United States. The two essays that conclude this section focus on the Western United States. Janet Worral's essay provides the reader with a comparative overview of the Hispanic and Italian experience in Colorado. While in many aspects the experience of the two groups is similar, several factors worked to ensure the more rapid assimilation of Italian immigrants. Martinelli's essay focuses on Italian workers at Theodore Roosevelt Dam in Arizona, where they formed part of a multi ethnic workforce that included Native Americans and Mexicans. The author distinguishes between racialized groups such as Mexicans, Native Americans and African Americans, and what she describes as semi-racialized groups — which include those European groups such as Italians or Jews — that share some of the lower status of the more completely racialized groups.

The section on the world of work covers Italian immigrants in California, New York, and Australia. Adele Maiello's paper focuses on Italian entrepreneurs of Genoese origin who were some of the first settlers in the San Joaquin Valley of California. The author suggests that various factors led to the success of the group including their early arrival, their ability to help each other, and most importantly the values of their culture of origin. Cinotto's essay on Italian American food importers and ethnic consumption focuses on the struggle between importers of food from Italy and local producers of Italian style food, for the control of the Italian American market of New York in the 1930s. Starting with large-scale importers of Italian foodstuffs in the 1890s, Cinotto traces the ultimate success of Italian American food producers in cornering the Italian American ethnic market. In the last paper of this section, Boncompagni focuses on those Tuscans — most of them Lucchesi — who emigrated to Western Australia between 1921 and 1939. Their increased presence in Australia (as the door to immigration closed in the United States in the early 20s), their desire to quickly accumulate capital to take back to their community of origin, the initial hostility of the Anglo-centric host country, all provide parallels with the Italian immigrant experience in the United States; their employment primarily in agriculture, woodcutting, and mining closely following the work pattern of their compatriots in the western U.S.

The last section, Italian Americans and Social Cultural Transformations, offers two essays on cinematic representation and one on the history of Italian American literary criticism. Esposito's essay delineates the parameters of the definition of the Italian American woman in general as well as how she is represented in cinema in her various roles. In so doing, Esposito examines the impact such representations may have on both the Italian American woman as well as the spectator of such films. Guida, in turn, examines the genre of mafia films and how they have raised the ire of Italian American intellectuals. He concentrates on films such as *Goodfellas* and the HBO series The Sopranos, and how such representations have exploited the identification of the spectator with the gangster, since the gangster figure in these films is usually similar to the average middle-class individual. Finally, Belluscio traces the development of Italian American literary voice through what he identifies as three distinct periods: beginning, transition, and maturation. He underscores how, with the transition from one period to the next, one witnesses a passage from an attempt at codification to that of theorization. All three essays in this section constitute significant contributions to the interpretive landscape of Italian America.

What this volume cannot do, unfortunately, is reflect the overall contribution made to the conference by the many interesting and provocative papers presented by the more than one hundred participants. Neither can it communicate the enthusiasm with which the packed audience received Diane Di Prima's and Lawrence Ferlinghetti's reading of their poetry. Ferlinghetti's concluding reading of "The Old Italians Dying" seemed to many of us an apt concluding statement for this the conference of 1999, as we now offer up the final verses:

> The old Italians with lapstrake faces
> are hauled out of the hearses
> by the paid pallbearers
> in mafioso morning coats & dark glasses
> The old dead men are hauled out
> in their black coffins like small skiffs
> They enter the true church
> for the first time in many years
> in these carved black boats
>         ready to be ferried over
> The priests scurry about
>        as if to cast off the lines
> The other old men
>          still alive in the benches
> watch it all with their hats on
> You have seen them sitting there
> waiting for the bocci ball to stop rolling
> waiting for the bell
>         to stop tolling & tolling
> for the slow bell

                    to be finished tolling
             telling the unfinished *Paradiso* story
             as seen in an unfinished phrase
                         on the face of a church
             as seen in a fisherman's face
             in a black boat without sails
             making his final haul

                    * * *

A successful conference is a communal effort and involves the work of many people. Paola Bagnatori and Annette De Nunzio of the Museo ItaloAmericano have to be thanked for the reception and presentation at the Museo as well as for the exhibit on Domenico Ghirardelli; Robert M. Gardner and Amy Mason have to be thanked for the technical support they provided to the conference web site; Larry di Stasi for organizing the poetry reading. Last and most important, organizers — and Paola in particular who worked most closely with her — as well as those who attended, owe the most profound thanks to Cheryl Kelly of Saint Mary's College whose work as Conference Coordinator was instrumental in ensuring a successful and inspiring conference. For the preparation of this volume, we thank Antonella Donadio and Deborah Starewich.

For the admirable professionalism they displayed in the grant application process, and for their continued support of Italian American causes, we are profoundly grateful to the Order of the Sons of Italy Foundation. When all other avenues closed before us, OSIA came forward with a most generous grant, without which this volume would not have been possible.

Paola Alessandra Sensi-Isolani
*Moraga, CA*
Anthony Julian Tamburri
*Boca Raton, FL*

# ITALIAN AMERICANS
# IN THE SOCIAL AND POLITICAL WORLDS

# Producerism's Last Gasp:
# G.B. DeBernardi and the Labor Exchange Movement, 1889–1901

Michael Magliari
California State University, Chico

G.B. DeBernardi (1831–1901) immigrò negli Stati Uniti nel 1858 e si sistemò in una fattoria nel Missouri. Profondamente influenzato dal pensiero socialista e anarchico, DeBernardi sviluppò un piano per proteggere gli agricoltori e gli artigiani colpiti dall'insorgente sistema capitalistico societario durante la rivoluzione industriale. Con a creazione di un nuovo sistema di carte-moneta e unendo agricoltori ed artigiani in una rete di cooperative di produttori-proprietari chiamate Labor Exchanges, DeBernardi sperava di rimpiazzare il capitalismo e di salvare il mondo in rapida estinzione dei produttori indipendenti. Durante la depressione degli anni 1890s, il movimento dei Labor Exchanges di DeBernardi attrasse un largo seguito, ma poi si dissolse rapidamente a seguito della sua morte e col ritorno della prosperità.

In 1890, G.B. DeBernardi of Independence, Missouri, published a rather curious three-hundred page book which he entitled *Trials and Triumphs of Labor*. In this work, DeBernardi unveiled an ambitious plan for a nationwide system of producer cooperatives that he hoped would save the thousands of small farmers and urban craftsmen across America being dispossessed and proletarianized by the rise of industrial capitalism, corporate monopoly, and a "tyrannical" wage system. According to DeBernardi, his so-called "labor exchange plan" would "abolish poverty, establish equity, promote peace and good will, create an atmosphere of prosperity, contentment and happiness." It would, he claimed, "do what has never been done before, viz.: Establish justice."[1]

---

[1] *Labor Exchange Monthly*, October 1894, and June 1894.

Despite its author's grand purpose, *Trials and Triumph of Labor* was not destined to become a best seller. For about five or six years, almost no one in America paid any attention to DeBernardi or his great scheme. As the nation entered the decade of the nineties and plunged into the worst economic depression it had yet known, those clamoring for economic reform pinned their hopes on the more popular alternatives offered by Henry George's Single Tax, Edward Bellamy's nationalism, the Populist party's Omaha platform, the trade unionism of the American Federation of Labor, or the cooperatives of the Farmers' Alliance. Suddenly, however, around 1895, the labor exchange movement sprang to life and DeBernardi's work began to attract considerable interest as many of its rivals began to falter. By the end of 1898, there were over 325 labor exchanges scattered across the country, doing business in at least thirty-three states and claiming over 15,000 members.[2] Then, even more suddenly than it had emerged, the Labor Exchange stalled and collapsed. When DeBernardi died in 1901, his name and work quickly vanished and today are virtually unknown to American historians.[3] In-

---

[2] *Progressive Thought and Dawn of Equity,* November-December 1898, January-February 1899, and March-April 1901.

[3] A good overview of the Labor Exchange is in H. Roger Grant, *Self-Help in the 1890s Depression* (Ames: Iowa State University Press, 1983): 41–58. The movement within Missouri is briefly treated in Michael J. Cassity, "Defending a Way of Life: The Development of Industrial Market Society and the Transformation of Social Relationships in Sedalia, Missouri, 1850–1890" (Ph.D. diss., University of Missouri-Columbia, 1973): 167–75. For the Labor Exchange in Kansas and the West, see H. Roger Grant, "Blueprints for Co-Operative Communities: The Labor Exchange and the Colorado Cooperative Company," *Journal of the West,* 13 (July 1974): 74–82; and Grant, "Portrait of a Workers' Utopia: The Labor Exchange and the Freedom, Kansas, Colony," *Kansas Historical Quarterly,* 43 (Spring 1977): 56–66. Regarding the relationship between the Labor Exchange and the Populist movement, see Michael Magliari, "California Populism, a Case Study: The Farmers' Alliance and People's Party in San Luis Obispo County, 1885–1903" (Ph.D. diss., University of California, Davis, 1992): 370–89.

deed, even his own followers soon forgot DeBernardi. Writing less than forty years later, prominent Pennsylvania labor leader and socialist James H. Maurer could recall only that, somewhere around 1896, "someone thought up a great scheme to eliminate the middleman through a system of organized barter, or direct exchange of products between groups of workers in different lines."[4]

Though forgotten and short-lived, DeBernardi's Labor Exchange movement is not without historic significance. When viewed in the larger context of nineteenth-century American radicalism, the Labor Exchange serves as an important milestone marking the last movement in the United States that perceived farmers and workers as members of a single class and which attempted to link them in a national organization based on their common identity as producers. The story of the Labor Exchange movement testifies to both the stubborn persistence of producerism among American farmers and workers, and to its increasing inapplicability in the rapidly industrializing United States.[5]

---

[4] James H. Maurer, *It Can Be Done: The Autobiography of James Hudson Maurer* (New York: The Rand School Press, 1938): 114. A member of both the Knights of Labor and the Populist party in Reading, Pennsylvania, Maurer was typical of DeBernardi's labor constituency. He became a Socialist in 1899 and a trade unionist in 1901, before going on to achieve national prominence as the President of the Pennsylvania State Federation of Labor (1912 to 1928) and as Norman Thomas's vice-presidential running mate in 1928 and 1932.

[5] Regarding the strength of producer ideology among late nineteenth century farmers and workers, see Chester McArthur Destler, *American Radicalism, 1865–1901* (New London: Connecticut College, 1946): 25–28, 76, 222; Bruce Palmer, *"Man Over Money": The Southern Populist Critique of American Capitalism* (Chapel Hill: University of North Carolina Press, 1980): 9–19, 28–38, 121–25, 199–221; and Richard Oestreicher, "Terence V. Powderly, the Knights of Labor, and Artisanal Republicanism," in Melvyn Dubofsky and Warren Van Tine, eds., *Labor Leaders in America* (Urbana: University of Illinois Press, 1987): 30–61.

Rooted firmly in pre-industrial values, producerism sought to maintain a society of economically autonomous individuals and households in both town and country, therefore appealing to farmers resisting tenantry and displacement, and to those skilled workers still struggling to avoid permanent dependency as wage earners. The uneven march of industrialism across the American landscape left enough of the latter to provide producer movements with sizeable, yet dwindling, constituencies within the ranks of organized labor throughout the entire nineteenth century.

In its essential form, producerism combined a firm belief in the labor theory of wealth with a simple, dualistic analysis of class structure. In the producerist world view, only two economic classes comprised human society: the honest, toiling producers and the idle, parasitic non-producers. Producerism championed the cause of the former (i.e. the farmers and workers) against the exploitations of the latter, who invariably included lawyers, corporate businessmen, and especially bankers.

Producerism's favorite strategy of defense against the forces of industrialism and monopoly capitalism was the formation of producer-owned and operated cooperatives. Cooperatives reunited labor and capital, enabling farmers to bypass the non-productive middlemen who dominated the modern marketplace, and providing skilled workers a practical means by which they could escape the wage system and reap the full reward of their labor.

As the last authentic producer movement in the United States, DeBernardi's Labor Exchange drew heavily from among veterans of the Grange, the Knights of St. Crispin, the Sovereigns of Industry, the Knights of Labor, and the Farmers' Alliance movement, all of which had enthusiastically embraced cooperative enterprise. Given such a constituency, it is not surprising that DeBernardi also attracted many members of the Populist party and earlier producer-based political groups such as the Greenbackers and the Union Labor party.[6]

Like most of these predecessors, the Labor Exchange linked cooperation with calls for fundamental financial reforms. In common with so many of his contemporaries, DeBernardi located the plight of America's producing classes in the nation's money system and its foundation upon the gold standard. For DeBernardi, the enshrinement of gold as legal tender was the root of all economic evil.

The relative scarcity of gold, coupled with the legal requirement that its paper representatives be redeemable upon demand in that precious commodity, resulted in what modern historians and economists generally agree was a serious inadequacy in the nation's money supply. The paucity of available cash was further aggravated by the National Banking system which discriminated against the rural South and West, and against small borrowers in general. The National Banks, backed by the authority of the federal government, formed the core of what financial reformers like DeBernardi decried as the "money power," monopolizing gold and controlling access to credit.

Upon the scarcity of money and the monopolization of the money supply, DeBernardi blamed all the economic woes that afflicted late nineteenth-century United States and espe-

---

[6] The cooperatives organized by these groups are discussed extensively in Clare D. Horner, "Producers' Co-Operatives in the United States, 1865–1900" (Ph.D. diss., University of Pittsburgh, 1978); Solon Justus Buck, *The Granger Movement: A Study of Agricultural Organization and Its Political, Economic, and Social Manifestations, 1870–1880* (Cambridge: Harvard University Press, 1913); D. Sven Nordin, *Rich Harvest: A History of the Grange, 1867–1900* (Jackson: University Press of Mississippi, 1974); Robert C. McMath, Jr., *Populist Vanguard: A History of the Southern Farmers' Alliance* (Chapel Hill: University of North Carolina Press, 1975); Lawrence Goodwyn, *Democratic Promise: The Populist Moment in America* (New York: Oxford University Press, 1976); and Joseph G. Knapp, *The Rise of American Cooperative Enterprise, 1620–1920* (Danville, Illinois: The Interstate Printers and Publishers, 1969).

cially its hardworking farmers and artisan producers. These included falling prices, appreciating debts, widespread strikes and labor violence, and the frequent financial contractions that drove down wages, caused interest rates to soar, destroyed small farms and businesses, and threw thousands of workers out of their jobs.

The legal tender system placed the indebted small producer at the mercy of the creditor who demanded repayment in cash, not in kind. Cash, however, was too often unavailable because of its scarcity and cost. When the producer tried to sell his goods in the market, he found that the dearth of money had devalued the price of his goods, again preventing him from acquiring the cash necessary to avoid further indebtedness or outright dispossession. "Who," asked DeBernardi, "has not witnessed hundreds of times, if not experienced it himself, instances of debtors who had made all possible efforts to convert other commodities and services into the legal tender one, and, failing in this, had tendered these commodities to the creditor at reduced value, only to see them refused and themselves pressed to ruin under the sheriff's hammer?"[7]

According to DeBernardi, the root injustice of the money system was that one commodity, gold, enjoyed a privileged status that gave its possessors command over all other commodities, and consequently over those who produced them. In recalling how he had arrived at this fundamental insight, DeBernardi, referring to himself as he often did in the plural, wrote that

> We have spent the best portion of a long life endeavoring to diagnose the social malady, viz.: why the vast majority of the human race should suffer want in a world of plenty, and why the producer of plenty should go empty-handed. We

[7] G.B. DeBernardi, *Trials and Triumph of Labor,* 2nd ed. (Independence, Missouri: Labor Exchange Publications, 1894): 17.

became confirmed in the belief that the cause of such anomalies is to be found in the universally spread dogma of legal tender money, making it impossible to come out of debt or develop the industries except at the will and pleasure of the owners of that royal commodity or commodities, gold, or gold and silver. We could plainly see that if a person was not permitted to pay his debts with the products of his craft or profession, but must procure an article he did not produce, or was even allowed to produce, he was at the mercy of the owner of that special legal tender commodity, and could thus be ruined and enslaved.[8]

De Bernardi boasted that few critics of industrial capitalism understood the centrality of the legal tender question as clearly as he did, not even Karl Marx. "Marx," wrote De-Bernardi, "never gave to the subject of money the attention it deserves and therefore did not fully understand its bearing upon the industrial affairs of the world. Money to him was simply a commodity" yet there is only one commodity "to which all [the others] yield precedence, the one crowned with the exclusive debt paying power — GOLD."[9]

DeBernardi's economic analysis led him to an obvious conclusion. To obtain justice for the producer, legal tender must be abolished or, as DeBernardi often preferred to put it, all real wealth must be made legal tender. He proposed to accomplish this not by political action but rather through the voluntary direct action of the producers themselves, joined together in a sweeping cooperative movement that would unite them across occupational lines. In sharp contrast to previous farmer and labor cooperative leaders, DeBernardi insisted that cooperation could only succeed through the joint efforts of all producers. "We regard true cooperation as impossible within one industry," declared DeBernardi. "We do not believe that farmers, for instance, can organize coop-

[8] *Labor Exchange Monthly,* May 1895.
[9] *Labor Exchange Monthly,* August 1897.

eration among themselves. They can only combine against other classes. What is true of farmers is true of manufacturers, of railroad men, of carpenters, tailors, cigar makers, etc. Each separate industry can only combine to raise the price of their labor or lower the price of others' labor to their own personal benefit."[10]

DeBernardi had much grander goals in mind. What he hoped to create was nothing less than an alternative economy in the United States, existing alongside of, and eventually replacing, the dominant capitalist system. This new cooperative order would reestablish and adapt to the modern age the essential features of the pre-industrial or simple market society in which the small-scale producer had once thrived. Capital and labor, separated by the rise of large-scale production and vastly expanded markets, would be reunited by private producer-owned cooperative enterprises. The abolition of legal tender would result in the end of banks and interest-bearing indebtedness, and a return to the direct exchange of goods between independent producers, liberated from the larcenous interventions of parasitic and non-producing middlemen. Production would be planned to meet social need rather than maximize the profits of individual market competitors, and the value of a given commodity would be determined not by the supply of gold, but by its usefulness and labor content. In short, honest, productive labor would reap the full reward of its effort and "the drones who are now preying on society and preventing the advancement of civilization will no longer live at the expense of the workers."[11]

When he spoke in more specific terms, DeBernardi described a nationwide network of local producer cooperatives engaged in purchasing, production, storage, marketing, and

[10] Edward W. Bemis, "Cooperative Distribution," U.S. Department of Labor, *Bulletin of the Department of Labor*, No. 6 (September 1896): 629.
[11] *Progressive Thought and Dawn of Equity*, August 1895.

even transportation, and whose transactions were carried out by means of a new non-interest bearing currency. The cooperatives, or "labor exchanges," would be linked together by a central exchange or national headquarters. DeBernardi's proposed currency took two forms ("certificates of deposit" and "labor checks") and, unlike legal tender, was confined to the performance of the only two functions he deemed proper for money: serving as a medium of exchange and as a means of keeping accounts.

In *Trials and Triumph of Labor,* DeBernardi spelled out the working details of his labor exchange plan. Membership was open to "any person, male or female, of good character, not addicted to intemperate or immoral habits, who is willing to engage in a useful occupation or calling, or to aid, by work or means, to advance the objects" of the association.[12] A minimum of fifteen such worthy recruits, each willing to pay the one dollar lifetime membership fee, could establish a local exchange. After sending $2.50 to DeBernardi's national headquarters in Independence, a new local was issued a branch charter and number.

The primary purpose of the local was to promote the exchange of goods between members. Accordingly, the first item of business for a newly organized branch, once it had elected a president and board of directors, was to secure or build a storage facility for saleable goods deposited by the membership. Members who deposited any of the goods they produced received from the Exchange "certificates of deposit" equivalent to whatever the Exchange officers determined as the prevailing local wholesale price for similar items. Printed on standard forms supplied by the national headquarters, the certificates could in turn be used to purchase other goods held by the Exchange, all of which had been marked up to the prevailing local retail prices. Certificates redeemed

---

[12] *Labor Exchange Monthly,* April 1895.

for goods at the Exchange were then cancelled and removed from circulation. In theory, the profits earned on any single item belonged to its original depositor but in practice all profits went toward the expansion of the Exchange into other fields of activity or to the assistance of sick and disabled members.[13]

Those members who contributed labor services instead of farm produce or finished goods received "labor checks" which functioned in exactly the same fashion as the certificates of deposit. Together, the certificates and checks circulated among the membership, providing a plentiful currency whose volume rose and fell with the amount of tangible wealth held by the Exchange. Successful locals sought to win the acceptance of DeBernardi's currency by neighboring private merchants who would thus be drawn into the Exchange system.

By studying the experiences of earlier and ill-fated cooperatives, DeBernardi tried to make sure that the Labor Exchange would not fall victim to the "money power." Thus, the charters he issued to his locals specifically forbade the contraction of debts. Locals had to rely instead upon the resources of their own members in order to begin operation. As DeBernardi explained, "The toilers' capital is labor, not money. . . . The Labor Exchange will risk no battle in the field of dollars . . . founded on labor, it is well equipped with labor . . . hence it applies to labor and not to money, nor to Congress for money, to set it in motion. . . . Let us trust in living labor.[14]

---

[13] The most readily available summary of DeBernardi's plan is in William D.P. Bliss, *The Encyclopedia of Social Reform* (New York: Funk and Wagnalls, 1897): 786. For a complete copy of the original charter issued to the Sedalia branch, see *Labor Exchange Monthly,* April 1897; or DeBernardi, *Trials and Triumph of Labor,* pp. 225-34.

[14] *Labor Exchange Monthly,* July 1894.

Similar concerns led the local exchanges to accept prevailing wholesale and retail prices rather than engage in direct commercial competition. DeBernardi warned his followers that

> To begin co-operation by starting a store . . . has been the blunder (of the) Grange, the Wheel, the Alliance, the Knights of Labor. This blunder costs those organizations millions of dollars. To keep store is to enter into competition with merchants. Competition is commercial warfare, and as in battle the largest and best equipped army will ever conquer. . . . The few dollars which the producing classes may combine are but toys compared to the thousands and millions of the capitalists. These capitalists can under buy and undersell us and thus drive us into bankruptcy.[15]

As long as followers avoided debt and direct competition with capital, DeBernardi remained certain that his plan could not fail and that the dawn of a new era was at hand. With supreme confidence, he predicted that "the moment when the workers shall rally under the flag of co-operation, the power of capitalism will vanish as the morning mist before rising sun."[16]

The precise origins of DeBernardi's Labor Exchange plan remain obscure. In his writings, DeBernardi always presented the plan as an original creation, the result of over forty years' study, travel, and experience. In a passing reference, historian Chester McArthur Destler classified DeBernardi as an anarchist and, although DeBernardi never applied that label to himself, his Labor Exchange plan does bear a striking resemblance to similar experiments launched by the American anarchist Josiah Warren during the late 1820s, and by Pierre Proudhon in France in 1849. However, DeBernardi's

[15] Ibid.
[16] *Labor Exchange Monthly,* September 1895.

scheme also shares many characteristics with French social-ist Louis Blanc's proposals for cooperative national work-shops, and especially with British socialist Robert Owen's National Equitable Labour Exchange stores established in 1832. To what extent these earlier projects served DeBernardi as models cannot be determined. A quick glance at his fascinat-ing career, however, indicates that he was probably quite fa-miliar with most, if not all, of them.[17]

Giovanni Battista DeBernardi was an Italian immigrant from Turin, the capital of Piedmont, in the Kingdom of Sar-dinia. The son of nobility, he was born in the small town of Zubiena on February 2, 1831. His formal education was de-signed to prepare him for the priesthood, but he soon devel-oped a taste for accounting and mathematics, and a desire to become a civil engineer. Reversals to his father's estate, however, ended his schooling and forced him to find employ-ment as a printer with the Pomba Printing Company in Turin. In the print shop, young DeBernardi's exposure to economic and political literature sparked a lifelong interest in social reform. Soon after, at the age of seventeen, DeBernardi left Turin for the revolutionary France of 1848.[18]

Settling in Paris, DeBernardi spent the next three years studying political economy in the turbulent and exciting at-mosphere of the new Second Republic and quickly developed

---

[17] Destler, *American Radicalism,* p. 74 (Destler mistakenly refers to DeBer-nardi as "B.G. Bernardi"); "Labor Exchange Banks," *Encyclopedia of the Social Sciences,* 8 (New York: MacMillan Co., 1932): 637–43; Knapp, *The Rise of American Cooperative Enterprise,* p. 18; Corinne Jacker, *The Black Flag of Anarchy: Antistatism in the United States* (New York: Charles Scribner's Sons, 1968): 48–67; William Sewell, Jr., *Work and Revolution in France: The Language of Labor from the Old Regime to 1848* (Cambridge: Cambridge University Press, 1980): 234–36.

[18] Biographical information on DeBernardi was drawn from *Progressive Thought and Dawn of Equity,* December 1897 and May-June-July 1901; *G.B. DeBernardi: A Sketch and Appreciation of His Life* (Independence, Missouri: Labor Exchange Publications, 1901); *Independence Examiner,* 11 October 1940; *Kansas City Star,* 15 August 1911 and 15 September 1942.

his own deep-seated and unorthodox opinions on economic issues. His new beliefs probably had something to do with his departure for London, where he soon fell in with groups of exiled 48'ers from all over the Continent and apparently met Mazzini, Kossuth, Blanc, and Alexandre Ledru-Rollin, among others.

Undoubtedly, young DeBernardi's experiences in London and Paris played a decisive role in shaping his political and economic views. Unfortunately, his reticence concerning these years allows only tempting speculations as to their precise importance. Certainly they lend credibility to speculation that his Labor Exchange plan was heavily influenced by Owen, Proudhon, Blanc, and other European champions of worker cooperatives such as Philippe Buchez in France and the Rochdale Equitable Society in England. In any event, DeBernardi never broke his contact with the Old World after leaving London and then Liverpool for America. For the rest of his life, he maintained a vigorous dialogue with members of the Rochdale society and prominent European reformers like Michael Flurscheim.[19]

Arriving in America in 1858, DeBernardi wandered through the North and into Canada before finally settling in Missouri where he took up a farm in Jackson County near Independence. In the summer of 1863, DeBernardi married Josephine Sale, Jackson County's first female public schoolteacher, and by the end of the decade was the father of one son and three daughters. For the next ten years DeBernardi successfully farmed his land and provided for his growing family. Then, in 1874, disaster struck western and central Missouri in the form of a drought, followed the next year by a devastating grasshopper plague that devoured the region's crops. These twin blows coincided with the depression that

---

[19] On Flurscheim, see Bliss, *Encyclopedia of Social Reform,* p. 617. On Buchez, see Sewell, *Work and Revolution in France,* pp. 203–04 and 211.

engulfed the United States following the Panic of 1873. Like thousands of farmers across Missouri and the rest of the country, DeBernardi watched helplessly as his farm "passed from his hands under the relentless suction of the devouring mortgage."[20]

The loss of all but a "few paltry acres" of his farm drove DeBernardi directly into agrarian politics. He joined the newly formed Patrons of Husbandry, better known as the Grange, and its electoral offshoot, the National Greenback Party. For the remaining twenty-seven years of his life, DeBernardi devoted himself to the struggle against the "money power" and fervently embraced one reform movement after another, often at the expense of his farm chores. As one of his followers later observed, "many a neglected crop can testify that self and pelf stood least in his thoughts where the good of reform was at stake."[21]

An enthusiastic Granger, DeBernardi organized at least thirty-seven locals and rose quickly to prominence in the Order which enjoyed spectacular early successes.[22] By January 1875, the Missouri Patrons had enrolled some 80,000 farmers and organized them into over 2,000 locals, more than any other state in the Union.[23] Despite its rapid growth, however, the Missouri Grange did not escape the precipitous decline of the Order toward the end of the decade.

Although the causes of this reversal were many and complex, an embittered DeBernardi placed the blame squarely on

---

[20] *Progressive Thought and Dawn of Equity,* December 1897; and Alma B. Wilkinson, "The Granger Movement in Missouri" (MA thesis, University of Missouri, 1926): 66.

[21] *Progressive Thought and Dawn of Equity,* December 1897.

[22] Oliver H. Kelley, *Origins and Progress of the Order of the Patrons of Husbandry in the United States: A History from 1866 to 1873* (Philadelphia: J.A. Wagenseller, 1875): 437.

[23] Buck, *The Granger Movement,* p. 58 ff.; David Thelen, *Paths of Resistance: Tradition and Dignity in Industrializing Missouri* (New York: Oxford University Press, 1986): 158-62.

the Grange's decision to adopt the English Rochdale plan of cooperative purchasing as the model for its own co-operative stores. The unhappy experience of most Grange co-ops confirmed DeBernardi's earlier doubts about the Rochdale plan which he had studied while in England:

> The result of the four fundamental principles which actuates the Roachdale [sic], viz: Dealing in cash, bearing down the prices of labor's products, paying interest on money, and rewarding consumers instead of producers, has been to draw to it the capitalists, the well-to-do classes, high salaried men, the non-producers, and to repel the moneyless, the producers, mound-builders, the creators of wealth. . . . We have lived in England and did not let these facts pass unobserved, and do not hesitate to say that the toilers of England today are comparatively worse off because of the existence of [the Rochdale] society. . . .[24]

Because Rochdale stores insisted on cash-only transactions in order to protect their tenuous solvency, they did nothing to help cash starved farmers who desperately needed credit to see them through the long months between harvests. Thus, poorer Patrons were effectively excluded from participation in the Grange co-ops, and soon dropped out of the movement altogether. As DeBernardi later recalled,

> Farmers, rich and poor alike, joined the Grange. In it both classes stood on an equality; all had equal rights. The equitable plan of England was adopted for the purpose of saving money by buying at wholesale for cash. But when a call was made to pool this cash, a small minority came forward and enjoyed the proffered benefit. A large minority heard the call, kept quiet or pensive or twisted awkwardly around in their seats, but failed to respond. They did not have the cash, and when the field needed plowing and the wheat was

---

[24] *Labor Exchange Monthly,* September 1895.

getting too ripe they went on the sly to the old store and submitted to the high priced [credit] accommodation, after which they felt ashamed to come to the Grange meeting and the Grange went down.[25]

In an unsuccessful attempt to offer an alternative to the Rochdale plan, DeBernardi decided to test a few of his own ideas on cooperation. In 1875, he organized a group called "The Industrials" and opened a co-op in Kansas City. After some initial success, the venture quickly folded, bringing to an end DeBernardi's first practical experiment with what eventually became his Labor Exchange plan. A second abortive attempt was made in 1884, when DeBernardi opened a "labor exchange" store in Kansas City. Like his first effort, a quick collapse followed a promising start, and the project never became more than a strictly local enterprise.

Undaunted, DeBernardi joined the Knights of Labor and was apparently active as an organizer in the great Southwestern railroad strikes of 1885 and 1886. During the latter year, DeBernardi won election as state lecturer of the Missouri Grange and used his new position to help push the remaining Patrons, along with the Knights, into the Union Labor Party movement of 1888. DeBernardi not only joined the new party, but received its nomination for Missouri state register of lands. In the Fall elections, DeBernardi went down with the rest of the ULP ticket to a resounding defeat that sealed his last venture into electoral politics.[26]

Sometime during this period, DeBernardi secured a dependable income as a subcontractor of the mails, a position that enabled him to travel across the country for the next several years. He also managed to put the finishing touches

---

[25] Ibid.

[26] Nordin, *Rich Harvest*, p. 179; Flora Carter, "The Grange in Missouri, 1878-1939" (MA thesis, University of Missouri, 1940): 133-35 and 216; Homer Clevenger, "Agrarian Politics in Missouri, 1880-1896" (Ph.D. diss., University of Missouri, 1940): 71-72.

upon his ever-evolving cooperative scheme and, in 1888, published an eighty-page pamphlet called *The Equitable Industrial Association of America. A Beneficent (!) Co-operative Association for the Employment of Idle Labor Through Mutual Exchange.*[27] This pamphlet, the first formal presentation of DeBernardi's Labor Exchange system, led directly to the publication two years later of his *magnum opus, Trials and Triumph of Labor.*

First published in 1890, *Trials and Triumph of Labor* is an odd and somewhat disjointed work which belongs to that genre of reform literature so popular in the late nineteenth century: the utopian novel. Literary historians have counted over 250 such works published in the United States between 1870 and 1901.[28] The greatest of these was Edward Bellamy's *Looking Backward* (1888), an immediate best seller that sold in the millions and generated the briefly flourishing Nationalist Club movement. *Trials and Triumph of Labor* was not nearly so successful, yet it spawned an organization twice as large as Bellamy's group.[29]

DeBernardi divided *Trials and Triumph of Labor* into four uneven and awkwardly connected parts. The first and longest consists of an allegorical financial history and economic analysis of the United States, focusing on the rise of banking and legal tender currency up through 1890. The second part features a fictitious account of the labor movement that

---

[27] *National Union Catalogue, Pre-1956 Imprints,* 136 (London: Mansell, 1971): 68.

[28] Walter F. Taylor, *The Economic Novel in America* (New York: Octagon Books, 1964): 59; Kenneth M. Roemer, *The Obsolete Necessity: America in Utopian Writings, 1888–1900* (Kent, Ohio: Kent State University Press, 1976): 186–208; Jean Pfaelzer, *The Utopian Novel in America, 1886–1896: The Politics of Form* (Pittsburgh: University of Pittsburgh Press, 1984): 181–88. Neither Taylor, Roemer, nor Pfaelzer include DeBernardi in their compilations of utopian authors and novels.

[29] Edward Bellamy, *Looking Backward,* 22nd ed. (New York: The New American Library, 1960): vi.

ends with labor embracing cooperation as the true remedy for the plight of the workers. Part three abruptly opens with a copy of the original charter of incorporation issued to the Labor Exchange by the state of Missouri in 1889. This is followed by a sudden leap into the future entitled "the Exchange in 1900." Here DeBernardi relates a series of fictional accounts taken from a mechanic, brick burner, farmer, merchant, physician, railroad worker, teacher, manufacturer, and carpenter. Each tells the story of how the Labor Exchange, which now "counts its members by the millions," brought economic prosperity and justice to his particular calling in just ten short years. "The Triumph" of the Labor Exchange is then summarized in a concluding fourth section that briefly describes a cheerful and productive America, with "the LEGAL TENDER obstruction removed from the path of human prosperity and progress" at last.[30]

Such a happy ending made "the textbook of the Labor Exchange" an effective recruiting tool for DeBernardi when he launched his third and final attempt to put his plan into action. Between 1890 and 1894, DeBernardi distributed thousands of copies of his book and won a number of valuable converts across the country. DeBernardi probably accomplished most of his proselytizing by preaching among local congregations of his fellow Knights and Grangers, as well as those of the newer Farmers' Alliance, which he also joined.

Meanwhile, back in Missouri, DeBernardi had already assembled a small cadre of followers in Sedalia, where he opened Labor Exchange Branch Number One toward the end of 1889. Incorporated under Missouri law as a benevolent association the following March, the Sedalia branch got off to a slow but satisfactory start. Hopes for further expansion as a national organization, however, remained largely frustrated. Over the ensuing four years, the Labor Exchange lan-

---

[30] DeBernardi, *Trials and Triumph of Labor,* pp. 257 and 298.

guished as reformers rallied to the banners of the Farmers' Alliance and the Populist party.

Disappointed but not discouraged, DeBernardi determined to redouble his efforts and devote his full attention to the Exchange. In 1894 he quit his mail service and began publishing a newspaper out of his home in Independence. The first edition of *Labor Exchange Monthly* came out in June 1894. It joined a second monthly publication that had already appeared the previous September, the *Progressive Thought and Dawn of Equity* edited by E. Z. Ernst of Olathe, Kansas. Ernst, a local Alliance lecturer in Johnson County, was DeBernardi's most important convert and became the General Organizer of the national Exchange. Johnson County had been a Granger stronghold and was the home of the most successful Grange cooperatives in the nation, some of which remained in business for over thirty-five years after their founding in 1876.[31] Operating in such a favorable environment, Ernst had little difficulty recruiting an active group of local supporters which included his wife and his assistant editor, Frank W. Cotton. Together, they provided the most influential leadership in the Labor Exchange movement after DeBernardi himself.

The *debuts* of the two Exchange papers could not have been better timed, for they appeared almost immediately after the great cooperative exchanges of the Farmers' Alliance had collapsed in state after state, and just prior to the electoral reversals that rocked the People's party in the fall of 1894. These disappointments, combined with the onset of the terrible depression triggered by the Panic of 1893, caused many reformers to look desperately for new alternatives. Within a year, the printed circulation of *Progressive*

---

[31] Knapp, *The Rise of American Cooperative Enterprise,* pp. 54–55; Buck, *The Granger Movement,* pp. 263–64 and 271; J. Harold Smith, "History of the Grange in Kansas, 1883–1897" (MA thesis, University of Kansas, 1940): 83–87.

*Thought* doubled from ten to twenty thousand copies per month, and Cotton boasted that over fifty Exchange branches now operated in twenty states.[32]

Naturally, Cotton and Ernst did all they could to encourage this sudden boom. So too did DeBernardi, who continually stressed the futility of political action and the inadequacy of Populist financial proposals that focused upon the free coinage of silver and the issuance of paper money, or "greenbacks." The People's party, DeBernardi complained, "still believes in a special legal tender and all it asks is the reabilitation [sic] of silver and to supplement the two metals with a very limited amount of treasury notes." Because it failed to strike at the root problem by calling for the outright abolition of legal tender regardless of form, the Populist platform, declared DeBernardi, "will rivet the chains of the money power on the people for another century."[33]

Similarly, when the Farmers' Alliance abandoned its famous subtreasury plan early in 1896, Ernst quickly seized the opportunity to attract angry Populists. The Alliance decision, he claimed, had "broken the backbone of that institution, as the sub-treasury plan was one of the best points in the movement. This action will have the tendency to make true co-operators look for 'something better.'"[34] The accuracy of Ernst's forecast was demonstrated in Lampasas County, Texas, the cradle of the Alliance movement. Calling for the establishment of local exchanges, the *Lampasas Journal* embraced DeBernardi's plan as "a practical illustration of the Alliance Sub-treasury proposition."[35]

---

[32] *Progressive Thought and Dawn of Equity,* November 1893 and January 1895; Frank W. Cotton, "The Labor Exchange," *The Arena,* 14 (September 1895): 143.

[33] *Labor Exchange Monthly,* July 1894 and August 1894.

[34] *Progressive Thought and Dawn of Equity,* March 1896.

[35] *Progressive Thought and Dawn of Equity,* January 1897.

Still more recruits flocked to the Labor Exchange following the Populists' controversial endorsement of Democratic presidential candidate William Jennings Bryan, who dragged their cause down to a disastrous defeat in November 1896. An Ozark, Missouri correspondent spoke for many when he reported to Ernst that, since the election, "I have hardly found a man of the People's party who does not admit that even relief is hopeless through political movement."[36] In Arroyo Grande, California, Populist David F. Newsom declared that "I for one will drop the hope of reform through political parties and do all that I can through the Labor Exchange.[37] Newsom was not alone. Within one year of Bryan's defeat, the Labor Exchange movement was in full bloom. Even a few nationally prominent Populists entered its ranks, including former Colorado governor Davis H. Waite, who helped organize Branch 162 in his hometown of Aspen.[38]

At its height from 1897 to 1901, the Labor Exchange united over 15,000 farmers and workers in a far-flung network of cooperatives that spanned thirty-three states plus the Oklahoma Territory and Canada. At least 326 local branches formed, each busy receiving goods and issuing De-Bernardi's new currency, which gained wide acceptance in many localities and circulated almost as freely as legal tender (see Table I). In Chicago, Cincinnati, Denver, and San Francisco, over one hundred private merchants in each city accepted Exchange checks, often at par.[39] Most transactions conducted through the Exchange involved local individual members, yet there is evidence of extensive long-distance trade between branches and even with cooperative stores in Great Britain. Inter-branch trade proved particularly attrac-

---

[36] *Progressive Thought and Dawn of Equity,* December 1896.

[37] *Labor Exchange Monthly,* August 1896.

[38] *Voice of Labor* (San Francisco), 15 May 1897.

[39] *Progressive Thought and Dawn of Equity,* October 1897, January 1898, March 1898; *Voice of Labor,* 5 March 1898.

tive to fruit growers in California still searching for an effective way to cooperatively market their produce, and helped make California, with almost sixty organized locals, the banner Labor Exchange state.

Exchange was not the only concern of DeBernardi's followers. In order to put unemployed members to work and to produce items with either high local demand or great potential for long-distance trade, many local exchanges entered into various lines of manufacture. In rural areas, this often meant the construction of cooperative sawmills, tanneries, brick kilns, warehouses, canneries, and grist mills, enterprises essential to the support of commercial farming. Meanwhile, in cities such as Lynn and Haverhill, Massachusetts, or Akron, Ohio, cooperative production usually developed among workers manufacturing shoes, barrels, textiles, cigars, hats, and brooms. Miners and timber workers also joined the Exchange. Washington and Louisiana lumberjacks, for example, organized cooperative sawmills and shingle mills, while miners in Kansas, Missouri, Pennsylvania, and Ohio operated their own coal mines. As in previous labor co-op movements, cooperative production in the Labor Exchange flourished among trades where skill requirements remained relatively high, while those for initial capital investment remained relatively low.

Though largely autonomous, the local exchanges were linked together by a small but active press (see Table II). Labor Exchange newspapers played a vital role in facilitating inter-branch trade, enabling locals to advertise surplus goods and to request items in short supply. Through such papers as the *Labor Exchange Monthly* and *Progressive Thought and Dawn of Equity,* members were kept appraised of the movement's growth and the progress of different branches. The papers also provided a vital educational forum in which DeBernardi, Ernst, and other leaders proffered practical advice on day-to-day operations and sermons on the superiority of

DeBernardi's plan over all other social reforms. Advertisements featured special deals on everything from Exchange literature printed in German to life-like busts of G.B. DeBernardi and Eugene V. Debs, available for only fifty cents each.[40]

The vigor of the Exchange movement at its height was best seen not in its papers, however, but rather in the daily operations of its local branches. DeBernardi often pointed to the wonderful miracle wrought in tiny Pfafftown, North Carolina, where "the Labor Exchange infused life and energy in a financially dead country." The Pfafftown branch, "situated in a village of one hundred souls, all poor, with no money or employment visible, went to work first at making brick, then building store-houses, then putting up a tannery, and tanning hides on shares, then a sawmill and gristmill, etc."[41] Pfafftown's revival required no borrowing and depended instead upon pooling the meager resources of its inhabitants. Branch founder and secretary Virgil A. Wilson reported that "there is no money here and consequently we have bought little. In the two years of our work we have not used $300 of legal-tender money."[42]

For DeBernardi, Pfafftown offered proof that his Labor Exchange plan worked. "Those few, very few, poor people of Pfafftown have done in one year what all the Labor Unions, Federations of Trades, Farmers' Granges and Alliances, and the reform political party have not been able to do in a quarter of a century agitation," crowed DeBernardi. "They have proven to the world that WORK is a greater power than lamentations, protests, strikes, boycotts and voting. . . . They have shown us 'THE WAY OUT.' We have only to follow their

---

[40] *Labor Exchange Monthly,* July 1896.
[41] *Labor Exchange Monthly,* February 1897.
[42] *Labor Exchange Monthly,* November 1895.

example and the dawn of a better day will burst upon the human race."[43]

Unfortunately for DeBernardi, Pfafftown's remarkable example, while not an isolated case, was not sufficient to sustain the Labor Exchange movement. Despite its impressive growth and activity, the heyday of the Labor Exchange proved quite brief. The return of prosperity after 1898, along with internal dissent, defections from the ranks, and poor management at many of the locals, led directly to the sudden and swift decline of the movement by the end of the century. Of far more importance, however, was the hopeless inadequacy of DeBernardi's plan. His small band of followers, eschewing political action and demands for government intervention in the economy, could not possibly have mustered by themselves the resources necessary to alter the course being taken by industrializing America. Frustration and defeat were inevitable. That DeBernardi's experiment received so much attention and support in the first place demonstrated both the severity of the 1890s depression, and the powerful grip producer values and goals still held on a large segment of the American public.

That segment was in rapid decline, however, especially in the cities. For most American workers, the dream of eventual self-employment had fled far beyond their grasp, and creating a world of direct exchange without middlemen and bankers seemed much less important now than securing more immediate and attainable goals like higher wages, improved conditions, and collective bargaining rights. When DeBernardi died on May 15, 1901, the fate of the Labor Exchange was sealed, although some local branches continued in business as late as 1906 and one, Branch 135 in Dos Palos, California, did not close its doors until 1920. Ironically, Branch 135 owed its

---

[43] Ibid.

longevity to its restructuring under the Rochdale plan in 1899.[44]

During the summer of 1897, DeBernardi had fallen seriously ill and one of his many correspondents wrote to him expressing concern for his health and that of his organization should he die. In his reply, DeBernardi reflected upon the failure of earlier reform movements and said, "I do hope that such will not be the fate of the Labor Exchange, for with it would vanish the hope of the toilers."[45]

As subsequent events proved, the failure of the Labor Exchange caused nothing quite so tragic. Nevertheless, it did represent an important larger development in the course of American history. Along with the collapse of the Knights of Labor, the Farmers' Alliance, and the Populist party all in the same decade, the demise of the Exchange provided one final sign that, as the United States entered the twentieth century, the once dynamic producer ideology had lost its vitality as a sustaining force of working-class dissent against the new industrial order.

[44] Florence E. Parker, *The First 125 Years: A History of Distributive and Service Cooperation in the United States, 1829-1954* (Superior, Wisconsin: Cooperative Publishing Association, 1956): 22-23.
[45] *Labor Exchange Monthly,* August 1897.

TABLE I: Locations and Branch Numbers of Known DeBernardi Labor Exchanges

Alabama
Branchville (43)
Pell City
Sylvan Glen
Thomasville (298)

Arkansas
Hot Springs (280)
Maple (82)

California
Alameda (190)
Armona
Arroyo Grande (41)
Bakersfield (64)
Ben Lommond
Boulder Creek
Calistoga (29)
Carpenteria (138)
Davisville (184)
Dinuba
Dos Palos (135)
Elgin (208)
Elsinore (77)
Escondido (128)
Eureka (133)
Exeter
Farmington (34)
Fortuna
Fresno
Hanford
Kingsburg
Langford
Los Angeles
Manton
Modesto (130)
Oakdale
Oakland
Pasadena
Paso Robles
Petaluma

Pleyto (146)
Plymouth (101)
Poplar
Porterville (136)
Potrero (196)
Red Bluff (32)
Reedley (267)
Riverside (53)
San Bernardino (95)
San Diego
San Francisco (26)
San Jacinto
San Jose (74)
San Luis Obispo (94)
Santa Ana
Santa Barbara
Santa Cruz
Santa Maria (177)
Santa Paula (88)
Springville
Stockton
Summerland
Traver
Tulare (97)
Ventura (92)
Visalia (127)
Williams (132)

Canada
Toronto (157)

Colorado
Aspen (162)
Boulder (81)
Canon City (259)
Del Norte (165)
Denver (158)
Fruita (104)
Hooper (153)
Hotchkiss (156)
Monte Vista (102)

Mosca (151)
Steamboat Springs
Trinidad (66)
Florida
Bunnell (308)
Ocala (55)

Georgia
Atlanta (16)
Fitzgerald (189)

Idaho
Idaho Falls (42)

Illinois
Chicago (179)
Englewood
Harvey (120)

Indiana
Elkhart (154)
Kingstown (240)
Richmond (211)

Iowa
Avery
Center Point (19)
High Creek (288)
Mapleton (186)

Kansas
Chanute
Edwardsville (197)
Fort Scott
Freedom Colony (199)
Fulton
Harding
Olathe
Osage City (223)
Pittsburg (54)

Salina (131)
Topeka

Kentucky
Science Hill (134)

Louisiana
Lake Charles (271)
Nugent (170)

Massachusetts
Boston
Chelsea (116)
Easthampton (291)
Haverhill (150)
Lynn (252)
Vineyard Haven (299)
Weymouth (303)

Michigan
Bay City (246)
Detroit (251)
Grand Rapids (249)
Lansing (35)
Manistee (233)
Saginaw (67)

Minnesota
Duluth (260)
Garfield (309)
Hubbard (172)
Long Lake (99)
Minneapolis (25)
New Ulm (225)
St. Paul (98)

Mississippi
Biloxi (260)

Missouri
Brookfield (78)
Chariton County (82)

Kansas City (4)
Malta Bend (268)
Marshall
St. Louis
Sedalia (1)

Montana
Florence (214)
Grantsdale (192)
Great Falls (226)
Hamilton
Lewistown (93)
Stevensville

Nebraska
Alliance (52)
Guide Rock (286)
McCook (169)
Niobrara
Omaha (254)

New Jersey
Jersey City (174)
Orange (125)
Paterson (121)
Phillipsburg (105)

New York
Jamestown (193)
New York City (295)

North Carolina
Kingston
Pfafftown (11)
Taylorsville (33)

Ohio
Alliance (224)
Akron (191)
Ashtabula (84)
Bellaire (265)
Cincinnati
Cleveland (109)
Columbiana (245)

Columbus (107)
Elyria
New Philadelphia (163)
Powell (213)
Salem (262)
Toledo (65)
Youngstown (210)

Oklahoma Territory
Aline
Bellmont (311)
Forrest (160)
Guthrie
Okarche (168)
Walthall (103)

Oregon
Amity (89)
Athena
Biddleton
Collier
Coquille (147)
Corvallis (200)
Detroit (118)
Dilley (14)
Empire City
Eugene
Falls City (203)
Forest Grove (14)
Harrisburg (244)
La Grange (122)
Lakeview (123)
Marshfield (253)
Medford
North Yamhill
Oregon City (185)
Pendleton (205)
Pittsburg
Portland (182)
Salem
Slayton (114)
The Dalles
Toledo (219)
Ukiah (85)

Vernonia

**Pennsylvania**
Allegheny
Brunswick Valley
Colony, Kepner
(230)
Corry (274)
Easton (105)
Erie (86)
Harrisburg
Johnstown (216)
Lancaster
Leechburg (171)
Lititz (12)
McKeesport (148)
New Brighton
(217)
Philadelphia (111)
Pittsburgh
Reading (119)
Sharpsburg
Sturgeon (231)
Trestle (31)

Wilkes-Barre
Wilmerding

**South Dakota**
Aberdeen (44)
Eureka (60)

**Tennessee**
Dixie Landing (175)
Harriman (91)
McEwen

**Texas**
Caddo (47)
Clifton (300)
El Dorado (261)
Gainesville (239)
Houston (287)

**Utah**
Salt Lake City (307)

**Virginia**
Danville (188)

Roanoke (143)

**Washington**
Anacortes (49)
Blaine (90)
Boise (285)
Buckley (61)
Clinton (68)
Colville
Kent (236)
La Center
Marysville (62)
Port Angeles (18)
Seattle (56)
Snohomish (75)
Spokane
Vancouver (180)
Whatcom (57)

**Wisconsin**
Maple Valley
Milwaukee (187)
Stetsonville (222)

TABLE II: The Labor Exchange Press

1. *Colorado Labor Exchange* (Mosca)
2. *The Co-Operative Age* (Chicago)
3. *The Director* (Stockton, California)
4. *Friend of Labor* (Mapleton, Iowa)
5. *The Inland Empire* (The Dalles, Oregon)
6. *Labor Exchange Accountant* (Oregon City, Oregon)
7. *Labor Exchange Guide* (Denver)
8. *Labor Exchange Monthly* (Independence, Missouri)
9. *The Labor Leader* (Lancaster, Pennsylvania)
10. *Pennsylvania Labor Exchange* (Leechburg)
11. *Progressive Thought and Dawn of Equity* (Olathe, Kansas)
12. *The Reformer* (Lake Charles, Louisiana)
13. *Self-Reliance* (Cincinnati, Ohio)
14. *The Utopian* (Ellensburg, Washington)
15. *Voice of Labor* (San Francisco, California)
16. *The Way Out* (Roanoke, Virginia)

# Italian Americans in World War One and World War Two: An Overview[1]

## Major Peter L. Belmonte, USAF

All'incirca 300.000 Italoamericani combatterono nelle forze armate statunitensi durante la prima guerra mondiale. Approssimativamente 12.000 di essi morirono durante la guerra, un mumero pari al 10% della totalità degli incidenti occorsi ai soldati americani. Le stime del numero degli Italoamericani che combatterono durante la seconda guerra mondiale variano da 500.000 a 1.500.000. Durante le due guerre essi combatterono su tutti i fronti e parteciparono a tutte le campagne. La loro storia merita di essere scritta e questo contributo è un primo tentativo di iniziare il percorso di ricostruzione storica necessaria. Esso consiste in una analisi generale del tema, comprendendo i tassi di incidenti, le decorazioni e le azioni rimarchevoli e inusuali che videro protagonisti i soldati italoamericani durante le due guerre.

Italian immigrants served in the United States armed forces during the Revolutionary War and during the Civil War, but they did so in very small numbers because immigration to the United States from the Italian peninsula was comparatively slight until the 1880s. And while Italian Americans served in the Army on the Western frontier during the Indian Wars, in the Spanish American War, and during the military campaigns of the early twentieth century, it was not until World War One that large numbers of them served in the armed forces of their adopted country.

When the United States entered World War One in April, 1917, there were about 750,000 men in the armed forces and National Guard. In May, 1917, President Woodrow Wilson, who felt conscription was essential to the nation's victory, signed the Selective Service Act which provided for

---

[1] This essay is in memory of Corporal Dean F. Belmonte, 292nd Engineer Combat Battalion, U.S. Army, European Theater of Operations, 1944–1945.

draft registration and conscription. All men, including non-citizens, between the ages of twenty-one and thirty-one would be required to register with their local draft boards. In the first draft registration day on June 5, 1917, "9,586,508 men between the ages of twenty-one and thirty-one registered with local civilian boards without commotion, riot, or organized resistance" (Link 127). In 1918, Congress expanded the age limits to include all men between the ages of eighteen and forty-five, and all told "draft boards registered 24,234,021 men, of whom 6,300,000 were found to be fit for service and 2,810,296 were inducted into the army" (Link 127).

Ultimately, by November, 1918, almost 4,800,000 men and women were serving in the Army, Navy, and Marine Corps. Of those, about 3,634,000 were in the U.S. Army, and about 1,971,000 were in the American Expeditionary Force (AEF), which was the fighting force in Europe (Link 126–128).

The number of Italians arriving in the U.S. from 1880 to 1915 — more than 4,140,000, including more than 1,000,000 in the decade before 1917 — insured the presence of a large number of first and second generation young Italian American men in the U.S. during the war (Glazier and Filby xii). The existence of conscription in the United States meant that many of those young Italian American men would serve in the U.S. military. Some men, arriving in the U.S. on the eve of war, found themselves drafted into the military of a country whose language they could not read, write, speak, nor understand. Still, they served their adopted country honorably, many of them paying the supreme sacrifice in defense of freedom and liberty.

Estimates of the number of Italian Americans serving in the U.S. armed forces during the War vary. Keeping in mind that the terms "Army" and "armed forces" do not necessarily mean the same thing, we can summarize the estimates. George Creel, Chairman of the Unites States Committee on

Public Information during the war, "estimated that more than 300,000 Italians served in the army during the war . . ." (Nelli 202). Major General Emilio Guglielmotti, former military attaché to the Royal Italian Embassy in Washington, DC, agreed with this figure, writing in 1920: "Three hundred thousand soldiers of the fighting Army of this great America . . . had Italian blood in their veins" (Guglielmotti, 1920). Justice Michael Musmanno, himself a World War One veteran, estimated that approximately 400,000 Italian Americans were in uniform during the war, and Richard Gambino wrote that "some ten to twelve percent of the American Army fighting in World War I were Italian-Americans" (1974, 113 and 290). Jerre Mangione and Ben Morreale also claim that "about twelve percent of the U.S. Army was made up of Italian immigrants and (to a lesser extent) their American-born sons" (1992, 340). Since there were 3,634,000 men serving in the Army in November, 1918, Gambino's and Mangione and Morreale's figure would be approximately 436,000 Italian Americans in the U.S. Army alone. This general assertion, that around ten percent of the nation's armed forces during World War One, more than 400,000 men, were of Italian descent, remains to be conclusively proven. If it is accurate, it shows that Italians, who were about 2.5 percent of the U.S. population at the time (although some claim a rate of approximately four percent), served in disproportionately high numbers, perhaps more than triple the amount expected (For population figures see, for example, Foerster 411, and Iorizzo and Mondello 220. George Creel and others have claimed a four percent rate for Italian Americans.).

In areas of high concentration of Italian settlement the percentage of Italian American draftees and volunteers would be expected to be proportionately high, sometimes even higher than their representation in the local population. The case of Kenosha, Wisconsin, is illustrative of this fact. Italians had been coming to Kenosha, by way of Chicago, located sixty miles directly south of Kenosha, since the 1880s. By World War One, Italians made up about six percent of Kenosha's population, yet, of the approximately 2,800 men from Kenosha who served in the U.S. armed forces during the War, 320, or about 11.4 percent, were Italian Americans (Simmons Library list and *Kenosha Evening News*, June 26, 1936). The numbers of men serving and war dead from Kenosha vary slightly among several sources.[2] In the small Connecticut village of Harwinton, sixteen out of the twenty-five men who served were Italian Americans (*Service Records, Connecticut Men and Women in the Armed Forces of the United States During World War, 1917–1920,* 1941).

Italian American servicemen also suffered a disproportionately high percentage of casualties during the war compared to their proportion of the U.S. population. According to George Creel, "the Italians in the United States are about four percent of the whole population but the list of casualties shows a full ten percent of Italian names" (Gambino 290, and Nelli 202). Generally, "the term casualties includes both battle and nonbattle casualties. The former are those killed, wounded, or missing in action (KIA, WIA, or MIA) while the latter encompass individuals who suffer from disease or illness while in the battle zone or from injuries not directly attributable to enemy action" (Maslowski 301). Creel may have been referring only to those who were killed in action or died of wounds. U.S. forces suffered approximately 320,500 battle casualties during the war, of which about 116,500 were killed in action or died of other causes, and 204,000 suffered non-mortal wounds. Thus, according to Creel, Italian American servicemen suffered about 32,000 casualties, including about 11,650 deaths.

---

[2] The numbers given here represent the author's best attempt to reconcile the various sources; still, the overall totals yield much the same picture regardless of source.

An analysis of some unit and local casualty lists confirms the general rate. For example, the 132$^{nd}$ Infantry Regiment was, before the war, part of the Illinois National Guard. Draftees from Chicago, other parts of Illinois, and other states joined the regiment prior to its departure for France as part of the American Expeditionary Force. Two hundred and seventy-three men of the regiment were killed in action, died of disease, or were missing in action during the war. Of these, twenty-one men, or 7.7 percent, were Italian Americans. If only combat deaths are counted, the numbers are 233 men killed, of whom nineteen men, or 8.2 percent, were Italian Americans (Davis, 1919).

We can examine the casualty rate in Kenosha, Wisconsin, as a further example. Of the 2,800 men from Kenosha who served, seventy-seven died from combat and non-combat causes during the war. Ten of the seventy-seven men were Italian Americans. This shows that they suffered almost thirteen percent of Kenosha's war deaths, slightly above the claimed national average for Italian Americans, and more than twice their representation in the population (about six percent) (Simmons Library list. Compare with Gregory 586–589).

An analysis of Connecticut casualty lists yields similar data for some cities. For example, of the thirty-three men from Torrington, Connecticut, who died during the war, eight, or almost twenty-five percent, were Italian Americans. Waterbury, another Connecticut city with a large Italian population, suffered 154 dead; twenty-four of them, almost sixteen percent, were Italian Americans. Two men from Harwinton, Connecticut, were killed in action during the war, both of them Italian Americans (*Service Records, Connecticut Men and Women in the Armed Forces of the United States During World War, 1917–1920,* 1941).

If Italian Americans suffered ten percent of U.S. casualties, this would seem disproportionate to their make-up of the World War One era U.S. population (about three to four percent). However, it is much closer to their expected "share" of casualties given the claim that they made up about ten percent of the U.S. armed forces. When discussing and analyzing casualty rates, it is important to consider the actual makeup of combat units versus support or stateside units. If a careful analysis of the rosters of front-line combat units reveal a composition of considerably less than ten percent Italian Americans, a claim of disproportionate suffering on the part of Italian Americans might be made. Of course, support and rear-echelon units occasionally suffered combat casualties during the war, so perhaps the best method of determining casualty rates would be to look at the composition of the AEF as a whole, thereby discounting stateside units of all types. And both stateside and overseas units suffered terrible losses from the influenza epidemic which ran rampant during the last few months of 1918.

Many Italian Americans, especially those who were drafted in the last few months before the November, 1918, armistice, served only in stateside training and replacement camps and never went overseas. Also, according to historian David M. Kennedy, initially the Army "relegated non-English-speaking recruits, along with others deemed unfit for combat, to 'depot brigades,' where they were assigned to menial chores in the various stateside camps" (Kennedy 158). Later, in an attempt to use military service as an Americanization agent, the Army placed "substandard but 'remediable' recruits" in "development battalions," where they received instruction in "the English language and American history and government" (Kennedy 158). In fact, of the 320 Italian Americans from Kenosha, Wisconsin, who served during the war, at least seventy-seven served some time in depot brigades and/or development battalions. Thus fully one-fourth of Kenosha's Italian Americans was prevented by official U.S. policy, at least temporarily, from serving overseas in combat.(Simmons Library list). However, not all men who served in Depot Brigades remained stateside. The records of Connecticut servicemen of Italian descent show that many men began training in Depot Brigades and were eventually transferred to units that served in combat overseas (*Service Records, Connecticut Men and Women in the Armed Forces of the United States During World War, 1917–1920*, 1941).

Given the fact that U.S. Army officials consciously placed many Italian Americans in these non-combat stateside units during the last four months of the war, it is possible that the casualty rate for Italian Americans does reflect a disproportionate share of suffering. This might also raise questions about the cause of the higher casualty rate. Was it due to a language barrier which hampered combat training or which made orders given in the heat of battle more difficult to understand? If so, an examination of soldiers of other non-English speaking nationalities should produce similar statistics.

Italian Americans served in all types of units. An analysis of Italian American veterans from Kenosha, Wisconsin, and from Connecticut shows that they served in infantry, artillery, engineer, and hospital units and in specialized units such as trench mortar batteries, machine gun battalions, bakery and butchery units, supply, quartermaster, salvage, and remount units, etc. (Simmons Library list, and *Service Records, Connecticut Men and Women in the Armed Forces of the United States During World War, 1917–1920*, 1941). Also, an Italian American, Giochino Varini, was in the first class of ten enlisted U.S. Navy pilots in 1917 (Tucker 25). Italian Americans also served in the American North Russian Expeditionary Forces in 1918–1919 (see Bozich 157 and 162).

Records of awards for valor indicate that Italian American servicemen made significant contributions on the battlefield. One man, Private Michael Valente, won the Medal of Honor, the nation's highest award for heroism. Valente, born in Cassino, Italy, in 1895, entered service at Ogdensburg, New York, and was assigned to Company D, 107th Infantry Regiment of the 27th Division. On September 29, 1918, Valente's unit was advancing against the Hindenberg line east of Ronssoy, France, when they encountered withering enemy machine-gun fire that held up the advance. Accompanied by another soldier, "Private Valente rushed forward through an intense machine-gun fire directly upon the enemy nest, killing two and capturing five of the enemy and silencing the gun. Discovering another machine-gun nest close by which was pouring a deadly fire on the American forces, . . . Pvt. Valente and his companion charged upon this strong point, killing the gunner and putting this machine-gun out of action. Without hesitation they jumped into the enemy's trench, killed two and captured sixteen German soldiers. Pvt. Valente was later wounded and sent to the rear" (*United States of America's Congressional Medal of Honor Recipients and Their Official Citations* 533). Out of a total of 124 recipients of the Medal of Honor for World War One, Private Valente was the only Italian American (Mangione and Morreale 340, mistakenly credit Private Joe Mastine, an Italian American who aided Private Valente during the action for which he was awarded the Medal of Honor, with also being awarded the medal.[3]).

General John J. Pershing, commander of the American Expeditionary Force in Europe during the war, included at least three Italian Americans on his list of *One Hundred Individual Acts of Extraordinary Heroism Performed by Officers and Soldiers of the American Expeditionary Forces*, compiled at the end of the war and designed to show typical acts of valor performed by American soldiers. All three men received the Distinguished Service Cross (DSC), the nation's second highest military award for valor, two of them posthumously (Wiley 27–31). During World War One, eighty-three

---

[3] See, Commission for Social Justice pamphlet, and *United States of America's Congressional Medal of Honor Recipients and Their Official Citations*.

Italian-born Americans and twenty Americans of Italian descent won the DSC (Gambino 290; Mangione and Morreale 340). One of the DSC recipients was Private First Class (PFC) Joseph T. Angelo. Angelo was Lt. Colonel (later General) George S. Patton's orderly while Patton commanded the 1st Tank Brigade, in September, 1918. During an attack near Cheppy, France, Patton was severely wounded; Angelo, who was the only other man left standing, administered life-saving first aide to Patton amidst a hail of enemy machine gun fire. Soon after the war, Patton recommended Angelo for the Medal of Honor, although the award was downgraded to the Distinguished Service Cross, and Patton himself won the Distinguished Service Cross for bravery during this action (See Blumenson for an excellent treatment of Angelo and Patton.).

Italian American doughboys received honors from their own local communities as well. Cities and states issued medals to returning veterans; they held parades and welcome-home ceremonies. Later, they erected service memorials to home-town boys in city halls, village squares, and memorial libraries all across the country. The names of Italian Americans on these monuments bear mute testimony to the service of these veterans; indeed, these monuments preserve the history of men whose deeds are slipping away with the sands of time. Perhaps unique is the city park in Bronx, New York, named after Private Vincent Ciccarone, Company B, 305th Infantry, 77th Division. Ciccarone died of wounds received at Argonne Forest in 1918; the park was named in his honor in 1934 (*NIAF* 7).

Of course, most Italian Americans who served did so honorably with no particular distinction, and returned home to resume their lives. Some veterans who later became prominent in other fields of endeavor include Michael Musmanno (future Pennsylvania Supreme Court Justice and author), who served in the infantry, Fiorello LaGuardia (future mayor of New York city), who served as a pilot in the

U.S. Army Air Service in Italy, Paul Gallico (future award-winning sportswriter and author), who served as a gunner's mate in the U.S. Navy, and Frank Capra (future award-winning motion picture director), who enlisted after graduating from college with a degree in engineering and served as a mathematics and ballistics instructor for artillery officers at Fort Mason, California, in 1918. Musmanno, Gallico, and Capra also served in the U.S. military during World War Two (Corte 82 and 176; Capra).

Many men, after having served in the U.S. military, returned to civilian life in the United States with a new feeling of pride and patriotism. They joined patriotic and veterans organizations such as the American Legion, Veterans of Foreign Wars, and the Italian American War Veterans. However, not all discharged veterans stayed in the United States; some men returned to Italy, their native country. The presence of these repatriated veterans in Italy strengthened the formal and informal ties between the U.S. and Italy — ties that remained strong despite World War Two and the two nations' belligerent status. Indeed, as late as 1947, U.S. Veterans Administration pension claims forms existed in bilingual editions for Italian American veterans of World War One; and there was a branch of the American Legion in Rome, Italy, no doubt made up of Italian American war veterans who had returned to Italy soon after World War One. One wonders how active this war veterans group was throughout World War Two. That these ties should have existed at the outset of America's entry into the war is not surprising given the comparative recency and volume of Italian immigration to the U.S. at the time. For example, of the twenty-one Italian American men in the 132nd Infantry Regiment who died or were missing in action during the war, at least seven listed their next of kin as family members still living in Italy. (Davis, 1919) Further, an analysis of World War One draft registration cards shows many Italian immigrants reported their next of kin (parents, siblings, and sometimes wives and children) as living in Italy.

Italian American veterans returned to their homes in 1919 after their service, ready to resume their lives and provide for their families. No doubt their experiences broadened their outlook and, perhaps, even aided in the process of "Americanization." But another war loomed on the horizon; and this war would involve many of the American-born sons of these same veterans.

By the eve of the United States' involvement in World War Two, there were approximately five million Italian Americans living in the United States. Despite the fact that the U.S. government declared Italian citizens living in the U.S. to be enemy aliens, a condition which lasted from December 8, 1941, to Columbus Day, 1942, the sons of many of these aliens flocked to military recruiting offices and induction centers. The exact number of Italian Americans who served in the United States armed forces during World War Two isn't known, but estimates vary from 500,000 to 1,500,000 (See, for example, Musmanno 206ff, and Mangione and Morreale 342). In any event, the number is large, and there is no doubt that Italian American families throughout the United States felt the impact of the war in a personal way.

For example, in Herrin, Illinois, eight brothers of the Faro family, whose father came to the United States from Italy in 1900, served in the U.S. armed forces during the war. Two brothers served in the Army, five in the Navy, and one as a bomber crewmember in the Army Air Forces. Incredibly, all eight brothers survived the war (*Illinois Post*). And eight brothers and one sister of the Scerra family from Gardner, Massachusetts, served in the U.S. armed forces during the war. One of the brothers, Joseph A. Scerra, later became the Commander-in-Chief of the Veterans of Foreign Wars, a prominent national veterans group (*VFW* 1999, 42).

Given the large numbers of Italian American servicemen in World War Two, it is not surprising that they were involved in every military operation in all theaters of war. From Europe to Japan, from Africa to Iceland, and from Brazil to Canada, wherever American men and women were stationed during the war, Italian Americans were to be found among them. World War Two unit histories and memoirs are replete with Italian surnames and references to the deeds and activities of Italian Americans. As is the case with World War One histories, names of Italian Americans are to be found on unit rosters, casualty lists, and lists of decorated soldiers. Since it would require a large volume to adequately tell the story of Italian Americans in World War Two, here we shall examine only some of the more noteworthy or unusual aspects of their service.

Italian Americans were among those who suffered the United States' first World War Two battle casualties at Pearl Harbor, Hawaii, on December 7, 1941. Out of 2,350 U.S. military members killed during the attack, at least forty-five were Italian Americans, and an unknown number were wounded during America's devastating entry into the global conflict. Italian Americans were also among the first to suffer privations as prisoners of war: Navy Pharmacist's Mate Anthony Iannarelli was captured by the Japanese, along with the entire small U.S. Navy garrison on Guam, on December 8, 1941. Iannarelli, who suffered unspeakable conditions during his four years as a P.O.W., survived to serve in the Navy until his retirement after thirty years of service in 1966. (see Iannarelli) Captain Sam Grashio, whose parents came from Calabria, was a pilot in the U.S. Army Air Forces who was captured early in the war and endured the horrific Bataan Death March. Later, he became part of the only successful escape from the Japanese during World War Two. It was the report of Grashio and his fellow escapees that brought to light the Death March. (Granata)

Many Italian Americans who were, or who later became successful in other fields served in the armed forces during the war. For example, professional baseball players who served included Joe DiMaggio, Dom DiMaggio, Yogi Berra, Phil Rizzuto, and Joe Garagiola. Some, like Joe DiMaggio, who served in the Army Air Forces, and Rizzuto, who served in the Navy, were given special treatment because of their fame or athletic abilities and were assigned to special services units where their main duty was to play exhibition baseball games for the benefit of other servicemen. Others, like Berra, who served in the Navy and fought at Normandy during the assault landings, did see extensive combat (See Berra, Rizzuto, Durso).

Other famous Italian Americans who served in the U.S. military during the war include singers Mario Lanza, Lou Monte, and Tony Bennett, composer Henry Mancini, actor Ernest Borgnine, boxer Rocky Marciano, poet John Ciardi (who served as an aerial gunner in B-29s in the Pacific Theater and was awarded the Air Medal), Penn State football coach Joe Paterno, and Congressman Silvio Conte who served in the U.S. Navy Seabees (Corte, Ciardi, Paterno).

The heroic exploits of some Italian American servicemen were reflected in various honors accorded them. Thirteen Italian Americans earned the Medal of Honor during the war, and at least three U.S. Navy warships were named for Italian American war heroes. The U.S.S Carpellotti (APD-136) was named for Private First Class Louis J. Carpellotti, a member of the First Marine Raider Battalion killed in action on August 7, 1942 on Tulagi in the South Pacific (Updegraph 105). The U.S.S. Damato was named for U.S. Marine Corps Corporal Anthony P. Damato who was killed in action on February 19, 1944, in the South Pacific and was posthumously awarded the Medal of Honor. The U.S.S. Basilone, a destroyer, was named in 1949 for Gunnery Sergeant John Basilone. Basilone was the first enlisted man to receive the

Medal of Honor during World War Two and is the only soldier in U.S. history to receive both the Medal of Honor and the Navy Cross, the nation's two highest awards for extraordinary heroism (Monaco 14-17). And Captain Don Gentile, from Piqua, Ohio, became one of America's leading air aces by downing thirty enemy aircraft during the war. Gentile won two Distinguished Service Crosses, eight Distinguished Flying Crosses, the Silver Star, and the Air Medal, among other decorations. Tragically, he was killed in a military flying accident in January, 1951 (Spagnuolo).

As in World War One, Italian Americans in World War Two served in all types of units. In addition to the myriad common combat and support duties, Italian Americans could be found performing some more unusual duties. For example, 1Lt Daniel A. Nigro became one of the U.S. Army's first helicopter pilots in 1944. Nigro served in an aircraft repair unit aboard a U.S. Army ship in the Pacific Theater (Baker 29-30). The Army also created special units, made up largely of Italian American soldiers and assigned to the Office of Strategic Services (OSS), which operated behind enemy lines in Italy. Other Italian American officers, such as Colonel Charles Poletti, former governor of New York, and Pennsylvania Supreme Court Justice Michael A. Musmanno, served in Italy as part of the Allied Military Government. (see Corvo, and Icardi for OSS activities in Italy) A Navy Lieutenant Commander DiGiannantonio was one of the officers in charge of producing special recordings of popular songs for distribution to Navy personnel worldwide during the war, thereby making an important, if unheralded, contribution to military morale (*GI Journal*). Many Italian American soldiers served in Signal Corps photographic units worldwide, risking their lives to record the war on film. At least one soldier-photographer, John Vita, was wounded; another, Benedetto James Mancuso, serving in the U.S. Navy, was cited for gallantry in action at Wadke Island in May, 1944 (Maslowski 18-19). And an Italian

American, Sgt. Frank Errigo, was the U.S. Army's first official color photographer.

After induction and training, Errigo, an advanced amateur photographer, was assigned to the Army Pictorial Service. Errigo was paired with Ardean Miller, and the two arrived in the Mediterranean to photograph the war in color in North Africa and Italy. After the liberation of Rome, Errigo and Miller became the first two photographers to have a private audience with the Pope. In the fall of 1944, Errigo, suffering from the effects of an artillery blast at Anzio, was sent to Washington, D.C., where he finished out the war taking pictures of military activities in the area (Gawne 2–3).

In addition to the relatively unknown Italian American men serving as still photographers in combat, a more well-known man served as an officer in the Army Pictorial Service where he made important films for the military and the American public alike. Sicilian-born motion picture director Frank Capra, a World War One veteran of the U.S. Army, re-joined the Army on December 8, 1941, the day after Pearl Harbor. Capra was awarded the Distinguished Service Medal and the Legion of Merit for his wartime services, and he was discharged in June, 1945, with the rank of colonel (Capra).

Second Lieutenant Theodore J. Boselli, who graduated in the first U.S. Army Air Corps navigator training class in 1940, also held a high-visibility position during the war. Because of his skill and excellent class record, Boselli was assigned to fly important military and diplomatic missions, including transportation for top U.S. government dignitaries. Following Pearl Harbor, Boselli flew hazardous missions evacuating aircrew members and technicians from the Philippines to Australia. After flying other special military missions, Boselli was chosen to be the navigator for the first U.S. presidential airplane, a C-54 named the *Sacred Cow*. The first flight of a U.S. president aboard an official military airplane occurred on February 3, 1945, when President

Franklin D. Roosevelt flew from Malta to Yalta; Boselli was the navigator on that historic flight (Whitcomb 139-150).

Two Italian American soldiers were among the first eighteen men to parachute into France just past midnight on D-Day, June 6, 1944. The men, Privates August M. Mangoni and Francis A. Rocca, of the 502$^{nd}$ Parachute Infantry Regiment, were in the lead element of the 101$^{st}$ Airborne Division Pathfinder Team which led the invasion of Europe (Howard 2-3, 11-15). Likewise, "Lt. Abe Condiotti, U.S. Naval Reserve (U.S.NR), [is] credited with commanding the first boat to hit Utah Beach about 0630 on 6 June [during the Normandy landings in 1944]" (Goldstein, et al 97). Among the many men killed on the beaches of Normandy on June 6, 1944, were at least forty Italian Americans. These men were a microcosm of the invasion itself; among the forty were army infantrymen in the assault waves, Rangers, combat engineers, field artillerymen, at least one man in one of the tank battalions making the dangerous landing, paratroopers and glider troops dropped behind the lines. One man was a pilot of one of the C-47s of the 91$^{st}$ Troop Carrier Squadron which dropped the paratroopers behind Utah Beach in the early morning hours of June 6. Also among the casualties were three Italian American naval personnel and one Coast Guardsman who were members of assault boat crews (Carlini).

Just as Italian American soldiers, sailors, airmen, and Marines were present at Pearl Harbor, and were among those who suffered the United States' first war casualties, so also did Italian Americans make their presence felt in the closing days of the war. Aside from the service of the many thousands of Italian Americans on duty throughout the world, there are some little-known aspects of their contributions to the war's end. For example, an Italian American soldier fired the last shots of the ground war in the European Theater. Private First Class Dominic Mozzetta, Company B, 387$^{th}$ Infantry Regiment, 97$^{th}$ Infantry Division, fired the last round at a German sniper near Klenovice, Czechoslovakia, on the night of May 7, 1945, only hours before Germany's unconditional surrender (*VFW* 1995, 30).

On April 21, 1945, an Italian American, Lt. Jack Perella, was on the last American bomber to be shot down over Germany during World War Two. Perella, the navigator on the ill-fated B-24 bomber of the 466th Bomb Group, and nine other members of his twelve-man crew were killed in action and were, in fact, the last combat deaths suffered by the entire 2nd Air Division during the war (Childers).

An Italian American from New York, Colonel Edward T. Imparato, piloted the first aircraft to land in Japan just prior to the end of the war. The aircraft carried a twenty-eight-man military negotiating team which was to prepare the way for Japan's unconditional surrender. Imparato, who has written extensively about his war experiences, also claims to have been the youngest colonel in the U.S. military during the war (Imparato).

And it was an Italian American who suffered what was probably the last combat death of the war. On August 18, 1945, nine days after the U.S. dropped an atomic bomb on Nagasaki, B-32 bombers from the 386th Bomb Squadron at Yontan, Okinawa, flew a photo-reconnaissance mission over Tokyo. Similar missions flown by the unit during the previous week had encountered hostile fire from Japanese fighters, and the crews were warned to expect resistance during this sortie. In the vicinity of Chosi, fourteen enemy fighters attacked the formation for twenty-five minutes. In one of the B-32s, as tail gunners fired at the attacking Japanese aircraft, two aerial photographers captured the action on film. One of the photographers, Sgt. Anthony J. Marchione, was wounded during one pass, and, as he was laying on the airplane floor being attended to by other crew members, he was mortally wounded by another fighter's shells as they pierced the stricken bomber. All U.S. bombers returned to their base, and the plane on which Marchione flew also shot down the last Japanese aircraft of the war during this mission (Y'Blood 68).

While there are no figures for the number of Italian Americans killed, wounded, captured, or missing during World War Two, there can be little doubt that most units engaged in combat suffered some casualties among these Italian American members. Further, in Little Italies across the United States the impact of the war was deeply felt. For example, of the ninety-four men from Rome, New York, who were killed during the war, twenty-four were Italian Americans. (Leonard 29–30) Kenosha, Wisconsin, home to a large Italian American colony, suffered 204 war dead. Of these, approximately eighteen, or 8.8 percent, were Italian Americans (*Kenosha Evening News*, 1946).

During the early wars and World War One, it could be said that Italian Americans were fighting for their adopted country because most of them had been born in Italy. However, during World War Two, Korea, Vietnam, and Desert Storm, most Italian Americans were native-born U.S. citizens fighting and bleeding, not for an adopted country, but for a beloved homeland. The participation and contributions of Italian Americans in World War One and World War Two are so vast and important that a complete volume should be dedicated to each topic. This present study is of necessity brief and general. Still, it is hoped that it brings to light some of the important contributions made by Italian Americans in this century's two greatest wars.

## BIBLIOGRAPHY

Baker, Sue. "Water Wings: 'Ivory Soap' helped to keep aircraft flying in World War II," in *Airman*, Vol. XLII, No. 3, March, 1998, Kelly AFB, Texas.

Berra, Yogi and Tom Horton. *Yogi: It Ain't Over. . . .* New York: McGraw-Hill Publishing Company, 1989.

Blumenson, Martin. *The Patton Papers: 1885–1940*. Boston: Houghton Mifflin Company, 1972.

Bozich, Stanley J. and Jon R. Bozich. *"Detroit's Own" Polar Bears: The American North Russian Expeditionary Forces, 1918–1919*. Frankenmuth, MI: Polar Bear Publishing Co., 1985.

Capra, Frank. *The Name Above the Title: An Autobiography*. New York: The Macmillan Company, 1971.

Carlini, Alessandro. E-mail to the author, March 8, 1999. Carlini transcribed the names of Italian Americans on memorials in Normandy.

Childers, Thomas. *Wings of Morning: The Story of the Last American Bomber Shot Down Over Germany in World War II*. Reading, MA: Addison-Wesley Publishing Company, 1995.

Ciardi, John. *Saipan, The War Diary of John Ciardi*. Introduction by Edward M. Cifelli. Fayetteville: The University of Arkansas Press, 1988.

Commission for Social Justice, Grand Lodge of New York, Order Sons of Italy in America. *Italian-American Recipients of the Congressional Medal of Honor*. Undated pamphlet.

Corte, Robert. *They Made it in America: A Celebration of the Achievements of Great Italian Americans*. New York: William Morrow and Company, Inc., 1993.

Corvo, Max. *The O.S.S. in Italy, 1942–1945: A Personal Memoir*. New York: Praeger, 1990.

Davis, Abel (Colonel, U. S. A.) *The Story of the 132d Infantry, A. E. F.* N. p., n. d., probably Luxembourg, 1919.

Durso, Joseph. *DiMaggio: The Last American Knight*. Boston: Little, Brown and Company, 1995.

Foerster, Robert F. *The Italian Emigration of Our Times*. New York: Arno Press, 1969. (Reprint of 1920 edition.)

Gambino, Richard. *Blood of My Blood: The Dilemma of the Italian-Americans*. Garden City, NY: Doubleday & Company, Inc., 1974.

Gawne, Jonathan. *U. S. Army Photo Album: Shooting the War in Color, 1941–1945, U.S.A to ETO*. Paris, France: Histoire & Collections, 1996.

*The GI Journal*. "V-Discs." Volume 1, Number 4, Winter, 1996. Jonathan Gawne, editor, Framingham, MA.

Glazier, Ira A. and P. William Filby, editors. *Italians to America: Lists of Passengers Arriving at U.S. Ports, 1880–1899. Volume*

*5, Passengers Arriving at New York, November 1890–December 1891.* Wilmington, DE: Scholarly Resources, Inc., 1995.

Goldstein, Donald M., Katherine V. Dillon, and J. Michael Wegner. *D-Day Normandy: The Story and Photographs.* Washington, D.C.: Brassey's (U.S.), 1994.

Granata, Fred. Letter to the author, November, 26, 1999. Granata is Capt. Grashio's cousin.

Gregory, John G., editor. *Southeastern Wisconsin: A History of Old Milwaukee County.* Volume I. Chicago: The S. J. Clarke Publishing Company, 1932.

Guglielmotti, Emilio, Major General, Italian Army. Letter to Order Sons of Italy in America, Grand Lodge of Ohio, 1920, copy in the author's possession.

Howard, Gary. *America's Finest: U.S. Airborne Uniforms, Equipment and Insignia of World War Two (ETO).* London: Greenhill Books, 1994.

Icardi, Aldo. *American Master Spy.* Pittsburgh, Pennsylvania: Stalwart Enterprises, Inc., 1954.

*Illinois Post (St. Louis Post-Dispatch).* "Family from Herrin sent 8 brothers to WW II," June 3, 1998. St. Louis, Missouri.

Imparato, Edward T. *Introducing Colonel Edward T. Imparato, Author.* Publicity pamphlet printed by Imparato, n.p., n.d. (but 1998).

Iorizzo, Luciano J. and Salvatore Mondello. *The Italian-Americans.* The Immigrant Heritage of America Series, Cecyle S. Neidle, editor. New York: Twayne Publishers, Inc., 1971.

Kennedy, David M. *Over Here: The First World War and American Society.* Oxford: The Oxford University Press, 1980.

*Kenosha Evening News.* "Library Board Asks Check of Roll of Honor," June 26, 1936. Kenosha, Wisconsin.

*Kenosha Evening News.* ". . . From These Honored Dead. . . ." July 2, 1946. Kenosha, Wisconsin.

Leonard, Peter M. "The Rome, New York, Medal of Honor: The Men, the Parade, the Medal," in *The Journal of the Orders and Medals Society of America,* Vol. 43, No. 5, May, 1992, Glassboro, NJ.

Link, Arthur S., William A. Link, and William B. Catton. *American Epoch: A History of the United States Since 1900.* Volume I:

An Era of Economic and Social Change, Reform, and World Wars, 1900–1945. New York: Alfred A. Knopf, 1983.

Mangione, Jerre and Ben Morreale. *La Storia: Five Centuries of the Italian American Experience*. New York: Harper Collins Publishers, 1992.

Maslowski, Peter. *Armed With Cameras: The American Military Photographers of World War II*. New York: The Free Press, 1993.

Monaco, Daniel. "The John Basilone Story: Above and Beyond the Call," in *Ambassador*, No. 24, Winter 1994/1995, Washington, D.C.

Nelli, Humbert S. *Italians in Chicago, 1880–1930: A Study in Ethnic Mobility*. The Urban Life in America Series, Richard C. Wade, general editor. New York: Oxford University Press, 1970.

*The NIAF News*. Volume 15, No. 4 (Fall 1999).

Paterno, Joe with Bernard Asbell. *Paterno: By the Book*. New York: Random House, 1989.

Rizzuto, Phil and Tom Horton. *The October Twelve: Five Years of New York Yankee Glory, 1949–1953*. New York: Tom Doherty Associates, 1994.

*Service Records, Connecticut Men and Women in the Armed Forces of the United States During World War, 1917–1920*. Office of the Adjutant General, State Armory, Hartford, Conn., 1941. Three volumes.

Simmons Public Library, Kenosha, Wisconsin. World War One Memorial and typewritten, unpaginated, undated list (but c. 1920s) of Kenosha County World War One veterans. Also included is an explanatory cover sheet from a later date.

Spagnuolo, Mark M., DDS. *Don S. Gentile: Soldier of God and Country*. East Lansing, MI: College Press, 1986

Tucker, Lester B. (CWO-4, U.S.N, Ret.) "Enlisted Pilots of the U.S. Navy 1916–1981," in *The Trading Post*, Vol. XLII, No. 1, October-December, 1982, Virginia Beach, Virginia.

*United States of America's Congressional Medal of Honor Recipients and Their Official Citations*. Columbia Heights, MN: Highland House II, 1994.

Updegraph, Charles L., Jr. *U.S. Marine Corps Special Units of World War II*. Washington, D. C.: U.S. Government Printing Office, 1977.

Van Osdol, William R. *Famous. Americans in World War II: A Pictorial History*. St. Paul, MN: Phalanx Publishing Co., Ltd., 1994.

*VFW*. "A GI's Combat Chronology: Europe, 1941-1945," May, 1995. Kansas City, Missouri.

*VFW*. "Past Commander-in-Chief Scerra Dies," December, 1999. Kansas City, Missouri.

Whitcomb, Ed (Colonel, U.S.AFR Ret.). *On Celestial Wings*. Maxwell Air Force Base, AL: Air University Press, 1995.

Wiley, Cliff. "General Pershing's Heroes of the Great War," in *The Journal of the Orders and Medals Society of America*, Vol. 49, No. 5, Sept.-Oct., 1998, Glassboro, NJ.

Y'Blood, William T. "Unwanted and Unloved: The Consolidated B-32," in *Air Power History*, Vol. 42, No. 3, Fall, 1995, Washington, DC.

# World War II and Italian–American Voters*

Stefano Luconi
Florence, Italy

La contrarietà dell'amministrazione Roosevelt per la decisione di Mussolini di dicharare Guerra alla Francia nel giugno del 1940 segnò una prima flessione del voto italo-americano per il partito democratico. I programmi assistenziali del New Deal riuscirono a contenere la disaffesione degli italo-americani nei confronti di Roosevelt nel 1940. Ma il partito repubblicano conquistò la maggioranza del voto italo-amnericano dopo che Italia e Stati Uniti si trovarono in Guerra tra loro e rafforzò il suo seguito ellettorale per lo scontento provocato tra gli italo-americani dalla politica di Washington nei confronti dell'Italia dopo la firma dell'armistizio tra i due paesi.

Scholarship on the developments of US ethnic politics during the first half of the twentieth century has focused primarily on the forging of a Democratic majority out of first- and second-generation immigrant voters in the Depression years. Conversely, the early stages of the demise of the Roosevelt ethnic coalition since 1940 have received relatively little attention.[1] This essay intends to cast some light

*Research for this essay was made possible in part by grants from the Franklin and Eleanor Roosevelt Institute, the Balch Institute for Ethnic Studies, and the Harry S. Truman Library Institute.

[1] John M. Allswang, *A House for All Peoples: Ethnic Politics in Chicago, 1890–1936* (Lexington: UP of Kentucky, 1971); Jack L. Hammersmith, "Franklin Roosevelt, the Polish Question, and the Election of 1944," *Mid-America* 59.1 (1977): 5–17; John W. Jeffries, *Testing the Roosevelt Coalition: Connecticut Society and Politics in the Era of World War II* (Knoxville: U of Texas P, 1979); Richard Jensen, "The Cities Reelect Roosevelt: Ethnicity, Religion, and Class in 1940," *Ethnicity* 8.2 (1981): 189–95; Nancy J. Weiss, *Farewell to the Party of Lincoln: Black Politics in the Age of FDR* (Princeton, NJ: Princeton UP, 1983); Leonard Dinnerstein, "Jews and the New Deal," *American Jewish History* 72.4 (1983): 461–76; James C. Mott, "The Fate of an Alliance: The Roosevelt Coalition, 1932–1952" (Ph.D., diss., University of Illinois-Chicago, 1988); Gerald H. Gamm, *The Making of the New Deal Democrats: Voting Behavior and Realignment in Boston, 1920–1940* (Chicago: U of Chicago P, 1989); Lizabeth Cohen, *Making a New Deal: Industrial Workers*

on such a neglected field of research. Specifically, it examines the timing and mechanics of the desertion of Italian-American voters from the Democratic Party in the aftermath of the outbreak of World War II.

On 10 June 1940, at the commencement of the University of Virginia at Charlottesville, President Franklin D. Roosevelt stigmatized Italy's eleventh-hour declaration of war on France by the metaphor "the hand that held the dagger has struck it into the back of its neighbor." His words not only brought shame on Italy. They also drew upon the notorious stereotype of Italians as stiletto-prone people that had haunted the members of this ethnic group since the beginning of mass immigration from Italy to the United States in the 1880s.[2]

The President's address was reprinted by the English-language press and fully translated by *Il Progresso Italo-Americano*. With an average circulation of 82,319 copies on weekdays and 76,832 on Sundays, this newspaper was the most influential Italian-American daily in the United States. Reaching a broad readership in Little Italies throughout the United States, Roosevelt's words struck a sensitive nerve among the American population of Italian descent. Italian Americans had previously basked in the glory of Italian dic-

---

*in Chicago, 1919-1939* (New York: Cambridge UP, 1990); Anna Maria Martellone, "Trent'anni di studi su etnia e politica," in *Una e divisibile: Tendenze attuali della storiografia statunitense*, ed. Ester Fano (Florence: Ponte alle Grazie, 1992): 170-77; Robert D. Ubriaco, "Bread and Butter Politics or Foreign Policy Concerns? Class Versus Ethnicity in the Midwestern Polish-American Community during the 1946 Congressional Elections," *Polish-American Studies* 51.2 (1994): 5-32; Patrick D. Kennedy, "Chicago's Irish Americans and the Candidacies of Franklin D. Roosevelt, 1932-1944," *Illinois Historical Journal* 88.4 (1995): 263-78.

[2] *The Public Papers and Addresses of Franklin D. Roosevelt*, ed. Samuel I. Rosenman, 13 vols. (New York: Macmillan, 1938-50), 9:263; Salvatore J. LaGumina, "Introduction," in *Wop! A Documentary History of Anti-Italian Discrimination in the United States*, ed. Salvatore J. LaGumina (San Francisco: Straight Arrow Books, 1973): 13.

tator Benito Mussolini's alleged achievements on the international scene. They therefore resented the President's derogatory characterization of their ancestral country. In addition, after experiencing decades of anti-Italian bigotry they feared that the implications of Roosevelt's statement would trigger off a new wave of ethnic discrimination against their own immigrant minority. For example, *Unione,* an Italian-language weekly published in Pittsburgh, denounced that "since President Roosevelt made his speech on 10 June, trying to drag America into the war, many of our people have been fired from their jobs and the members of their families, though born in America, have been deprived of all protection." Similarly, the Philadelphia-based *Il Popolo Italiano* accused the "stab-in-the-back" address of fanning the flames of anti-Italian prejudice. Indeed, Democratic Congressman James A. Shanley from Connecticut wrote Roosevelt that, following his speech at Charlottesville, not only "there is a wave of sentiment in New England particularly against Italians" but "under the cover of false patriotism certain Italians are being dropped from jobs." Likewise, an English-language neighborhood newspaper serving the Little Italy in South Philadelphia, cried out that "already in the name of patriotism some of our citizens [. . .] are leading the attack on aliens, refusing them relief, denying them ordinary civil rights, taking away their work."[3]

[3] *Boston Globe,* 11 June 1940; *New York Times,* 11 June 1940; *Philadelphia Inquirer,* 11 June 1940; *Il Progresso Italo-Americano,* 11 June 1940; *N.W. Ayer and Son's Directory of Newspapers and Periodicals* (Philadelphia: N.W. Ayer and Son, 1941): 666; Philip V. Cannistraro, "Fascism and Italian Americans," in *Perspectives in Italian Immigration and Ethnicity,* ed. Silvano M. Tomasi (New York: Center for Migration Studies, 1977): 51–66: Alexander De Conde, *Half Bitter, Half Sweet: An Excursion into Italian-American History* (New York: Charles Scribner's Sons, 1971): 240–41; John Morton Blum, *V Was for Victory: Politics and American Culture during World War II* (New York: Harcourt Brace Jovanovich, 1976): 149–50; *Unione,* 28 June 1940; *Il Popolo Italiano,* 12 October 1940; James A. Shanley to Roosevelt, Washington, DC, 9 July 1940, Franklin D. Roosevelt Papers, President's Personal File

Italian Americans had been a pivotal cohort of the ethnic coalition that contributed to Roosevelt's election to the White House on the Democratic ticket in both 1932 and 1936. Therefore, as Roosevelt was running for a third term in 1940, his denunciation of Italy's entry into World War II also became a liability for the Democratic Party among voters of Italian descent in the forthcoming presidential contest.[4]

Democratic workers complained that they were unable to campaign in New York City's Little Italy without police escort because of local residents' anger at Roosevelt. Other Democratic activists wired the White House and called upon the President to say anything in praise of Italian Americans and make, thereby, amends for his speech at Charlottesville in the eyes of the electorate of Italian descent. Mark A. Bogart, for instance, warned that the Italian vote was at risk throughout New York State and advised Roosevelt to utter "some statement adequate to offset the whispering campaign actively being conducted within the City of New York to the effect that the President is anti-Italian." Emanuel F. Schifano, the chairperson of the Italian Democratic Committee in Pittsburgh, urged the President to "make some favorable comment about the Italians in America" because "we need the Italian vote for Roosevelt." Herman P. Kopplemann wrote from Hartford that

> in a conference with several outstanding and loyal Italian Democrats, it was suggested that the boss take advantage of Columbus Day for some kind of laudatory statement concerning the Italians here in America. They are very strongly of the opinion that the Italians here in this coun-

---

6735, Franklin D. Roosevelt Library, Hyde Park, NY; *South Philadelphian*, 28 June 1940.

[4] Phylis Cancilla Martinelli, "Italian-American Experience," in *America's Ethnic Politics*, ed. Joseph S. Roucek and Bernard Eisenberg (Westport, CT: Greenwood, 1982): 221-22.

try could be turned away from their opposition to the boss on account of the "stab in the back" statement. They feel that everything would be forgiven if in some manner the Italians of America were given some praise.

On 9 October 1940, a memorandum for the President about his forthcoming Columbus Day address similarly remarked: "Would it not be helpful if an indirect reference was made to the fact that Columbus was an Italian? Reports are that some of the Italian groups in New York are still shakey [*sic*]."[5]

Indeed, Roosevelt seized the opportunity of his Columbus Day message and made efforts to become reconciled with Italian Americans. His requisite celebration of the brave Genoese navigator's deeds on 12 October 1940 was intended to extol the contribution of Italian immigrants to America and to acknowledge once and for all that they were no longer aliens but a key component of US society. The President further elaborated on these concepts in an address he gave in Dayton on the same day,

> Many and numerous have been the groups of Italians who have come in welcome waves of immigration to this hemisphere. They had been an essential element in the civilization and make-up of all the twenty-one Republics. During these centuries Italian names have been high in the list of statesmen in the United States and in the other Republics — and in addition, those who have helped to create the sci-

---

[5] *F.D.R.: His Personal Letters, 1928–1945*, ed. Elliott Roosevelt, 3 vols. (New York: Duell, Sloane, and Pearce, 1950), 2:1072; Mark A. Bogart to Marguerite Le Hand, secretary to Roosevelt, New York, 24 October 1940; Emanuel Schifano to Stephen Early, secretary to Roosevelt, Pittsburgh, 1 November 1940; Herman P. Kopplemann to Henry Kannee, Hartford, CT, 3 October 1940, all in Roosevelt Papers, Official File 233a, folder "Miscellaneous 1938–40;" James Rowe, Jr. to Roosevelt, Washington, DC, 9 October 1940, ibid., Official File 781, folder "1937–40."

entific, commercial, professional, and artistic life of the New World are well known to us.[6]

The President's words found a large echo in the Italian-language press. Yet the GOP continued to hammer away at the point that Roosevelt was anti-Italian and that, therefore, Italian-American voters should cast their ballots for Republican presidential candidate Wendell L. Willkie in November. For example, in the opinion of the secretary of the Italo-American Republican League of Pennsylvania, Herman E. Carletti, "the reason why the Italians must vote for Willkie is simply obvious. [. . .] The insult against the Italians in Virginia, when he [Roosevelt] uttered those infamous words — stab in the back — can never be forgiven by Italian Americans and shall never be excused." GOP activist Alfred R. Pacini from Buffalo notified the Columbia Republican League of New York State that "we shall be able to garner most of the [Italian] votes in behalf of Mr. Willkie and one of our main arguments which is meeting with enthusiastic response is the reference to the President's speech at Charlottesville, the infamous 'Stab in the back' speech." According to a report of the Office of War Information, former Republican State Senator Eliodor Libonati "invited the Italians of Chicago to vote against Roosevelt because Roosevelt was against Fascist Italy."[7]

Actually, the Republican propaganda also played on the implications of the "stab-in-the-back" address for US foreign policy. GOP workers maintained that the President's angry words had paid the way for American participation in

---

[6] *The Public Papers and Addresses of Franklin D. Roosevelt*, 9:459-60.

[7] *Il Progresso Italo-Americano*, 13 October 1940; *Il Popolo Italiano*, 20 October 1940; Alfred R. Pacini to Anthony Maisano, Buffalo, NY, 21 October 1940, Anthony Maisano Papers, box 1, folder 2, Balch Institute for Ethnic Studies, Philadelphia, PA; Renzo Sereno to Eugene Katz, Washington, DC, 27 October 1942, Philleo Nash Papers, box 23, folder "Italian-American Memoranda," Harry S. Truman Library, Independence, MO.

World War II against Italy. As their argument went, a vote for Roosevelt was a vote for war, while a vote for Willkie was a vote for peace.[8]

Italian Americans were sensitive to this latter issue, too. Most of them still retained relatives and friends in their native land and, therefore, regarded a conflict between their native and adoptive countries as an awesome prospect. For instance, a member of Pittsburgh's community has recalled that "we were sad about the situation that brothers would be fighting against brothers, 'cause there were many of our Italian boys in the United States army." Likewise, as soon as Italy surrendered to the United States, most Italian Americans rejoiced because — as one of them put it — "now our boys in the American army won't have to kill their own kind." Sergio Campailla has properly pointed out that to Italian Americans fighting against Italy was like fighting against themselves. Indeed, as sociologist Joseph S. Roucek has remarked, after a war actually broke out between Italy and the United States "most American Italians looked for a mirage: American victory without Italian defeat." Similarly, Renzo Sereno, of the Office of War Information, reported that "people of rank and file are in an altogether pathetic situation. They are sincerely attached to America and many of them have children and relatives in the United States army. At the same time they have a keen and noble attachment to the country that gave them birth."[9]

---

[8] *Rhode Island Echo*, 5 July 1940; *Il Popolo Italiano*, 29 October 1940; *La Gazzetta del Massachusetts*, 26 October 1940.

[9] Transcript of an interview with Angela Silvioni Baccelli, 1 December 1975, Ethnic Fraternal Organization Oral History Project, Archives of Industrial Society, Hillman Library, University of Pittsburgh; *Philadelphia Record*, 9 September 1943; Sergio Campailla, "Little Italy," in *Il sogno italo-americano: Realtà e immaginario dell'emigrazione negli Stati Uniti* (Naples: CUEN, 1998): 61; Joseph S. Roucek, "Italo-Americans and World War II," *Sociology and Social Research* 29.6 (1945): 468; Renzo Sereno to Eugene Katz, Washington, DC, 26 August 1942, Nash Papers, box 23, folder "Italian-American

Willkie's campaign gained momentum not only among Italian Americans but also in the eyes of the US electorate as a whole thanks to the increasing characterization of Roosevelt as a warmonger in Republican propaganda. As a result, the President tried to defuse his own opponent's most profitable issue. After Willkie stated that the United States could expect to be at war by April 1941 in case Roosevelt was reelected, the President retorted by promising American "mothers and fathers" that "your boys are not going to be sent into any foreign wars."[10]

Despite this statement, many Italian Americans remained skeptical about Roosevelt's real intentions. Even his closest associates and staunchest supporters of Italian descent distrusted the President as for the war issue. This was the case of Ernest Cuneo, a counsel to the Democratic National Committee and a member of the Office of Strategic Services at the time of World War II. As Cuneo later recalled, "the only time I winced was when the President [. . .] assured the electorate 'again and again and again that their sons would fight in no foreign war,' when as a matter of fact we were in it by reason of uncountable number of belligerency."[11]

Pro-Fascist Italian-language newspapers also contributed to encourage Italian-American voters to go over to the Republican Party in the 1940 presidential elections. Domenico Trombetta's New York City-based *Il Grido della Stirpe*, Mus-

---

Memoranda."

[10] Robert E. Burke, "Election of 1940," in *History of American Presidential Elections, 1789-1984*, ed. Arthur M. Schlesinger, Jr. and Fred L. Israel, 5 vols. (New York: Chelsea, 1971–86), 4:2942; Ross Gregory, "Seeking the Presidency: Willkie as a Politician," in *Wendell Willkie: Hoosier Internationalist*, ed. James H. Madison (Bloomington: Indiana UP, 1992): 63; Kenneth S. Davis, *FDR Into the Storm, 1937-1940: A History* (New York: Random House, 1993): 611-21; *The Public Papers and Addresses of Franklin D. Roosevelt*, 9:517.

[11] Ernest Cuneo, untitled memoirs, Ernest Cuneo Papers, box 98, folder "Enemies Foreign," Roosevelt Library.

solini's most outspoken mouthpiece in America, advised its
own readers that Roosevelt's reelection would cause the
United States to enter World War II against Italy. Likewise,
after having endorsed Roosevelt since 1932, Ettore Patrizi's
L'Italia, San Francisco's leading Italian ethnic newspaper,
bolted to Willkie on the grounds that the President had of-
fended Italy at Charlottesville and that the Republican candidate would keep the United States out of the European
conflict.[12]

An opinion poll, ordered by Patrizi, predicted that 92
percent of Italian-American voters in California would cast
their ballots for Willkie. It was a gross exaggeration. Still,
when ballots were counted, it turned out that a significant
number of Italian Americans had gone over to the Republican
Party throughout the United States between 1936, the year
of the previous presidential contest, and 1940. The Italian-
American vote for Roosevelt fell from 85 percent to 72 percent in Hartford, from 85 percent to 63 percent in Boston,
from 83 percent to 74 percent in Pittsburgh, from over 70
percent to 54 percent in New Haven, and from 65 percent to
53 percent in Philadelphia. A slump in the Democratic vote
also occurred in Buffalo, Chicago, and Detroit. In addition,
support for the GOP rose from 9 percent to 42 percent in
San Francisco. Yet it was only in New York City that the Democratic Party lost its pre-war majority among Italian
Americans. These latter cast 79 percent of their ballots for
Roosevelt in 1936 but as little as 42 percent four years
later.[13]

---

[12] *Il Grido della Stirpe*, 24 August 1940; *L'Italia*, 24 October 1940. For
Trombetta and *Il Grido della Stirpe*, see also Department of State, Record
Group 59, 865.20211/Trombetta Domenico, series LM 142, reel 41, National
Archives II, College Park, MD. For Patrizi's stand, see also Patrizia Salvetti,
"La comunità italiana di San Francisco tra italianità e americanizzazione negli
anni '30 e '40," *Studi Emigrazione* 19.65 (1982): 19-20.
[13] Gabriella Facondo, *Socialismo italiano esule negli USA (1930-1942)* (Foggia:
Bastogi, 1993): 148; Jeffries, *Testing the Roosevelt Coalition* 88-89, 201;

The average Italian-American vote for Roosevelt in cities with more than 10,000 residents declined from 88 percent to 75 percent nationwide between 1936 and 1940. Therefore, despite Italian Americans' indignation for the "stab-in-the-back" speech and their worries about the course of the foreign policy set by the President, a majority of the voters of this ethnic group stuck to the Democratic Party in 1940. Indeed, a number of Italian-American organizations endorsed Roosevelt's unprecedented bid for a third term on the grounds that individuals of Italian ancestry had largely benefited from the social and labor legislation of the New Deal. As *Unione* pointed out,

> The major portion of our people belongs to that section of society known as the wage-earning class, and no one can doubt that the wage earners of America have progressed more during the last eight years than they had in the preceding fifty years. [. . .] if it had not been for an unfortunate phrase in a speech which had nothing to do with the Italians in America, there would be no doubt that 95 per

---

Gamm, *The Making of New Deal Democrats* 83; Robert A. Dahl, *Who Governs? Democracy and Power in an American City* (New Haven: Yale UP, 1961): 49; Frederick W. Williams, "Recent Voting Behavior of Some Nationality Groups," *American Political Science Review*, 60.3 (1946): 530, 532; Frederick M. Wirt, *Power in the City: Decision Making in San Francisco* (Berkeley: U of California P, 1974): 235; Ronald H. Bayor, *Neighbors in Conflict: The Irish, Germans, Jews, and Italians of New York City, 1929-1941* (Baltimore: Johns Hopkins UP, 1978): 147. For Pittsburgh and Philadelphia, here and henceforth, it has been assumed that the election returns of the precincts in which at least 52 percent of the registered voters in the former city and 80 percent of the registered voters in the latter were of Italian descent are representative of the vote of each community. The ethnic concentration of the precincts has been calculated through a name check of the *Street Lists of Voters*, held by the Archives of Industrial Society for Pittsburgh and by the Philadelphia City Archives for Philadelphia. The row votes for the 1936 and 1940 presidential elections are from *The Pennsylvania Manual* (Harrisburg: Commonwealth of Pennsylvania, 1937 and 1941).

cent of the voting Italians in America would be for Roosevelt.[14]

Interestingly enough, however, Roosevelt obtained his lowest political following among Italian Americans in major urban areas in two cities under Republican administrations, Philadelphia and New York, although this latter city's mayor — Fiorello H. La Guardia, a politician of Italian ancestry himself — was an outspoken supporter of the President. Moreover, the GOP made its second highest gain over 1936 (33 percent), after the 46 percent of New York, in San Francisco, another city under Republican rule. Conversely, Pittsburgh — where Roosevelt won his largest plurality in 1940 — was the seat of a recently established but solidly entrenched Democratic machine. Indeed, in 1940, support for the President usually overcame the Republican vote nationwide in those districts where the Democratic organizations were particularly strong and effective in the allotment of patronage among ethnic voters.[15]

The unemployment rate was still as high as 22.2 percent in Pittsburgh in April 1940. The economic crisis particularly affected construction activities, which had long been a major source of jobs for local Italian Americans. Pittsburgh showed no striking departures from other major cities that were home to large Italian-American communities. For instance, in

---

[14] Louis P. Bilotta to Roosevelt, Pittsburgh, 30 October 1940, Roosevelt Papers, President's Personal File 7007; Charles H. Sansone to Roosevelt, Detroit, 31 October 1940, ibid., President's Personal File 7031; *Unione*, 1 November 1940.

[15] Jensen, "The Cities Reelect Roosevelt" 192; Thomas Kessner, *Fiorello H. La Guardia and the Making of Modern New York* (New York: McGraw-Hill, 1989): 480–82; Bruce M. Stave, *The New Deal and the Last Hurrah: Pittsburgh Machine Politics* (Pittsburgh: U of Pittsburgh P, 1970); Michael P. Weber, *Don't Call Me Boss: David L. Lawrence, Pittsburgh's Renaissance Mayor* (Pittsburgh: U of Pittsburgh P, 1988): 65–105; Harold F. Gosnell, *Champion Campaigner: Franklin D. Roosevelt* (New York: Macmillan, 1952): 188.

that year, unemployment was 13.6 percent in Boston and 17.0 percent in Philadelphia. It was 14.4 percent in the country as a whole.[16]

With the United States still in the grip of the Depression, in the 1940 elections relief jobs and the patronage controlled by the Democratic party played a leading role in curbing the defection of voters of Italian descent from Roosevelt's ranks out of retaliation for the President's attitude toward Italy in foreign policy. In Philadelphia, the local Republican administration prevented the city from qualifying for an adequate share of jobs with the Works Project Administration (WPA) in the late 1930s because it was afraid that the Democratic party would cash on federal relief at the polls. Conversely, in the same years, the mayors of Boston and Pittsburgh — Maurice Tobin and Cornelius D. Scully — were able to secure enough New Deal projects in order not only to fight the economic crisis but also to enable the local Democratic machines to strengthen their control over ethnic voters through federal patronage. Specifically, between 1934 and 1940, the percentage of Italian Americans working on government projects rose from 3.0 percent to 11.3 percent in Boston's North End and from 5.0 percent to 11.3 percent in East Boston. Actually, unlike his predecessor Michael Curley, who had been in conflict with Roosevelt, Tobin was on good terms with the President and succeeded in having the local WPA rolls increase in 1940 notwithstanding a nationwide drop in relief projects after 1938. A Democratic committeeman acknowledged that machine politics was central to the allotment of federal relief jobs in Pittsburgh in 1936. In both

---

[16] US Department of Labor, *Impact of the War on the Pittsburgh, Pennsylvania, Area* (Washington, DC: US Government Printing Office, 1943): 6, 26; Charles H. Trout, *Boston, the Great Depression, and the New Deal* (New York: Oxford UP, 1977): 177; US Bureau of the Census, *Population and Housing: Statistics for Census Tracts, Philadelphia, Pa.* (Washington, DC: US Government Printing Office, 1942): 58.

Boston and Pittsburgh, however, the brokerage of Democratic politicians remained necessary for Italian Americans to obtain WPA positions until the entry of the United States into World War II boosted the employment rate through a further development of war industries.[17]

Only one third of Italian Americans had a favorable opinion of Roosevelt in Boston's North End as late as June 1941. Most of them were recipients of federal relief as well. Indeed, the city's low-income Italian Americans in wards 1 and 3 went over to the GOP in 1940 to a lesser degree than their more affluent fellow ethnics who lived in other districts. It is also significant that the decline of the Roosevelt vote among Italian Americans in Philadelphia between 1936 and 1940 was lowest where relief rates were highest. Support for the Democratic Party in this city dropped by 17.5 percent in the Italian neighborhoods of ward 34, in which only 1.9 percent of the Italian-American residents were on relief in 1940. By contrast, Roosevelt lost 8.3 percent of the Italian-American vote in the Little Italy of ward 3, where 4.4 percent of the workers of Italian ancestry held federal emergency jobs in 1940.[18]

---

[17] Thomas H. Coode and John F. Bauman, *People, Poverty, and Politics: Pennsylvanians during the Great Depression* (Lewisburg, PA: Bucknell UP, 1981): 176–99; Bruce M. Stave, "Pittsburgh and the New Deal," in *The New Deal: State and Local Levels*, ed. John Braeman, Robert H. Bremner, and David Brody, 2 vols. (Columbus: Ohio State UP, 1975), 2:393–94; Trout, *Boston* 177; Vincent A. Lapomarda, "Tobin, Maurice Joseph," *Biographical Dictionary of American Mayors, 1820–1980: Big City Mayors*, ed. Melvin G. Holli and Peter d'A. Jones (Westport, CT: Greenwood, 1981): 365; Lyle W. Dorsett, *Franklin D. Roosevelt and the City Bosses* (Port Washington, NY: Kennikat, 1977): 32; Priscilla Ferguson Clement, "The Works Progress Administration in Pennsylvania, 1935 to 1940," *Pennsylvania Magazine of History and Biography* 95.2 (1971): 246; William F. Whyte, *Street Corner Society* (Chicago: U of Chicago P, 1955): 197. For the influence of federal relief on the Democratic vote, see in general Wesley C. Clark, "Economic Aspects of a President's Popularity" (Ph.D. diss., University of Pennsylvania, 1942).

[18] Jeanette Sayre Smith, "Broadcasting for Marginal Americans," *Public Opinion Quarterly* 6.4 (1942): 589; Trout, *Boston* 296. For Philadelphia, it

Similarly, in New York City, Roosevelt received his highest support among Italian Americans in lower-class districts where people were more likely to rely on federal relief than their fellow ethnics who resided in more affluent areas. In particular, 44.3 percent of Italian Americans cast their ballots for Roosevelt in lower-class voting units as opposed to 39.3 percent in middle-class voting units.[19]

American participation in World War II after the Japanese attack on Pearl Harbor not only brought about full employment in the country but it also made the United States and Italy fighting enemies. The end of the Depression freed many Italian Americans from reliance on federal relief in order to make a living. As a result, a larger number of voters of Italian ancestry could express their anger at Roosevelt at the polls. Of course, ethnic defensiveness led Italian Americans to flood the White House with pledges of allegiance to the United States as soon as Washington received Italy's declaration of war on 11 December 1941. Yet they did resent Roosevelt's stand against their mother country in their hearts. As an Italian-language newspaper pointed out, the patriotic sentiments toward the United States that Italian Americans showed off in public following the Pearl Harbor attack were nothing more than "rhetoric [. . .] necessary [. . .] in order to be in harmony with the times."[20]

Democratic politicians were fully aware of Italian-American voters' wrath at Roosevelt. For instance, it is hardly by chance that, while campaigning in Philadelphia's Italian dis-

---

has been assumed that each voting precinct of the sample of the Italian-American vote had the same percentage of residents on relief jobs as the census tract in which it was included. The raw data on relief jobs are from US Bureau of the Census, *16th Census of the United States: Population and Housing, Statistics for Census Tracts, Philadelphia* (Washington, DC: US Government Printing Office, 1942): 59, 89.

[19] Bayor, *Neighbors in Conflict* 148.

[20] Roosevelt Papers, Official File 233a, folder "Miscellaneous 1941;" *Il Popolo Italiano*, 9 March 1943.

tricts in 1942, incumbent Democratic Congressman Leon Sacks made a point of stressing that it was Italy which had declared war on the United States in compliance with her alliance with Japan, whereas Roosevelt had excluded Italy from the American declaration of war on Japan because she took no part in the Pearl Harbor attack. Sacks had carried the Italian-American community by 52 percent of the vote in 1940. Two years later, however, such qualifications did not prevent him from losing a majority of the Italian-American electorate to his Republican opponent, James Gallagher, who won 66 percent of the Italian-American ballots.[21]

While the United States and Italy were fighting one another, the Roosevelt administration made additional war-related decisions that contributed to further alienate the Italian-American electorate. Unnaturalized Italian immigrants were classified as enemy aliens and subjected to a number of restrictions in everyday life. Enemy aliens, for instance, needed special permits to travel and could not possess certain articles like firearms, ammunition, cameras, and short-wave radios. Moreover Executive Order 9066 authorized the relocation of Italians from designated military areas, especially along the Pacific coast, for security reasons.[22]

Italian-American voters were US citizens and, therefore, could not be affected directly by such measures. Still they were concerned about those provisions. Both the enemy-alien classification and executive order 9066 touched the unnaturalized relatives and friends of Americans of Italian background. Furthermore they helped spread distrust in people of

---

[21] *Il Progresso Italo-Americano*, 25 October 1942. The row votes are from County Board of Elections of Philadelphia, 1940 and 1942 elections for Representatives in Congress, unpublished worksheets, Philadelphia City Archives.

[22] John P. Diggins, *Mussolini and Fascism: The View from America* (Princeton, NJ: Princeton UP, 1972): 399–401; Rose D. Scherini, "Executive Order 9066 and Italian Americans: The San Francisco Story," *California History* 70.4 (1991–92): 367–77; Dan A. D'Amelio, "A Season of Panic: The Internments of World War II," *Italian Americana* 17.2 (1999): 147–62.

Italian descent who were characterized as potential fifth columnists in the eyes of the US society at large.[23]

Once again, in a last-minute attempt to regain the support of Italian Americans for the 1942 mid-term elections, Roosevelt instructed Attorney General Francis Biddle to revoke the enemy-alien status for Italian citizens who lived in the United States. In the President's opinion, the country had nothing to fear from Italians. "They are a lot of opera singers," he told Biddle. A few Italian-American leaders had already known of the forthcoming reclassification of their unnaturalized fellow ethnics by late May 1942 and the Committee on War Information recommended that Italians be eliminated from the enemy-alien category in June. However, the official announcement was delayed on purpose until 12 October, Columbus Day. According to Roosevelt's election-campaign strategists, the postponement would let the President's decision have a broader echo in Italian-American communities nationwide and a deeper impact on the vote, which was scheduled for early November.[24]

Biddle himself called the repeal of the enemy alien designation "an important weapon of political warfare" and a deed of "good politics." The reclassification pleased many Italian Americans but it turned out to be of little avail for Roosevelt's party at the polls. Between 1940 and 1942, the rise in the Democratic vote among Italian Americans was only 1 percent in Pittsburgh. The Democratic candidate for Governor, Herbert H. Lehman, had carried New York City's Little Italy

---

[23] Walter Firey, "Problems Concerning Italian Morale," 15 May 1942, Nash Papers, box 23, folder "Italian-American Memoranda."

[24] Francis Biddle, *In Brief Authority* (Garden City, NY: Doubleday, 1962): 207; Maddalena Tirabassi, "Enemy Aliens or Loyal Americans? The Mazzini Society and Italian-American Communities," *Rivista di Studi Anglo-Americani* 3.4-5 (1984-85): 424-25; memorandum for Elmer Davis, director, Bureau of Intelligence, 2 October 1942, Nash Papers, box 23, folder "Italian-American Memoranda." See also Elena Aga-Rossi, "La politica degli Alleati verso l'Italia nel 1943," *Storia Contemporanea* 3.4 (1972): 851.

by 60 percent in 1938. But his would-be Democratic successor, John J. Bennet, obtained only 41 percent of the Italian-American vote four years later, which meant that he lost an additional 1 percent over Roosevelt's 1940 performance. Bennet's failure to gain a majority among Italian Americans was key to his defeat against his Republican opponent Thomas E. Dewey. Moreover, in Pennsylvania's 1942 gubernatorial contest, the GOP carried Philadelphia's Italian-American districts by 65 percent, as opposed to the 46 percent Willkie had received two years earlier.[25]

The 1942 election outcome can be easily explained. On the one hand, the United States and Italy were still at war. On the other, as an Italian-language daily pointed out, it was a Democratic president who had initially applied the enemy-alien classification to unnaturalized Italians. Conversely, the only opponent of the measure in Roosevelt's cabinet was Republican Secretary of War Henry Stimson. These issues added to the wound of the President's speech at Charlottesville, which had not yet healed. For instance, a report by the Office of War Information maintained that Italian Americans in Cambridge, Massachusetts still "resented Roosevelt's 'stab-in-the-back' remark" as late as May 1942 because it "implied that Italians are cowards." Likewise, Democratic activist Nicholas J.A. Tumolo complained that the GOP was still

---

[25] Francis Biddle to Roosevelt, Washington, DC, 7 October 1942, Francis Biddle Papers, box 1, folder "Aliens and Immigration," Roosevelt Library; Biddle, *In Brief Authority* 229; Roosevelt Papers, President's Alphabetical File, box 216; Ugo Carusi Papers, scrapbooks, folder 2, Roosevelt Library; Marjorie Ferguson et al., "Survey of the Italian-Language Press, 7 October 1942 to 21 October 1942," Nash Papers, box 16, folder "Italian-Language Press;" Bayor, *Neighbors in Conflict* 47; William Spinard, "New Yorkers Cast Their Ballots" (Ph.D. diss., Columbia University, 1948): 82; Ennio Di Nolfo, "The Italian-Americans and American Foreign Policy from World War II to the Cold War (1940-1948)," in *The United States and Italy: The First Two Hundred Years*, ed. Humbert S. Nelli (Staten Island, NY: American Italian Historical Association, 1977): 98. The row votes for Pittsburgh and Philadelphia are from *The Pennsylvania Manual* (1943).

able to make inroads into Philadelphia's community in 1942 "by poisoning the minds of the Italian-American voters, particularly the Democrats, with respect to [. . .] the 'stab-in-the-back' propaganda."[26]

After the fall of Mussolini and the collapse of his dictatorship on 25 July 1943, the Badoglio government, which had replaced the Fascist regime, signed an armistice with the United States in September and declared war on Nazi Germany the following October. However, not even Italy's new role as a cobelligerent of the United States prevented a further decline in the Democratic vote nationwide in 1944.

In a post-election analysis of the outcome of the 1944 contest for the White House, S. Samuel Di Falco, the chairperson of the Italian-American Division of the Democratic National Committee, assured Roosevelt that "in districts comprised principally of voters of Italian extraction your majority ran anywhere from 60 percent to 90 percent." His data were decidedly wrong. That year, Republican presidential candidate Dewey swept New York City's Italian-American districts with 67 percent of the vote, while support for Roosevelt reached a low of 33 percent. The President managed to carry Pittsburgh's and Hartford's communities in 1944. But, in four years, his majority dropped from 74 percent to 68 percent in the former and from 72 percent to 65 percent in the latter. This also meant that the Democratic vote underwent a 7-percent decline in Pittsburgh between 1942 and 1944. Likewise, Roosevelt's following fell by 2 percent in San Francisco's community between 1940 and 1944. Moreover the President won only 41 percent of the Italian-American vote in Philadelphia in 1944, as opposed to the 53 percent of 1940. In 1944, Roosevelt failed to carry another Italian-American community where he had come on top in his previous reelec-

---

[26] *Il Popolo Italiano*, 26 October 1942; Firey, "Problems Concerning Italian Morale;" circular by Nicholas J.A. Tumolo, Philadelphia, 11 October 1943, Nicholas J.A. Tumolo Papers, box 5, Balch Institute for Ethnic Studies.

tion campaign. He had obtained a 54-percent majority in New Haven's ward with the highest proportion of Italian-born residents in 1940, but he lost this district to Dewey four years later.[27]

Many Italian Americans were still dissatisfied with Roosevelt's policy toward Italy in 1944. They wanted the US government to upgrade the status of Italy from cobelligerent to ally and to provide the Italian provinces occupied by the American and British armies with large amounts of humanitarian and economic aids. These two claims were strictly related because, as an ally of the United States, Italy would have been entitled to American assistance under the Lend-Lease Act. Such issues also cut across ideological cleavages in Italian-American communities. Remarkably, American Labor party US Representative Vito Marcantonio and former Fascist leader Eugene V. Alessandroni worked side by side in the fruitless effort to have the United States recognize Italy as an ally. Indeed, the Roosevelt administration refused to take such a step because the Badoglio government had not signed a peace treaty with the United States yet. Similarly, the quantity of US relief for Italy fell short of Italian Americans' expectations, although the so-called "Hyde Park Declaration" of 26 September 1944 committed the US government to the recovery of Italy and granted her economic assistance through the United Nations Relief and Rehabilitation Administration (UNRRA).[28]

---

[27] S. Samuel Di Falco to Roosevelt, New York, 17 November 1944, Roosevelt Papers, President's Personal File 9007; Spinard, "New Yorkers Cast Their Ballots" 82; Jeffries, *Testing the Roosevelt Coalition* 201; Wirt, *Power in the City* 235; Dahl, *Who Governs?* 49. The row votes for Pittsburgh and Philadelphia are from *The Pennsylvania Manual* (1945).

[28] *Il Popolo Italiano*, 8 October 1944; *Ordine Nuovo*, 21 October 1944; *New York Times*, 28 October 1944; *Unione*, 2 November 1944; James Edward Miller, "The Politics of Relief: The Roosevelt Administration and the Reconstruction of Italy, 1943–44," *Prologue* 13.3 (1981): 193–208; Nadia Venturini, "Italian American Leadership, 1943–1948," *Storia Nordamericana* 2.1 (1985):

Like the repeal of the enemy alien designation for un-naturalized Italians in 1942, the "Hyde Park Declaration" was part of Roosevelt's strategy to win the Italian-American vote. But in 1944, too, his efforts were in vain. Edward Corsi, for example, argued that the fifty-million-dollar UNRRA aids to Italy were "only a drop of water in the desert." Partisan-ship may have biased his statement since Corsi was New York State's Commissioner of Labor in the Republican administra-tion of Governor Dewey. Yet even such a staunch supporter of the Democratic Party as Generoso Pope, the owner of *Il Progresso Italo-Americano*, shared Corsi's worries.[29]

Contrary to Roosevelt, Republican presidential candidate Dewey seemed more responsive to Italian Americans' claims. He stated that "freed Italy is now a friend and an ally, not a mere cobelligerent." He also remarked that "the Italian peo-ple deserve something better than the improvised, ineffi-cient administration which personal New Deal government is giving them."[30]

The devastating impact of the US military operations in Italy also contributed to alienate the bulk of the Italian-American electorate from Roosevelt. The reaction of novelist Gay Talese's father to the news that the Allied had razed the Benedictine Abbey of Monte Cassino well epitomizes the attitude of his fellow ethnics toward the Roosevelt admini-stration. When Joseph Talese learnt of the bombing raid, he destroyed two dozen replicas of American fighter planes that were his son's pride.[31]

---

43–45, 48–49.

[29] Elena Aga-Rossi, "La politica estera americana e l'Italia nella Seconda Guerra Mondiale," in *Italia e America dalla Grande Guerra a oggi*, ed. Giorgio Spini, Gian Giacomo Migone, and Massimo Teodori (Venice: Marsilio, 1976): 168–69; *Il Popolo Italiano*, 8 October 1944; Gregory Dale Black, "The United States and Italy, 1943-1946: The Drift Toward Containment" (Ph.D. diss., University of Kansas, 1973): 185.

[30] *Il Popolo Italiano*, 11 October 1944; *New York Times*, 19 October 1944.

[31] Gay Talese, *Unto the Sons* (New York: Alfred A. Knopf, 1992): 627–29.

It was only in the 1948 presidential elections that the Democratic Party eventually managed to regain a significant share of the Italian-American votes that Roosevelt had begun to lose in 1940 in the aftermath of his "stab-in-the-back" speech. At that time, the war had been over for more than three years and the bulk of the Italian-American electorate nationwide was glad to join again the Democratic ethnic coalition of the New Deal era in appreciation of the Marshall Plan by which the Truman administration had made a major contribution to Italy's postwar economic reconstruction and had allegedly saved this country from communism.[32]

---

[32] Samuel Lubell, *The Future of American Politics* (New York: Harper & Row, 1965): 202-03, 216; Dahl, *Who Governs?* 49; Jeffries, *Testing the Roosevelt Coalition* 248.

# The Italian-American Community in the 1950s: A Case of Political Assimilation

Marie-Christine Michaud
Université Bretagne-Sud, France

Questo contributo esamina la situazione degli italoamericani durante I primi anni 1950, e compie un paragone con la loro espe-
rienza durante gli anni 1920. I due contesti sono paragonabili dal
punto di vista politico, ma mentre gli italomaricani furono considerati pericolosi per la stabilità politica durante la "Grande Paura
Rossa" successiva al primo conflitto mondiale, dopo il secondo conflitto mondiale e durante il maccartismo essi furono considerati
sostenitori dell'anticomunismo o addirittura utilizzati come agenti
pro-americani. Un tale cambiamento ci rivela la misura della loro as-
similazione nella società americana.

Literature covering the Italian-American community in the United States during the 1950s is rather scarce compared to that dealing with Italians before World War II. Nevertheless, in the 1950s, Italians still represented one of the largest ethnic groups in the U.S., comprising more than 4.5 million people (Hutchinson). It is thus surprising to note the paucity of studies concerning the experience of the community at that time. Does this imply that after World War II the Italian-American community was no longer considered as a specific group because of the progress of assimilation? By comparing the situations of the political experience of the community in the 1950s and the 1920s, we shall see that the Italian-American community no longer represented a political menace for American authorities, which confirms the fact that the process of political assimilation had been accomplished. Taking the example of the political experience of Italians at these particular periods is significant since both periods mark turning points in the political construction of the United States. Both were characterized by the government's distrust of the policies of foreign governments, most especially of those that were Communist, as well as the need for foreigners to prove their acceptance of the American political system.

## TWO COMPARABLE POLITICAL CONTEXTS

The twenties and the fifties have been chosen to draw a parallel between the experiences of the Italians in the U.S. because they are highly comparable from a political point of view. Both are postwar eras, and in both cases allied forces were victorious, and the United States as the leader, stood for the champion of liberty, which was an essential psychological factor in the building of postwar society. The U.S. was regarded as a model for the allied countries in their recovery and an arbiter in the settlement of peace, standing as the protector of the free world.

In both cases, the Republicans were in power. Presidents Harding's and Coolidge's foreign policies (1921-29) as well as President Eisenhower's (1953-61) were characterized by the desire to protect the nation from any external influence, their policies marked by isolationism. Besides, even President Truman (1945-53), a Democrat, adopted a suspicious attitude toward foreign countries and set up the principles of the Cold War, whose underlying principles were distrust of foreign nations as well as in any non-American ideals.

Postwar administrations took up domestic policies designed to contain the potential spread of Communism within the United States. Post World War I was marked by the Big Red Scare that Attorney General Mitchell Palmer launched in 1919-20 and the adoption of Quota Laws in 1921 and 1924 designed to limit immigration. Post World War II was characterized by a witch-hunt against Communists that Senator Joe McCarthy organized in 1950 and that President Truman had already introduced as early as 1947, thanks to the adoption of the Federal Employee Loyalty Program.

The two wars, the image of the American WASP democracy as the model, and the social agitation in Europe during the postwar eras were at the basis of such anti-Communist campaigns. But the discrepancies in the implementations of these measures within the United States, however, implied that American public opinion — and its government — had adopted very different attitudes towards Italians.

## THE ITALIAN COMMUNITY AND THE BIG RED SCARE

As LaGumina explains in *WOP*, anti-Italianism reached its peak by the turn of the century. Prejudice and violence developed as Italian immigration increased. The Italian was seen as a criminal, a poor peasant belonging to an inferior race. This prejudice had reached a climax by the time World War I broke out. During the decade 1900–10 the number of Italian immigrants had exceeded two million and during the next decade more than one million had arrived (Bureau of the Census). American public opinion saw the coming of the Italians as a dreadful invasion. After World War I and the Russian Revolution, it was felt that new European immigrants were bringing un-American principles such as Russian Bolshevism and Italian anarchism that had spread throughout Europe. The perception of the Italian immigrant as a revolutionary agent coupled with the traditional stereotype of the Italian, who seemed inassimilable since he resented being naturalized,[1] and could not speak English, emphasized the possibility of this menace to national security.

While peaceful means such as the Americanization Bill of 1920 were adopted, more repressive and drastic measures were also passed since, as President Harding declared *"it was time to keep America American."* In fact the Big Red Scare was a response to the idea that the Americanization move-

---

[1] In 1920 only thirty percent of Italians over twenty-one had acquired American citizenship compared to more than sixty-five percent of British or seventy-three percent of German aliens.

ment was a failure. The political assimilation of those immigrants was not yet completed, and this was why anti-American principles were likely to develop within the national boundaries. Thus, radical associations, labor organizations such as the Industrial Workers of the World or the "Galleanistas," the supporters of Luigi Galleani, an Italian anarchist who was deported in 1919 because of his political convictions, became the targets of Palmer's raids. The Big Red Scare was waged to submit radicals to American political ideals. Those who did not follow the American model, and particularly its political system, were suspected of representing a threat to the established order. The Espionage Act of 1917 and the Sedition Act of 1918 were only preparatory steps to sterner measures to contain any subversive activism. In fact, Palmer launched an anti-Bolshevik crusade to prevent the U.S. from being influenced by the revolutionary swirl that was destabilizing such European countries as Russia, Hungary, Germany and Italy. In fact, Mussolini's increased power pushed anti-fascists and radicals to flee their country, with the result that many came to the United States, the traditional land of freedom.

These new immigrants were said to introduce subversive ideals into the U.S. a perception that underlay Palme's war on Communism, and which in essence amounted to a war on immigrants. Furthermore the growth of political awareness among immigrants led to the idea of the introduction of a "red" danger through immigration: trade-unionists and anti-fascist leaders such as E. Grandinetti, C. Tresca, L. Galleani and A. Capraro were said to be trying to prevent their fellow immigrants from Americanizing and acquiring the principles of American democracy. Little Italies were seen as cradles of political unrest, with Italian unionists as well as Russian immigrants highly involved in the 1919 strikes in Lawrence, Seattle or New York, considered agents of the 1917 Russian revolution. These were the Communists that Palmer was chasing in order to save American democracy.

On January 2, 1920, more than five thousand aliens were arrested. By the end of the month, some three thousand foreign-born people had been deported. In June 1920, the Sterling-Johnson Act authorized the exclusion of any alien advocating or favoring the overthrow of the American government. This year also marked the climax of this anti-Communist crusade. The arrest of the two Italian anarchists, Sacco and Vanzetti, for burglary and murder illustrated the hysteria and the depth of anti-Italian prejudice. The social disorder that the strikes produced in addition to the stereotype of Italians' lack of morality and propensity for criminal activity strengthened the image of Italians as dangerous. It justified Palmer's concern over their community and the adoption of the quota laws of 1921 and 1924.

The political organization and successes of the Italian community, mainly revealed during the 1919 strikes and local elections, were also felt as a possible threat since they showed the emergence of political awareness. Even if their political militancy was not strong, some Italians were gradually elected, at the local level especially, which meant integration in the American political system. The best example of their increasing involvement was the career of Fiorello La Guardia who became the mayor of New York City in 1933.

Therefore, after the war, Italians appeared a political menace because of their association with radicalism. They were seen as not having submitted to American political ideals, and still needing to prove their loyalty to their foster country.

## THE ITALIAN-AMERICAN COMMUNITY AND THE COLD WAR

Even more than World War I, World War II accelerated the political assimilation of Italians. The Italian community in the United States became an Italian-American community.

The aftermath of World War II was marked by American fear of the introduction of a spy ring, and the fear of sabotage on behalf of the Soviets. Several cases of treason during the late 1940s and early 1950s (the Alger Hiss case in 1948, the Klaus Fuchs case in 1950, and the case of the Rosenbergs in 1950) seemed to confirm such fears.

When Italy declared war on the United States, Mussolini lost his prestige among Italian Americans who preferred to support the country that had given them economic and social opportunities and that stood for democracy. More than 500,000 Italian-Americans joined the military forces, thus proving their attachment to the United States.

During the 1950s, Joe McCarthy launched a witch-hunt against Communists or any person associated with radicalism. This was the domestic counterpart of the foreign policy of containment that the Cold War had established. Since the traditional stereotype of the Italian was the image of a radical and a criminal, which the specter of Sacco and Vanzetti had immortalized, and which the political attitude of Congressman Vito Marcantonio embodied, they would have been expected to be the targets of this post-World War II Big Red Scare. But no association of the Italians to Communists was openly made. On the contrary, many Italian Americans turned to conservatism, and the administration even used them to prevent the expansion of Communism in the United States as well as in Europe (Rossi 108–29).

Italian Americans even gained noteworthy political victories when McCarthy was waging a war on traitors, which is evidence of Italian integration into the political system. The elections of Vincent Impellitteri as the mayor of New York City (1950), congressmen such as Anthony Tauriello (from 1949 to 1952), John Torquato (since the 1940s) and John Vincent Volpe (who will be nominated to the government by President Eisenhower in 1957) and the nomination of Michael Musmanno as Associate Justice at the Supreme Court in

1952 are significant examples of this integration. Fiorello La Guardia or Salvatore Cotillo led the path to political success as soon as the late 1920s, and by the 1950s it seemed that Italian-American leaders could be relied upon to defend American ideals.

The establishment of the Cold War pushed Italian Americans to exhibit their loyalty, which led to their becoming "superpatriots." Two main events (the letter campaign of 1948 and Impellitteri's trip to Rome in 1951) corroborated such a shift in the Italian-American milieu. By then, it was clear in American public opinion that the Italian community had become an Italian-American community. It had chosen its ideological side, denouncing Communism and promoting American principles.

President Truman used the mayor of New York City, Vincent Impellitteri, and the whole Italian-American community in the U.S. to enforce the policy of containment in Italy. In order to prevent Communism from spreading he encouraged interference in Italian political affairs. In 1948 President Truman asked V. Impellitteri to lead an anti-Communist movement among his compatriots in Italy where general elections were to take place. In Italian-American communities a letter writing campaign was launched to defeat the Communist menace. As a matter of fact, the American government became very concerned by the political situation in Italy as it comprised the largest Communist party in the western world, which it was feared, would threaten the balance of power in Europe and could, as well, eventually influence the Italian-American community. Thus Italy was the country which received the greatest amount of financial aid through the Marshall Plan.

The fear of a Communist takeover during the 1948 elections induced the American government to concentrate its efforts on the Italian situation. Before Italians went to the polls, Italian Americans were urged by the leaders of their community to send letters to their families and their friends in Italy to convince them to vote for the pro-American Christian Democrat, De Gasperi. Italian Americans were highly mobilized: the community even provided some pre-written letters to be sent more quickly and more easily; the press publicized the campaign and associations such as the Order of the Sons of Italy as well as the Catholic Church urged individuals to write home. The campaign was a success, leading to the defeat of the Communist Party.

Italian immigrants who had been naturalized and who had voted in Italy at the time of the election lost their American citizenship. But in 1951, in order to prove its trust of the Italian-American community, the American government allowed naturalized Italians who had lost their citizenship by voting in this election, to regain it. They could do so if they had not supported the Communist party.

These 1948 Italian elections were a test of the anti-Communism of Italian Americans. They had chosen to stand on America's side, which was reconfirmed during the 1953 Italian election and the new letter campaign that it brought about. In the 1950s, instead of importing Italian political principles to the United States, which was the perception in the 20s, Italian Americans were seen as exporting American ideals to Italy.

In 1951, V. Impellitteri, the mayor of the largest city of Italians outside Italy, traveled to Rome to promote the policy of containment on behalf of President Truman. The trip was to cement relations between the two countries and reaffirm that Italy was ready to help the United States contain Communist expansion. But V. Impelliteri, who sought to be reelected against Carmine De Sapio, the leader of Tammany Hall, also used this trip as an instrument in his own political campaign among Italian-Americans who were supporting the Republican party.

As president Truman relied upon V. Impellitteri, the FBI and Edgar Hoover appealed to Gaetano Salvemini, the socialist leader of the 1920s and the 1930s who strove to promote democratic principles against Fascism, into praising containment and obtaining information on Communist as well as Fascist activities in the United States (Killinger 190). The attitude of G. Salvemini, who became an informant for the FBI as early as the 1940s, was symbolic of the commitment of Italian Americans to defend American ideals and to contain so-called un-American activities. The loyalty of the Italian-American community was proven.

## POLITICAL ASSIMILATION?

After World War II, the Italian-American community gave a new political image of itself, which coincided with increased social assimilation. The second generation of Italian immigrants, that is the children of those who came during the period of mass immigration at the turn of the century, was then leading the organization of the community. The progressive disappearance of the first generation along with the Americanization of the second generation led to the destruction of traditional life and its cultural, social, and political characteristics. While during the 1920s Italian communities still attempted to transplant their way of living, by the 1950s, Italian-American communities had adopted an American model that they were trying to impose on the parents' neighborhoods. The assimilation of Italians, brought about in part through their educational advancement (the GI bill enabled many Italians who had joined the armed forces during the war to attend college), their economic and occupational positions (they tended to belong to the middle class whereas the first generation of Italians were concentrated in the working class) was the beginning of the end of the image of the Italian as a radical.

Italian Americans in the 1950s no longer attacked American institutions but supported the American system and policies since they owed the host society their social improvement, hence acquiring a "cult of gratitude" (Lopreato 124). The upward mobility of the immigrants of the second generation was related to the postwar prosperity and their ability to adapt to the core society. Social assimilation coincided with the end of overt conflicts and isolation. The proportion of Italians in professions and technical positions in 1950 among white workers was thirty-two percent for the first generation compared to seventy-nine percent for the second generation. The figures of the census of the turn of the century showed that very few Italians had professional positions during mass migration. The younger generation had managed to understand the values of the American system and had integrated into the host society. Indeed, Italian Americans felt they shared the general postwar prosperity and the availability of opportunities, which reinforced the cult of gratitude. They did not feel any sense of injustice as their social status had improved and as they participated in national prosperity. They did not identify with an underprivileged or oppressed group, which is a political form of social marginality and a prerequisite to radicalism (Rossi 108–29). Therefore they adopted a conservative attitude. While they used to shift between the Democratic and the Republican parties, they now massively supported the Republican Party (seventy-one percent registered as Republicans in 1952) which symbolized prosperity and which had led the anti-Communist crusade.

Immigrants of the second generation relegated political issues to secondary importance as they tried to secure their social status first. Social integration was prevailing over political considerations that might divide, isolate or even exclude them from American society. The Italian-American community was more interested in its social position in the prosperous post-war society than in ethnic issues or political characteristics that could prevent them from improving their standard of living. Hence, Italian Americans became conservative, their primary concern to shift from working class to a middle class status. This is what Richard Hofstadter (97–104) called "status anxiety," which urged a conservative attitude of the individuals, enabling them to enter the American mainstream.

Their conservatism is a product of Italian Americans' eagerness to integrate since a radical political attitude would keep them out of the system. Adopting such a behavior tends to decrease their ethnic awareness and their marginality, while increasing their feeling of belonging to American society. They supported the Republican Party, which symbolized postwar prosperity. The Democratic Party was seen as the stronghold of the poorest, of new immigrants, of minorities, such as Blacks and Puerto Ricans. As a result, it could no longer attract those who wished to get into the mainstream. Thus, the influence of conservative Italian-American leaders such as John Volpe or Vito Batista rose while simultaneously radicals such as Vito Marcantonio lost credit. Moreover the increasing number of naturalizations (about nine thousand each year during McCarthyism) also testifies to the desire of belonging to American society and can be seen as a proof of loyalty.

It seemed that the Italian-American community became indistinguishable from the American core society. Thus, the relative scarcity of literature for this period in the field of immigration studies is further proof that the Italian American community had moved toward total Americanization.

CONCLUSION

The political assimilation of Italians in the U.S. corresponds to the disappearance of the stereotype of the Italian as a radical immigrant. During the witch-hunt against Communists that Senator McCarthy led when American national security was said to be at stake, Italians were no longer considered a threat and even gained some political victories. This reveals the progress of their political assimilation since the 1920s when they had been the target of the Big Red Scare.

After World War II, Italians were no longer marginalized and their presence was neither resented nor threatened. The contexts of the postwar eras accelerated their political assimilation and the Big Red Scare urged them to prove their political compliance. The Cold War helped them re-affirm this. The very fact that by the 1950s Italian Americans were no longer harassed proved that their political assimilation had come about: they had adopted American political ideals. Their mobilization to export American principles and to support the policy of containment of Communism is surely one of the most significant examples of the success of political assimilation in the United States.

## Works Cited

Bureau of the Census, Department of Commerce.

De Conde. Alexander. *Half Bitter. Half Sweet.* Scribner's inc. New York, 1971

Femminella. Francis. *Italian-Americans and Radical Politics.* AIHA. New York, 1971

Gambino. Richard. *Blood of my Blood.* Doubleday. Garden City, 1974

Gordon. Milton. *The Assimilation in American Life.* Oxford University Press. New York, 1964

Henderson. Thomas. *Immigrant Politician: Salvatore Cotillo. Progressive Ethnic.* International Migration Review. CMS. New York. Spring 1979. vol. 13. n°1

Hofstadter, Richard. *The Pseudo-Conservative Revolt Revisited* in D. Bell. *The Radical Right.* Garden City. Doubleday Anchor Books. 1964, p.97-104

Hutchinson, E.P. *Immigrants and Their Children*. J. Wiley & Sons. New York, 1956.

Killinger, Charles, *Wartime Anti-Fascism: G. Salvemini and the American Authorities*. AIHA. New York, 1986, p.190

LaGumina. Salvatore. *Ethnicity in American Political Life: the Italian American Case*. AIHA. New York, 1968

_____. *The New Deal. the Immigrants and Congressman Vito Marcantonio*. International Migration Review. CMS. New York. Spring 1970. vol. 4

_____. *WOP*. Straight Arrow Books. San Francisco, 1973

_____. *Mayor Vincent Impellitteri. Anti-Communist Crusader*. AIHA. New York, 1993

_____. *WOP*. Straight Arrow Books. San Francisco, 1973

LeMay. Michael. *From Open Door to Dutch Door*. Praeger. New York, 1987

Lopreato, Joseph. *Italian Americans*. Ramdom House. New York, 1970, p.324

Mangione. Jerre and Ben Morreale. *La Storia*. Harper publishers. New York, 1992

Nelli. Humbert. *From Immigrants to Ethnics*. Oxford University Press. New York, 1983

Parenti. Michael. *Ethnic and Political Attitudes*. Arno Press. New York, 1975

Penicone. Nunzio. *Anarchism in Italy*. AIHA. New York, 1972

Rossi. Ernest. *Italian Americans and U.S. Relations with Italy in the Cold War*. AIHA. New York, 1976

Vecoli. Rudolph. *Italian Immigrants in the U.S. Labor Movement from 1880 to 1929*. F. Angeli editore, 1983

# Italian Ethnics in a Multicultural United States

# We Are All Multiculturalists Now:
## From Melting Pot to Cosmopolitanism

James M. Wallace
Lewis and Clark College

"We Are All Multiculturalist Now" è basato sulla vita e la carriera di Angelo Patri e tende a dimostrare che il multiculturalismo ha una lunga ed onorata storia nell'educazione scolastica americana. Patri, il primo amministratore scolastico italoamericano negli Stati Uniti, diresse dal 1908 al 1944 due grandi scuole nel Bronx che prepararono gli studenti ad avere successo nella società americana senza dimenticare gli elementi essenziali delle proprie radici culturali. Patri diede inizio a classi e club dove si insegnava l'Italiano e creò una delle prime "scuole di comunità" americane, in parte anche invitando i genitori immigrati a condividere le loro storie, cultura e "saper fare" con tutti gli studenti. Egli utilizzò ampiamente e con successo nelle scuole pubbliche urbane degli approcci alla diversità non troppi distanti da quelli proposti da Randolph Bourne e John Dewey.

*W*e Are All Multiculturalists Now is the title of a 1997 book by Nathan Glazer, in which he asserts that multiculturalism is pervasive in American society, particularly in education: "We all now accept a greater degree of attention to minorities and women and their role in American history and social studies and literature classes in schools" (Glazer, 1997, 14). What we now call multiculturalism has a long and tangled history, and the version of it expressed in Glazer's book has many antecedents. In order to personalize an often-abstract topic, I will explore themes of multiculturalism, inclusion, and diversity through the life of one Italian immigrant, Angelo Patri, and his extended family. In 1881, Carmela Petraglia migrated to the United States with her infant daughter, five-year-old son Angelo, and brother, to join her husband, Nicolas Petraglia, who had already emigrated. The daughter died shortly after their arrival in New York City, and Carmela's brother, like many newcomers, returned to Italy after a few years (Patri, 1943). Angelo Patri, although sickly as a child, grew up to become a leading progressive educator and writer of advice for parents. He was the first Italian-American school administrator in New York City and was well known for leading two diverse inner-city schools in the Bronx from 1908 to 1944. A student and disciple of John Dewey, he applied progressive principles in his work with students.

Throughout Patri's life he experienced cultural exclusion and inclusion, thought deeply about these experiences, and in true Deweyan form, added meaning to them for himself and others. He thought about such issues as he wrote thousands of newspaper columns, gave radio addresses, and wrote five books for children and nine for parents. I will describe selected events of Patri's life to connect his experiences with broader developments and to explore issues of inclusion and diversity. Paraphrasing a statement by David Hollinger, I will "inquire outward" from Patri's experience (Hollinger, 1995, 60). We may thus see a process through which Patri and his family were increasingly included in the mainstream of American life; this then enabled them to help other families accommodate to the increasing diversity of metropolitan America. (In this essay I draw on information and quotations from three previous articles: Wallace, 1994; Wallace, 1997a; Wallace, 1997b. To promote clarity and continuity, I have occasionally updated Patri's sometimes antiquated spelling, added punctuation, and linked paragraphs.)

Patri was born in Piaggine, Salerno Province, in Southern Italy, on 27 November 1876, the son of Nicola and Carmela Petraglia di Angelo. (The family later had the common immigrant experience of having their names changed in America by public officials.) Nicola was a farmer in Italy and then a laborer in New York City. Patri learned to read and write Italian from an uncle, but because of illness, didn't begin school until 1887, when he was eleven years old. He was an avid student, however, and by 1897 had completed his public schooling as well as a bachelor's degree at City College of New York. He taught in various New York City schools from 1897 to 1908, meanwhile earning in 1904 a Master's degree at Teachers College, Columbia University.

In 1908 he was appointed principal of Public School (hereafter PS) #4 in the Bronx, where he worked with a diverse group of students until 1913. During the summer of 1909 he returned to Teachers College to take John Dewey's course, "Logic Applied to Education." He was appointed principal of PS # 45 in the Bronx in 1913, and served there until 1944. PS 45 was one of the Gary Schools (Platoon Schools) which became centers of controversy in 1915 (Ravitch, 1988, ch. 18). Patri and his staff made the school effective and well known, and it attracted many visitors, including Maria Montessori and Theodore Roosevelt.

Patri's reputation as a progressive administrator was later overshadowed by his activity as a writer and speaker. His column, "Our Children," which he began in 1923, was published in hundreds of newspapers and reached millions of readers, and his speeches and radio addresses reached millions more. He married Dorothy Caterson in 1910, and although they had no children of their own, they helped raise other people's children and maintained an active social life with Patri's siblings and their families. They retired in 1944 to a home in Pawling, NY, and lived a comfortable life gardening, writing, and collecting art. Dorothy Patri died in 1961 and Patri in 1965 (Wallace, 1997a).

With that background, I will examine in more detail some events of Patri's life and interpret them in terms of inclusion and diversity. Patri's first five years of life took place in an Italian peasant culture. By comparison with his later American life, existence in Piaggine was simple, integrated, and poor. After moving to Manhattan's "Little Italy," the family was able to maintain much of its Italian culture, but it was necessary to learn English (Wallace, 1997a). When Patri began attending what he called an "American school" in 1887, and when his family moved to a more "American" neighborhood, their assimilation became more rapid. Patri went through a period of alienation from his parents, but realized what was happening, and developed a renewed appreciation for his family and its heritage. This experience helped him later to deal with similar situations in the lives of his students (Patri, 1917). Patri progressed rapidly through school, and in 1892 he and his friend Anthony Pugliese entered the City College of New York in the "sub-freshman" Classical class in 1892. Patri and Pugliese completed a traditional Euro-American program and graduated in 1897, among the earliest Italian-American graduates of CCNY.

The Patri and Pugliese families did not share the common Southern Italian immigrant resistance to schooling. Stephen Lassonde explains that this resistance was based in part on the realization that schooling often alienated children from their families and native language. These two families, however, came early in the great Italian immigration and acquired the more traditional "American" assumption that education could be a source of social mobility and family pride (Lassonde, 1998, 45–47). According to Lassonde, another reason for resisting education was the loss of income that the children might otherwise be earning. In Patri's case, his father supported him through CCNY; then the father fell fifty feet off a ladder and could not work, so Patri took a teaching job to help support the family (Patri, 1917, 5). In so doing he took a further step toward inclusion in the larger culture by becoming an employee of the New York City school system, already an avenue to mobility for earlier immigrants (Ravitch, 1988, 102, 180). The opportunities provide by school jobs benefited the entire Patri family. Patri, his wife, two of his sisters, and other relatives all worked for the New York City School system.

In *Schoolmaster of the Great City* and other writings Patri described his decade of teaching in several New York City schools. He began at $1.20 a day as a substitute in a new school in the Bronx, but was soon appointed a regular teacher (Patri, 1955). After experiencing student boredom and discipline problems, Patri discovered that his father's stories from Italy captured the interest of students and motivated them to study. Patri's one course in Pedagogics at CCNY had provided meager preparation for his work, so after three years of teaching, he began classes at Teachers College, Columbia University, where he completed his MA degree in 1904. In his General Methods course Patri read Dewey's "Ethical Principles Underlying Education," which helped move him from traditionalism to progressivism. Patri's most intense learning occurred as he wrote his thesis "Educational Forces Outside of the Public School, Considered from the Standpoint of School Administration." Patri's preface shows how "Americanized" he was. He hoped that the school might "become as it should be — the most potent factor for the uplifting of the race, the Americanizing of the foreigner, the perpetuation of our American traditions and ideals" (Patri, 1904, 2).

Patri gives stereotyped descriptions of various groups, starting with the Jews, with their strong attachment to education and learning. "The Italian is proud, liberal, frugal, emotional, revengeful, ambitious," but has become "careless of his religion. . . . The Chinaman . . . is so secluded, and his Eastern ways are so different from ours that it is as hard for him to be assimilated as it is for us to find grounds upon which to Americanize him. . . . Where the negro congregates, thence the white man flees. No matter how much we talk about negro rights and privileges, as long as inherent prejudices hold sway the negro will be compelled to live by himself. . . . He must be taught the art of work through the institutions of Free Labor, Free School, and the Christian

Religion. Through these he must learn the lessons of self-help, self-advancement, self-respect. Our public schools do but a small part of this work. Cannot the activities of the school and its co-operation with outside forces be so increased as to accomplish more for him?" (Patri does not capitalize "negro" here, but does so later in the thesis.)

"In our very poor East and West side districts . . . we find another very dangerous and ignorant element . . . the poor Irish. Here ignorance and poverty are the result of drink. . . . The schools in what are known as the Gas-house District, the Slaughterhouse, Hell's Kitchen, present more problems of school management in a day than other schools do in a month. . . ."

After this depressing summary, Patri falls back on noblesse oblige for help: "Of the better classes, it is scarcely necessary to speak. Together they must solve the problem which confronts the city. . . . In their hands lies the administration of the schools and we trust of the government. They should therefore be thoroughly acquainted with the great social problem before them, and go about its solution consistently and without faltering" (Patri, 1904, 7–16).

Patri continued to teach while studying at Teachers College, and after ten years in multi-ethnic classrooms, was appointed principal of PS #4 in the Bronx. In *Schoolmaster* he described the school population. "There were people who had come from various countries of Europe and they differed in their attitude toward ethics, society, religion, education, cleanliness. These differences isolated the various groups, the families, and the blocks" (Patri, 1917, 78). But Patri made successful efforts to connect parents with the school. He organized a Parents' Association, had a member of its executive committee appointed to the local school board, and saved the local park from the incursion of a proposed armory and firehouse (Patri, 1917, ch. 4).

From his own experience, Patri was familiar with the pattern in which schooling alienated children from their families and original language, and thus looked for ways to maintain children's respect for their parents. "Here were children and parents living their lives apart. These children were ashamed because their parents did not speak or look like Americans. How could I help the children in my school respond to the dreams of their fathers? How could I get the fathers to share in the work of building a school for their children?" (Patri, 1917, 81) He described his efforts to make teaching more humane and effective and to involve parents in the school. "I had learned that education was a matter of cooperation between parents and teachers. . . . To save the school and the home from becoming cloistered, self-centered, the culture of children would have to be a co-operative effort between the people and the teachers" (Patri, 1917, 86).

Patri and his faculty looked for ways to bring family culture into the schools. In assemblies they began with readings from English and American poets, but soon went on to "folk tales, not scattered, but in terms of people, Russian, Irish, German, Norwegian, and Indian. . . . These were dramatized and the songs and dances introduced. We gave the children a sympathetic appreciation of people and taught them to take home these folk stories, tell them to their parents and get the parents to tell their own folk tales. So would the children be kept close to their parents, giving and receiving values that were human" (Patri, 1917, 166).

On issues of inclusion and diversity, the most significant part of *Schoolmaster* comes at the end when Patri writes: "I have been a part of many movements to Americanize the foreigner, but I see that the child is the only one who can carry the message of democracy if it can be carried at all. . . . Americanize the foreigner, nay, through the child let us fulfill our destiny and Americanize America" (Patri, 1917, 218-19). The children then, were to link immigrant parents with the school, and they could do so only by learning to respect the values and culture of both home and school. Patri had come a long way from the stereotyped statements in his 1904 thesis. His work as a principal had given him a broader view of the place of the school in the community, and a greater respect for the varied communities from which his students came.

Dewey's writings, encountered at Teachers College, had also helped Patri extend his vision of democracy. His studies with Dewey during the summer of 1909 had deepened his understanding of Dewey's views on democracy and education. It is significant that one of the most positive reviews of *Schoolmaster* was written by Randolph Bourne, a leading interpreter of Dewey's ideas. In an August 1917 review Bourne wrote that Patri "knows from his own experience the life that is behind the children who throng the city schools. There was no one better fitted than he to know how much the congested city home needed the ministrations of the school, and how effectively the school could spread out its functions until it touches and stimulates the home" (Bourne, 1917).

Bourne's "Trans-National America" had been published in *The Atlantic* the previous year. One of the earliest critiques of the "melting pot" approach to Americanization, it supported policies of respect and inclusion for the various groups that made up the country. Bourne wrote: "We cannot Americanize America worthily by sentimentalizing and moralizing history. When the best schools are expressly renouncing the questionable duty of teaching patriotism by means of history, it is not the time to force shibboleth upon the immigrant. . . . The inflections of other voices have been drowned. They must be heard" (Bourne, 1964, 264). Patri, an avid reader, may well have read Bourne's essay, and found in "Americanize America" words that helped him express his own views.

A personal example of Patri's own participation in transnational America was his marriage in 1910 to Dorothy Caterson, from an Irish Protestant background. There are different perspectives among Patri's surviving relatives on his marrying out of the faith. One niece says that there was grumbling among his sisters about his marriage and rare attendance at church, but other relatives feel that it was a minor issue. In fact, only the oldest of Patri's three sisters married an Italian Catholic. The next married a Catholic from a French-German background, and the youngest an Irish Catholic. Decades later, long after her first husband died, this sister married a Jewish educator who worked closely with Patri (Wallace, 1997a).

These intermarriages may be seen as examples of flexibility in religious and ethnic matters accompanied by occupational integration. We are familiar with the idea of schools acculturating students; in this and similar families we may see also how schools continued the acculturation process for ethnic adults who worked in them. Education was very much a family affair for the Patris. Angelo and his wife were lifelong educators. Josephine, the second sister, taught special education, and Carmine, her husband, was a truant officer. The youngest sister, Jane, was a school secretary for decades and eventually married Abraham Kroll, a member of the New York Board of Examiners. These jobs provided family members with financial resources, middle-class status, and connections with one another and with the larger world. The Patris were able to maintain desired essentials of their heritage while becoming successful in the American economy and society (Wallace, 1997a).

In 1913 Patri transferred to a new intermediate school, PS 45, where he served as principal from 1913 to 1944. This was an unusually long tenure for a principal, but Patri survived through changes in superintendents, educational fads and panaceas, war, depression, and yet another war. Unfortunately, he never wrote a book about his much longer and more influential career in this school. For insight into his work there we must turn to other sources, including an unpublished memoir he wrote ten years after retiring.

Patri wrote in this memoir that PS 45 was in "the kind of neighborhood I knew as a boy. . . . The new school was in an Italian colony, a sparsely settled corner of the Bronx. . . . To the south [was] a neighborhood of second and third generations of Americans. These two groups were as far apart in language, customs and manners as if they were living on opposite sides of the world. The Italian group [was] self-contained, aloof, and the American group . . . well content to leave it so (Patri, 1954, 19–28). The ethnic conflicts of the neighborhood inevitably entered the school. Patri wrote about one such encounter: "In the yard I came across a teacher escorting two loud, angry boys to the office. . . . One had a very bloody nose and the other a rapidly swelling black eye. 'What's the matter?' The boys eyed me. 'He hit me,' said the one with the bloody nose. ' Yeah — he called me a Kike so I hit him. I'll do it every time he calls me names.' ' He called me a Wop,' said the one with the black eye. 'Anyone who calls me a Wop gets a bloody nose.' " In response to such ethnic conflicts and to academic stress, Patri gradually persuaded the teachers to listen to their students, teach them more imaginatively, and help them deal with their group conflicts (Patri, 1954, 44–45).

Patri was very concerned about what he called "the non-bookish child," who could not adapt to the rigid curriculum. He wrote: "It was time, as John Dewey put it, that the active way of learning, the child's way of acquiring knowledge instead of the teacher's way of imparting information, became the basic principle, if the children were to grow in grace and power." Patri learned from Maria Montessori, who visited PS 45 in 1915: "Her emphasis was laid on sense training, on hand training, as a necessary background to understanding what the books said" (Patri, 1954, 52–60). Montessori talked with Patri "about the Gary system then being introduced in the public schools, praising the newly installed workshops and gardens that were part of the Gary Plan," and said, "You are preparing children to meet the realities of life" (Kramer, 1976, 213).

Patri had been heartened in 1913 by the election of John Purroy Mitchel, an anti-Tammany reformer, as Mayor (Patri, 1954, 63). Mitchel appointed a committee to find a better model for the New York Schools, and found it in William Wirt's "platoon schools" in Gary, Indiana. Patri's PS 45 was one of the schools selected to try out the plan; Patri went to Gary to see it in action, and returned ready to use the program in his own school. Wirt was hired to help implement the Gary plan in twelve New York schools, and Patri and his faculty struggled to put it into effect in PS 45 (Levine & Levine, 1977; Patri, 1954, 63). Working closely with Wirt, Patri acquired land where children worked in a garden and learned about soils and plants. A wood shop, pottery shop, and print shop were created, and craftsmen hired to teach in these areas. But students were not being narrowly prepared for specific careers; they cycled through all of the arts and crafts as well as through physical education and five periods of academic work. Patri wrote: "In the classrooms for academic studies the children were grouped into traditional grades, but in shops, studios, laboratories, gym, playground, the grade groups were ignored and children were together irrespective of grades or ages, irrespective of I.Q.'s. . . ." In spite of over-crowding and resistance by some administrators and teachers, the program worked remarkably well in providing meaningful education to a wide range of students (Patri, 1954, ch. 6).

Italian was introduced as an elective in the seventh and eighth grades, and students passed the Regents tests as well as those who had taken two years of high school Italian.

Nonetheless, rigid high schools made these students start over with first year Italian. Bureaucrats and others who didn't understand what the school was doing attacked the school. Protests against the Gary schools reached the point where Patri was called before a Bronx grand jury to answer questions about the school. Patri was heard politely, but just before the election the grand jury reported that the "work-study-play school idea was undeveloped and entirely un-adapted to the requirements of a city community" (Patri, 1954, ch. 7). In 1917 reform mayor Mitchel was voted out and Tammany mayor John Hylan elected; progressive superinten-dent William Maxwell was replaced by traditionalist William Ettinger. The fear of immigrant parents that their children could not prepare for professions undermined the Gary plan in the New York City schools system (Ravitch, 1988, ch. 20). However, without using the Gary label, Patri and his faculty managed to preserve successful parts of the system.

Journalist Ida Tarbell, who visited PS 45 in 1922 and wrote a long, positive article for *Collier's*, confirmed the per-sistence of sound elements of the Gary plan. She described the vibrant life of the school in classrooms and shops, but was most impressed by the connections with the community and parents: "One of the realest things School No. 45 is able to do is occasionally to make children see the value of their parents. Many of these foreign-born fathers and mothers, handicapped by inability to speak English, to 'get on,' come to be half despised by their own children. School No. 45 knows them. It works itself patiently into the homes, finds the pe-culiar talent, skill, knowledge in father or mother, and con-trives to use it" (Tarbell, 1922).

Patri's school of 4000 students, from kindergarten through ninth grade, was selected in 1923 to become a junior high school and was reduced to 3000 students. Patri ac-cepted the change as it enabled him to maintain much of the program of the platoon school. A new district superintendent imposed a rigid classifying system based on IQ scores that sorted students into college-bound, commercial, and vocational programs. Patri wrote: "This thing that we were entrusted and ordered to do ignored both the nature of the child and the needs of society. It burdened the children with a program that was an affront to them and it embarrassed society by training its children to fit into a groove which might be non-existent by the time the child was ready to follow it. . . . Was this class stratification and narrow education anything but a lopsided training for lopsided living?" (Patri, 1954, 172–77).

Patri satisfied the bureaucrats by submitting reports showing that students had been "classified as ordered — industrial, general, commercial, rapid, normal, slow." But reports did not reflect the complete reality — that Patri maintained the Gary program and gave children important choices: "Each child selected or was assigned an art or a science or a craft, and in this activity, he worked with other children irrespective of whether they were in grades seven, eight, or nine, and irrespective of whether they had been classified in the monthly report as commercial, general, industrial, rapid, normal, slow." Children continued activities they liked or shifted to new ones they wanted to try out (Patri, 1954, 181–83).

While leading his school, Patri continued to write on Americanization, as he had in *Schoolmaster*. Stimulated perhaps by the patriotic fervor of World War I, he wrote a series of essays titled "Americanisms" (Patri, 1919). In 1925 the essays were gathered into a text, *The Spirit of America*, that presented an optimistic impression of this country. Patri began with recollections of his Italian village birthplace, of the steamer crossing to America, of playing in the streets, and of eventually attending "an American school. That was where my life in the new country began." Here he heard the stories of American heroes. "And it happened to me, as it did to thousands of foreign-born children, that after many years, I was graduated from an American school and then from an American college. I became a teacher, an American teacher in an American Public School. I belonged" (Patri, 1925, 1–2).

Patri wrote: "Every people under the sun is represented here in America. How then can America be a nation?" Immigrant groups maintained their old-world habits, but "America is too big to be measured by food or dress or custom. America is an idea, a way of living." And the idea "lies at the heart of what we call America, "Our country," — the right to be different while being useful and happy: free as common brotherhood allows one to be free" (Patri, 1925, 12). Patri's understanding of democracy kept him from being a single-minded advocate of superficial unity: "The man who leads the minority is necessary in this government of ours. He calls attention to the things that are not as they should be. He keeps us alive and growing." Majorities eventually learn that minorities "are bearing the heart of America with them" (Patri, 1925, 90). Patri recognized that intolerance was based on fear, but optimistically claimed: "We have begun to learn the lesson of tolerance. . . . We are learning, as the years go by, that intolerance is but another way of saying: 'We're afraid.' " And, in a statement much like that in Franklin Roosevelt's inaugural speech eight years later, Patri wrote: "What have we to fear? Nothing but our own fears" (Patri, 1925, 93).

While making his school more inclusive ethnically and educationally, Patri never neglected his particular connections with the Italian-American community. Indeed, given the population of PS 45, it would have been hard to do so. In 1933 half of the pupils had parents born in Italy, but over four-fifths of the pupils had been born in the United States. By that date, with the Depression and restrictive laws limiting immigration, the school was very much one for second-generation immigrants, but the faculty worked to maintain ethnic connections, and forty percent of the students studied Italian.

Novelist Dorothy Canfield Fisher visited PS 45 in 1940 and wrote about Patri and his work. She was critical of schools which favored only bookish students: "Our machine world is withering for lack of what children with gifts not now in fashion could give us if we gave them a chance. We go on scorning children who cannot make a good showing in the kind of examinations now in favor, but who have gifts of personality which would regenerate our society if they could be developed." To develop those gifts, Patri and his colleagues had created a school with many shops " full of tools for weaving, printing, carving, gardening, painting, sewing, leatherwork — all the arts of the human hand." In a society that valued speed, Fisher was impressed by the comfortable pace of Patri's school: "The opportunity for continued effort, with no feeling of haste to finish a project and begin another, is one of the finest elements in the life of P. S. 45. For another dangerous mistake American education makes is to subject children to hurry, to judge by their ability to live and produce at speed. . . ." Fisher emphasized Patri's sensitive response to one of the most fundamental differences among students — the pace at which they work. By encouraging students to take their time he helped many of them to achieve truly creative results (Fisher, 1940).

Fisher's article demonstrated that, four years before his retirement, Patri continued to lead a school that responded to the diverse talents of his students. The essentials of the platoon school, with its variety of shops and study areas, were still alive in PS 45. Further testimony to this fact was provided by a former student who attended Patri's school during World War II. Anthony Vilhotti told the story of disruptive, aggressive student Julius Garfinkel, who was sent to Patri's office when teachers could no longer manage him. Patri talked with Julius, listened to him, discovered in him, in spite of a nervous stutter, a talent for acting, and steered him to drama classes. Julius succeeded, lost his stutter, completed school, and became the popular film actor John Garfield.

Vilhotti's own experience with Patri came about because, as he said, "a polio condition in early childhood had left me with a limp in my left leg and an overly sensitive reaction to the jibes of my classmates. I was constantly in fights when in school or not in school at all." When sent to Patri for threatening a teacher, Patri asked him: "Anthony, do you have any pain in your leg now?" They talked about his polio and what he could and could not do. They had further discussions, which inspired Vilhotti to settle down and use his talents. Patri helped Vilhotti to transcend his handicap and become a useful citizen. Vilhotti regretted that he never thanked Patri for his support, but took great satisfaction years later in working with the Teacher Corps in the Bronx school named after Patri (Vilhotti, 1976).

World War II gave Patri a renewed appreciation for American diversity. In radio addresses he said: "Since the war started we have begun looking at things and people, especially people, with sharpened understanding and heightened emotion. Our crowded neighborhood of folk from many lands of every race and creed and color seems more human and friendly than ever before. . . . We have discovered a common need of understanding and help while in practice we prove to be as different as different can be. Each has his oddity which the rest of us treasures, knowing that if he surrenders it and takes on colorless unanimity we shall lose something rare in the quality of our living and so will he. . . . We are all for good government and each has his ideal and supports it loudly. We present a veritable rainbow of shaded opinion but the returns on Election Day prove that we voted for what we believed to be the greatest good for the greatest number.

The next evening the arguments begin all over again, as loud as ever."

Patri concludes: "Strangely enough there are still people in the world asking, 'what are you fighting for?' Make no mistake. We know. We are fighting for this way of life, for the right to differ, for the right to live according to our feeling and our good conscience. . . . We want to rear our children in the vision of a world where everyone counts his full value whoever he is, wherever he goes, whatever he does for a livelihood. We want to create a world that makes room and actually enjoys men's delightful differences" (Patri, 1942). Having made his contribution to such a world, in 1944, after 47 years in the New York City schools, Patri retired.

I now turn to selected scholars for insights that will help us interpret Patri's experiences and those of millions of immigrants like him. The word "selected" must be emphasized here. As I "inquired outward" from Patri's experience, I followed from author to author, citing those whose writings connected most clearly with Patri, and ignoring most of the vast literature on inclusion, diversity, and multi-culturalism. Other writers have surveyed that material thoroughly; I choose to focus on Patri himself and on a few writers who add meaning to his experience and that of other immigrants.

The other leading Italian American educator during this period was Leonard Covello. A decade younger than Patri, he was from 1924–37 principal of Benjamin Franklin High School in Manhattan. Both Patri and Covello had enough initiative and energy to carry on activities broader than running their own schools. Patri became a writer and speaker on parenting; Covello became an activist and scholar, and wrote an influential thesis on Italian-American education, later published as *The Social Background of the Italo-American School Child.* Perhaps because of similar background, they reached parallel conclusions on assimilation. Covello identified various approaches to assimilation, contrasting the "melting pot" with the "cultural pluralism" advocated by writer Horace Kallen. He firmly rejected the melting pot but also disagreed with what he saw as Kallen's separatism, saying that pluralism should lead "toward an integration of cultural patterns created from valuable elements in all foreign cultures. This should lead to a harmonious American culture which would be developed from an *interaction* among cultural groups, involving changes in these groups in language, in the creative arts, in social patterns, and in political ideology. . . ." Covello concluded that "an understanding of the reciprocal character of the process of assimilation is a basic principle in social planning for this process." He acknowledged that a variety of institutions were involved in assimilation, and, like Bourne, Patri, and Dewey, put his own emphasis on the role of the public school (Covello, 1967, 411–12).

Several historians can also help put Patri's cosmopolitan pluralism in perspective. In 1989 Paula Fass published *Outside In: Minorities and the Transformation of American Education*, which gives a persuasive interpretation of the educational experiences of European immigrants and of progressive responses to the diversity issues which these experiences presented. "Weaned on values derived from cohesive, organically integrated communities, the progressives discovered a cacophony of different cultural modes, family economies, attitudes, and traditions. All the progressives found this disturbing, but some also found vitality and hope in this diversity, and their curiosity was titillated about how a new and better society could grow from the energy of new forces and new contributions" (Fass, 1989, 267).

Fass notes Patri's response to diversity, quoting from *Schoolmaster*: "The school must open its doors. It must reach out to spread itself, and come into direct contact with all its people. Each day the power of the school must be felt in some corner of the school district. It must work so that everybody sees its work and daily appraises that work." Fass adds: This idea of a community school required more than an adaptation to the perceived needs of its immigrant constituents. It required that the school respect the culture of the students and act in such a way as to produce pride in self, family and past." But Fass is not uncritical, adding: "Nevertheless, this open-door school policy was ambiguous. Like the social settlements upon which it was modeled, it was at once an expression of democratic aspiration and an intrusion upon the community it was meant to serve" (Fass, 1989, 57–58). Patri, actively involved in the community, was willing to gently intrude into the lives of families in order to promote the "democratic aspirations" which were central to his work

Years earlier, in 1967, David Tyack had noted Patri's willingness to run an activist, intrusive school. He wrote: "The community expected the school to be policeman as well as parent-surrogate. One principal, Angelo Patri, heard all sorts of complaints from people who thought the school should do something about children's misbehavior . . . Patri accepted the notion that the teacher was 'responsible for what the child does out of school.' How otherwise, he asked 'can the teacher ever know that her world counts in the life of the child?'" (Tyack, 1967, 113).

David Hollinger, in *Postethnic America*, presents a history and interpretation of American ethnic experience, as part of which he clarifies the distinction between Kallen's pluralism and Bourne's cosmopolitanism: "Both shared the basic idea that unites cultural pluralism with multiculturalism — that the nation should be home to a diversity of cultures, especially those carried by ethno-racial groups — but Bourne envisioned a dynamic interaction while Kallen stressed the autonomy of each group" (Hollinger, 1995, 11).

Hollinger continues: "Multiculturalism is rent by an increasingly acute but rarely acknowledged tension between cosmopolitan and pluralist programs for the defense of cultural diversity. Pluralism respects inherited boundaries and locates individuals within one or another of a series of ethno-racial groups to be protected and preserved. Cosmopolitanism is more wary of traditional enclosures and favors voluntary affiliations. Cosmopolitanism promotes multiple identities, emphasizes the dynamic and changing character of many groups, and is responsive to the potential for creating new cultural combinations" (Hollinger, 1995, 11, 3, 93). Hollinger brings Patri's intellectual mentor, Dewey, into the dialogue, noting that Dewey, while sharing Kallen's resistance to co-erced assimilation, "warned Kallen against the danger of en-dorsing 'segregation' and of promoting a program whereby traditional cultural differences would be too rigidly 'fastened upon people" (Hollinger, 1995, 93).

The term "postethnic" in Hollinger's title unfortunately may suggest that people leave their ethnicity behind as they move into new cultural settings. I prefer an adaptation of Bourne's term "trans-national." We live in a "trans-ethnic" America — one in which our social and political structure permits some degree of ethnic choice, many choose to cross ethnic boundaries, and intermarriage among racial and ethnic groups is increasingly common. Our continuing tragedy as a country is our failure to make these choices available to all people and to make them acceptable in all American communi-ties.

Patri was effective in meeting a major challenge of his time — helping the children of European immigrants maintain their language and heritage while becoming part of a multi-ethnic America. Nathan Glazer, lamenting America's particu-lar failure to provide equity to African-Americans, reminds us of the challenge facing us now: "The 'culture wars' reflect many things, but when it comes to the divisions of blacks and others, they reflect a hard reality that none of us wants, that all of us want to see disappear, but that none of us knows how to overcome. It is only a change in that larger re-ality that will reduce multiculturalism to a passing phase in the complex history of the making of an American nation from many strands" (Glazer, 1997, 160–61).

We may extend some definitions of multi-culturalism to encompass related perspectives and to incorporate Hollinger's emphasis on voluntary affiliations. There is room within America's broad versions of schooling for those who cheerfully experience being "melted down" into bland suburbanites; for pluralists who emphasize difference; for the separatism of such disparate groups as the Amish and the Afrocentrists; and for cosmopolitans who appreciate creative interaction among our subcultures. We need not force students into one version of multi-culturalism, but instead can help them participate in this ongoing dialogue. We cannot teach them one answer to our complex cultural questions, but can, as Gerald Graff proposes, "teach the conflicts" (Graff, 1992). We can invite students into this fascinating, essential discussion of what it means to be an individual, an American, a group, and a nation, and thus, in the words of Bourne and Patri, we may help "Americanize America."

It is important finally to recall that Patri's sense of inclusion went far beyond race and ethnicity. Being as inclusive as possible in those fundamental areas enabled Patri to focus on differences that were equally important to him and to colleagues, students, and families: differences in personality, talent, energy, abilities and disabilities, and even in the pace at which students worked. Patri was one in a long historical line of people who have learned to respond to diversity as inclusively as possible. This essential effort continues in new and more challenging ways as we currently see students dividing themselves into distinct groups, some of them dangerous to themselves and others. It is glaringly evident, in spite of Glazer's optimistic title, that we are neither all multiculturalists nor cosmopolitans now, and we are far indeed from dealing with one another with full sensitivity to our many differences. In this new millennium our schools and communities will need many more thoughtful, concerned, active citizens who are able to confront our challenges as vigorously and humanely as Patri faced the problems of his own time.

## Works Cited

Bourne, R. (1917, August 11). Review of *Schoolmaster of the Great City*, by Angelo Patri. *The Survey*, 38, 422–423.

Bourne, R. (1964). Trans-National America. In C. Resek (Ed.), *War and the Intellectuals: Collected Essays, 1915–1919* (107–123). New York: Harper and Row.

Covello, L. (1967). *The Social Background of the Italo-American School Child*. Leiden, Netherlands: E. J Brill.

Fass, P. S. (1989). *Outside in: Minorities and the Transformation of American Education*. New York: Oxford University Press.

Fisher, D. C. (1940). Angelo Patri's public school. *Reader's Digest*, 36(1940, June), 101–105.

Glazer, N. (1997). *We are all Multiculturalists Now*. Cambridge, MA: Harvard University Press.

Graff, G. (1992). *Beyond the Culture Wars: How Teaching the Conflicts Can Revitalize American Education*. New York: Norton.

Hollinger, D. A. (1995). *Postethnic America: Beyond Multiculturalism*. New York: Basic Books.

Kramer, R. (1976). *Maria Montessori: A Biography*. New York: Putnam's Sons.

Lassonde, S. (1998). Should I go, or should I stay? High school attainment and attitudes toward extended schooling in southern Italian immigrant families for New Haven, Connecticut, 1900–1940. *History of Education Quarterly* 38(1), 37–60.

Levine, A., & Levine, M. (1977). The social context of evaluative research: A case study. *Evaluation Quarterly* 1(4), 515–542.

Patri, A. (1904). *Educational Forces outside of the Public School, Considered from the Standpoint of School Administration*. Unpublished Masters Thesis, Special Collections, Milbank Memorial Library, Teachers College, Columbia University, New York.

Patri, A. (1917). *Schoolmaster of the Great City*. New York: Macmillan.

Patri, A. (1919, ). Americanisms. *Red Cross Magazine*, n.p.

Patri, A. (1925). *The Spirit of America*. New York: American Viewpoint Society.

Patri, A. (1942). *Alike and so Different* Patri papers, Library of Congress, Box 81, File 6.

Patri, A. (1943). *The Teacher Goes to War* (Unpublished, WWII) : Patri papers, Library of Congress, Box 81, File 3.

Patri, A. (1954). *Memoir*, untitled (344): Patri papers, Library of Congress.

Patri, A. (1955). *A Teacher Sees the Light*; undated draft of article . Patri papers, Library of Congress, Box 82.

Ravitch, D. (1988). *The Great School Wars: A History of the New York City Public Schools*. New York: Basic Books.

Tarbell, I. M. (1922, ). The Man Who Discovers Children. *Collier's: The National Weekly*, 70, 7-8,19.

Tyack, D. B., editor. (1967). *Turning Points in American Educational History*. Waltham, MA: Blaisdell.

Vilhotti, A. (1976). Dr. Angelo Patri: The man. In A. Weisberg (Ed.), *The Making of the Angelo Patri School*, District 10 (9-13). New York: Fordham University Teacher Corps.

Wallace, J. M. (1994). Angelo Patri: Immigrant educator, storyteller, and public school progressive. *Vitae Scholasticae*, 13(2), 43-63.

Wallace, J. M. (1997a). Interviews by James M. Wallace with Patri relatives, 1997-1999 : Tapes and transcripts in possession of James M. Wallace.

Wallace, J. M. (1997b). The last day, by Angelo Patri. *Vitae Scholasticae*, 16(2), 23-37.

Wallace, J. M. (1997c). Reconsideration: Angelo Patri, Schoolmaster of the Great City. *Educational Studies* 28 (Summer, 1997), 99-110.

# A Comparative Study of Hispanics
## and Italians in the Southwest

### Janet E. Worrall

Verso la fine del 19mo secolo e i primi del 20mo molti immigrati si sistemarono nelle zone agricole e nelle aree di nuova urbanizzazione nel Sud est degli Stati Uniti. Fra di essi furono gli Italiani e gli Ispanici ad esercitare la maggiore influenza nel settore. Gli Ispanici erano presenti nella zona già da tre generazioni, ma il loro numero crebbe in maniera drammatica a causa della dislocazione causata dall Rivoluzione Messicana e dalla crescente necessità di lavoratori nell'area. Un paragone fra queste diverse culture in termini di modelli d'insediamento, occupazione, discriminazione, come anche potenziali conflitti ed altri fattori ci offre un interpretazione che ci consente di esaminare le dinamiche del multiculturalismo nell'America del 20mo secolo.

In the late nineteenth and early twentieth centuries while thousands of European immigrants entered the United States through New York City, a growing number of Mexican immigrants began arriving in the southwest. As the Europeans moved west, interesting dynamics of cultural mixing developed between the different ethnic groups. A comparison of Mexicans with one of these European groups, Italians, makes for some instructive cross-cultural observations. To avoid confusion in terms, this paper will use Mexican and Hispanic interchangeably to refer to those people from Mexico of Spanish and Indian heritage. Only in discussing the period after 1960 will the term Chicano be used, although some authors use it interchangeably with Mexican-American. This author is of the persuasion that Chicano has the connotation of the more vocal and perhaps militant Mexican-Americans who emerged in the 1960s.[1] Comparisons will be made in the areas of push factors, settlement patterns, occupations, as-

[1] Manuel G. Gonzales, *Mexicanos A History of Mexicans in the United States* (Bloomington: Indiana University Press, 1999), 135-38.

similation, discrimination, women's roles, religion, and ethnic conflicts.

The southwestern part of the United States had been part of Mexico until the Mexican War and ensuing Treaty of Guadalupe Hidalgo in 1848. Given several options, most Mexicans living in the newly acquired area of the United States chose to remain. In the following decades unemployment, poverty, political unrest, and eventually revolutionary rumblings in northern Mexico caused thousands of Mexicans to cross over the border into the United States. By the 1880s and 1890s construction and maintenance on railroads provided jobs to newly arriving Mexicans. The Atchison, Topeka, and Santa Fe Railroad went as far as El Paso by 1881 and hired 32 Mexicans to extend the line west. By 1900 the Southern Pacific Railroad hired 4,500 Mexicans in California, taking the lead from the Irish as the largest ethnic group in railroad work in the West. As industrial jobs became more readily available in the East, fewer European immigrants were willing to travel West for railroad work, thus leaving much of the building and maintenance to Mexicans. From 1900 to 1940 they made up 60 to 90 percent of the railroad gangs on eighteen western railroads.[2]

As the 1910 Mexican Revolution approached, northern Mexico became a battleground among potential revolutionary leaders. Families fled the violence, especially in the state of Chihuahua where Pancho Villa raised his army, often taking men off the street to fill its ranks. Between 1910 and 1917, 300,000 Mexicans fled to the United States. Most went to Texas, Arizona, and California, with smaller numbers settling in New Mexico, Utah, Nevada, and southern Colorado.[3]

[2] Carey McWilliams, *North from Mexico The Spanish-Speaking People of the United States* (Philadelphia: J.B. Lippincott Company, 1949), 186.

[3] M. L. Miranda, *A History of Hispanics in Southern Nevada* (Reno: University of Nevada Press, 1997), 75–77; Richard L. Nostrand, *The Hispano Homeland* (Norman: University of Oklahoma Press, 1992), 6.

Because such large numbers entered, the estimate is nearly one million between 1900 and 1930, employers hired Mexicans en masse. They lived in company towns or in areas on the edge of towns referred to as *colonias*. This segregation retarded their assimilation and also led to charges of clannishness. In addition most of the newcomers had no intention of forfeiting their citizenship and fondly hoped to return to their homeland. This sojourner mentality further delayed assimilation.[4]

Mines — silver, copper, and coal — attracted thousands of Mexican immigrants. Carey McWilliams states that from 1900 to 1940, Mexicans contributed 60 percent of the labor in the mines in the Southwest.[5] Colorado Fuel and Iron Company (CFI) was a leading employer of immigrants for its southern Colorado coal lands. Here Mexicans worked alongside Italians in particular, and Slavic, Polish, Greek, and Irish with less frequency. Of all jobs available to Mexicans, those in the mines were the worst due to the dangerous working conditions, payment in scrip, poor housing, and abuse by the company store.[6]

Growth of the sugar beet industry coincided with the onset of Mexican immigration. Colorado was quickly becoming the number one sugar producing state in the Union, a position it gained by 1909. In the first decade of the twentieth century Great Western Sugar Company built over fifteen factories and hired a Spanish American recruiting agent to bring families to several northern Colorado towns including

---

[4] McWilliams, *North from Mexico*, 215–221; Mario T. Garcia, "La Frontera: The Border as Symbol and Reality in Mexican-American Thought," in *Between Two Worlds Mexican Immigrants in the United States*, ed. David G. Gutierrez (Wilmington: Scholarly Resources, 1996), 90–92.

[5] McWilliams, *North from Mexico*, 186.

[6] Sarah Deutsch, *No Separate Refuge: Culture, Class, and Gender on an Anglo-Hispanic Frontier in the American Southwest, 1880-1940* (New York: Oxford University Press, 1987), 88–89; Gonzalez, *Mexicanos*, 122.

Greeley, Loveland, Fort Collins, Longmont, and Brighton. The entire family engaged in the planting, hoeing, weeding, blocking, and topping of sugar beets. The demand for sugar of course increased once war broke out in 1914. Many Hispanics left their jobs on the railroads or in the mines for work in the beet-fields and worked during the off-season on the former two. At first Hispanics were out-numbered by Japanese and German-Russians, but with the immigration legislation of the teens and 1920s, Hispanics became the majority in the beet-fields. So desperate were the sugar companies for labor that they won suspension of the contract-labor law between 1918–1920. By 1927, 30,000 of the 58,000 sugar-beet workers were Mexicans.[7]

While literature on the experience of Italian immigrants in the West is not nearly as abundant as that for Hispanics, one can still make comparisons from the available sources. Economic factors accounted for the emigration of most Italians — population increase, primitive agricultural conditions, outbreaks of diseases, and a general desire to provide a better life for their children. Italians populating western states came from northern as well as southern Italy. Many had origins in the Tyrol, Piedmonte, and Lombardia, as well as Abruzzi, Basilicata, Calabria, and Sicilia. No single pattern existed; some came as "Birds of Passage" with a sojourners mentality, but after several trans-Atlantic journeys decided that their long term options were better in the United States. Others hop-scotched across the United States working a few years in eastern industrial areas, then trying several western mining sites before permanently settling in the West, often near *paesani*. Letters from relatives and the

---

[7] McWilliams, *North from Mexico*, 181; United States Immigration Commission, *Reports*, Vol. XXIV, (41 vols., Washington, 1911): 533–548.

resulting chain migration further explains the movement of Italians westward.[8]

Italians, as did Hispanics, found employment building and maintaining the railroads of the West. Indeed Italians probably gained prominence in the industry a decade or two before the Hispanics came in sizeable numbers.[9] In some cases railroads in the East sent Italians to work on extensions out West, only to have the workers decide to remain there rather than return to the crowded, less desirable immigrant communities of the East. Mining attracted numerous Italians — coal mines in Colorado, Utah, Wyoming, and Idaho; copper mines in Arizona, Montana, and Nevada. Fewer in number than Hispanics, Italians mixed more with other European immigrants and as a result were not as segregated in living accommodations as were the Hispanics. It was not uncommon for men and families to move from camp to camp. One husband and wife started in Cripple Creek, Colorado and subsequently moved to Deadwood, South Dakota, Denver, Colorado, and finally to the copper mines of Miami, Arizona.[10] Another example is that of Lorenzo and Anna D'Amato who left Petina, Italy around 1908 for Lebanon, Pennsylvania. There, Lorenzo worked in the steel mills before he and Anna joined friends from Petina in the mining town of Sunrise, Wyoming.

---

[8] Nicholas P. Ciotola, "From Agriculturalists to Entrepreneurs: Economic Success and Mobility Among Albuquerque's Italian Immigrants, 1900-1930," *New Mexico Historical Review* 74.1 (1999): 5; David Kathka, "The Italian Experience in Wyoming," in *Peopling the High Plains*, ed. Gordon Hendrickson (Cheyenne, Wyoming State Archives and Historical Dept., 1977) 68-69; Philip F. Notarianni, "Utah," in *The Italian American Experience An Encyclopedia*, eds. Salvatore J. LaGumina et al. (New York, Garland Publishing, Inc., 2000), 655-56.

[9] Robert F. Foerster, *The Italian Emigration of Our Times* (New York, 1919): 358-62.

[10] Phylis C. Martinelli, "Italian Immigrant Women in the Southwest," in *The Italian Immigrant Women in North America: Proceedings of the Tenth Annual Conference of the American Italian Historical Association*, eds. Betty Boyd Caroli, R. F. Harney, L. F. Tomasi (Toronto, 1978), 326.

After World War I, when the mining industry declined, the family moved to the outskirts of Denver to join friends from Petina who had preceded them. There they bought land, and along with other Italians in the Denver area, grew vegetables to serve the growing urban population. While Italians did not follow Hispanics in the sugar beet fields, many did make their living off the land as truck gardeners.[11]

Italians also displayed an entrepreneurial bent satisfying the needs of their ethnic community with grocery stores, saloons, barber shops, drugstores, and general merchandise stores. This was particularly true in the western cities of Denver, Albuquerque, Cheyenne, and Rock Springs, Wyoming. Throughout the West there is considerable evidence to suggest that Italians did better economically than their counterparts in the East.

The Italian mindset differed from that of Hispanics, which influenced the more rapid assimilation of Italians. While men outnumbered women immigrants from Italy, this was often only a temporary situation. Once men established themselves they sent for their wives and families, or returned to wed a childhood sweetheart before coming to America permanently. Once settled, the overwhelming desire was to learn English. While parents might continue to speak Italian, they wanted their children to become Americans. Italian newspapers also urged assimilation.[12] The sojourner

[11]. Interviews with Genevieve Fiore, April 29, July 23, 1995; letters from G. Fiore dated May 11 and July 26, 1995; Giovanni Perelli, *Colorado and the Italians in Colorado* (Denver, n.p., 1922); *Reports*, Vol. XXIV, pp. 549–554.

[12] For details on where Italians settled throughout the West, see Andrew F. Rolle, *Westward the Immigrants Italian Adventurers and Colonists in an Expanding America*, (University Press of Colorado, 1999). For Italians in western cities see, David Kathka; Judith L. DeMark, "Occupational Mobility and Persistence within Albuquerque Ethnic Groups, 1880–1910: A Statistical Analysis," *New Mexico Historical Review*, 68 (4): 389–398; Janet E. Worrall, "Work and Community: Italians in Denver, Colorado 1900–1940," *Proceedings* Xth International Oral History Conference, (Rio de Janeiro, June, 1998) I:

mentality of the Hispanic had no parallel in Italian homes — but then an ocean separated them from their homeland rather than a few hundred miles.

The mindset on the part of the receiving society hampered the efforts of Hispanics to improve their economic situation and promote their assimilation. Until the 1920s many Hispanics lived comfortably in communal villages or on small acreages in rural New Mexico. But then a culmination of factors: the expanding cattle industry, railroad land grants, homesteaders, and development of national forests pushed them off the land. Some left for the New Mexican towns of Grants and Albuquerque, and those who chose not to, entered the wage labor market, primarily the beet-fields of Colorado. Hispanics were trapped in a no-win situation surrounded by blatant racial prejudice from the dominant Anglo culture. Recruiters for the sugar beet companies told Hispanics that they would, "rake in the money," and have a garden plot, decent housing, and a clean water supply. While this was true for a few, far more lived in one or two room shacks often supporting a family of ten or twelve. The prevailing opinion of landowners was that whatever they gave the Hispanic was better than conditions he had left and he should be grateful. Such comments as, "the peon has always lived like a pig and he will continue to do so," were not uncommon.[13] Colonias grew up around towns in northern Colorado. The Ku Klux Klan marked the edges of these areas with burning crosses. Shops displayed signs in their windows, "No Mexican Trade Wanted" or "White Trade Only."[14]

---

15-25; Ciotola, "From Agriculturalists to Entrepreneurs." For a comparative study in one city, see Karin Sporleder Chapman, "An Overview of Gender and Ethnicity in Pueblo, Colorado; 1900-1950" (M.A. thesis, University of Northern Colorado, 1996).

[13] *Il Grido del Popolo*, Denver, Colorado, Oct. 2, 1907.

[14] Deutsch, *No Separate Refuge*, 128-134.

Several factors contributed to the discrimination suffered by Hispanics: low job status, language, skin color, and the relatively large number in a concentrated area. The darker skin of Hispanics made them readily identifiable; racial prejudice of westerners had been documented back in the mid-nineteenth century.[15] Interestingly German Russians also worked in the beet fields and faced similar discriminatory acts of burning crosses, exclusion from shops, and taunting for their unusual dress. They had the added stigma of speaking German when the country was in arms against the hated "Hun." Yet within two generations the German Russians became owners of the land and by the next generation had assimilated completely. Their lighter skin color was a factor, plus their numbers declined rapidly in the 1920s as noted above while the number of Hispanics increased dramatically as they continued to be a visible, identifiable group.

Italians settling in the southwest at the same time faced racial prejudice, but not on the same scale as did Hispanics. While Italians found jobs on the railroads and in mines, as noted above they were not recruited for the beet fields. This was due to several reasons. Unlike the Hispanics and German Russians, there was no single entry point where large numbers could be recruited (German Russians usually came through Omaha where recruiters greeted them). Italian migration to the West was diffuse and more of a chain migration with contacts already made before their arrival, especially after 1910. This is evident from the lack of Italian boardinghouses in cities. Instead, newly-arriving Italians stayed with relatives in established "Little Italies." Through these contacts they often found jobs on an individual basis rather than depending on recruiters. And their relatively lower numbers simply did not make them attractive to re-

---

[15] Ibid., 134. See Eugene H. Berwanger, *The West and Reconstruction* (Urbana: University of Illinois Press, 1981) for documentation of racism in the West.

cruiters. Many of them worked in unskilled labor in the lowest status occupations, but again because their numbers were lower, they did not constitute a visible minority.

But Italians still suffered their share of ethnic slights. The Ku Klux Klan targeted them for their Catholicism. Their somewhat darker complexion brought comment and on occasion kept them out of dance halls and other public places. Discrimination was more one of attitude by Anglos who made disparaging remarks regarding the "lower intelligence" and "dirty" habits of Italians. In places like Albuquerque, Hispanics and Native Americans bore the brunt of racism, sparing the Italians.[16] In California, Chinese, Japanese, Hispanics, and Native Americans outnumbered Italians and thus attracted the racism of nativists. Indeed Italians sometimes harassed Chinese.[17]

Early in the twentieth century Hispanic and Italian women in towns and cities had similar experiences. The majority stayed at home to raise children and contribute to the family's livelihood in a number of ways. They raised vegetables for summer consumption and canning in the fall, took in laundry, processed butchered livestock, sewed the family clothing, and on occasion did seasonal labor. Relatives living nearby gave support, and the village church provided a means for socialization. Life was often hard, but women had an important role and a degree of respect in the community. If they earned small change by taking in laundry or sewing, it was theirs to manage as they wished.

The Hispanic women whose families went north to work in the beet fields discovered that the above pattern would not continue. In most cases garden plots did not exist, and if they did, women did not have the time to raise vegetables

16 Citola, "From Agriculturalists to Entrepreneurs," 19.

17 Micaela di Leonardo, *The Varieties of Ethnic Experience Kinship, Class, and Gender Among California Italian-Amerians* (Ithaca: Cornell University Press, 1984), 56.

when they were working in the beet fields. The communal sharing of produce and visiting while crocheting and knitting disappeared, and with it the woman's sense of belonging to a community. Women had no opportunity to earn extra money on their own and lost all control of the income paid directly to their husbands. Even the church ceased to be much of a comfort. The Catholic churches in the north did not serve the same function as elsewhere. Often they were too distant for regular attendance and did not have the same social functions as village churches. Being in rural areas denied the second generation the opportunity to get work other than in the beet fields. When families wanted an education for their children, the attitude of Anglos in the area was less than encouraging. Referring to Mexicans, one former school board member remarked, "They're needed in the fields and the school don't do them any good anyway." A sugar company employee justified the attitude with, "If every child has a high school education, who will labor?"[18] Some girls escaped by finding domestic service, but once again faced ethnic barbs as one housewife told a Hispanic worker, "People of your nationality are just terrible; I can't stand them, they're so crude, lazy, and so uncultured." Hispanic women often lost out to the more desirable domestic servants of Norwegian, Swedish, and Danish heritage. On the rare occasion when an Hispanic woman desired to become a teacher, a classmate responded with, "If I were you, I wouldn't waste my time here for they'll never permit girls of your race to teach in our American schools."[19]

The experience of Italian women, not having to leave their ethnic communities, was entirely different. Women found satisfaction in their lives at home and encouraged their daughters to get the education they had been denied.

[18] Deutsch, 141.
[19] Ibid., 147.

Much of the difference came from being in an urban as opposed to rural area. Italian daughters found jobs in small factories producing boxes, trunks, soap, clothing, biscuits, candy, and pasta. A few went on to college to become teachers. Vincenza D'Amato obtained her teaching certificate from the Colorado State Teacher's College in Greeley, Colorado and immediately found a job in the area where she was raised. Her mother received her share of negative comments regarding her daughter's advanced education, but probably in equal amounts for being a woman as well as an Italian.

A study of Black, Chicano (here referred to as Hispanic), and Anglo women in Atlanta, New Orleans, and San Antonio in the 1930s gives another perspective on the issue of women. For purposes of this paper, only women in San Antonio will be considered. There, the majority of Hispanic women listed as employed by the 1930 census worked in the pecan shelling industry, primarily because of its availability in non-harvest periods. Otherwise the women were apparently involved in migratory labor. Another avenue for Hispanic women in San Antonio was the garment industry. They contracted to do piecework of children's and infants' clothing at home. Contractors avoided federal regulations of the 1937 Fair Labor Standards Act by selling the materials directly to the workers and then buying back the finished product. Hispanic women did engage in domestic work in San Antonio although it was viewed as more appropriate for blacks. What is particularly interesting about this study is that Anglo leaders in the city viewed the "Mexican problem" as the city's major issue and Mexicans were perceived as the lowest class. The Depression exacerbated the problems of large Mexican families. During the decade the number of female headed households increased as husbands abandoned their families or died prematurely. Mexicans had a higher disease rate, poorer living conditions, and lower incomes than blacks. Further studies are needed to determine how typical this was of Hispanics in other urban areas in the 1930s.[20]

The Depression brought hardship to both Hispanics and Italians. At first beet-workers returned to their villages in northern New Mexico to seek refuge with family and relatives. But due to the severe economic distress and lack of jobs, the villages were unequal to their task. Family networks helped when possible, but ultimately Hispanics left for the cities hoping to find work or become eligible for relief. In Denver the number of Hispanics tripled as they joined other unemployed beet-workers. Between 1930 and 1935 acreage in beets dropped from 242,000 acres to 140,000; four-fifths of the beet-growers in the Arkansas Valley went bankrupt. Thousands of Mexicans and their children, born in the United States, were "repatriated" to Mexico. Colorado's Governor Johnson tried to seal the state's border with New Mexico. These callous actions were discriminatory as well as illegal. As relief agencies, state and local, ran out of funds, the unemployed looked for new strategies for survival that led to organizational efforts in the 1930s.[21]

Italians in the southwest had established themselves in towns and cities or had already purchased tracts of land when the Depression struck. They were spared the blatant hostility directed toward Hispanics. But Italians still had to adopt different strategies to survive. For example, in order to save their home in Denver's "Little Italy," the Leprino family rented it and moved to a much smaller house which had neither electricity nor indoor plumbing. In the late 1930s they could afford to return to their original home. Italian railroad workers and street cleaners were cut back to two days of work a week The garden plots that most Italians had

[20] Julia Kirk Blackwelder, "Women in the Work Force Atlanta, New Orleans, and San Antonio, 1930 to 1940," *Journal of Urban History* 4.3 (1978): 345–56.

[21] Deutsch, *No Separate Refuge*, see Chapter 7.

in their front and backyards offered the daily food supply, and grocery stores let patrons in "Little Italy" purchase staples on credit. The local coal merchant gave fuel to residents asking only that they pay when they could. The Italian community had an established support system that saw them through difficult times. In addition while there had been a generational numerical increase, virtually no new immigrants had arrived after the middle of the 1920s. In short, most Italians had part-time work and the support of a community to see them through the Depression. Hispanics were not as fortunate.

After World War II conditions changed almost overnight for Mexican workers. Only a few years earlier, cursed for their presence on relief rolls, they were now welcomed for their strong backs. With the outbreak of World War II, a formalized pattern of migrant workers began in 1942 with the *bracero* program. This perpetuated an earlier practice of male laborers working in agriculture, sending part of their salary back home, and eventually returning to their families in Mexico. With the constant demand for workers during the war, many Mexicans ignored the formality of the *bracero* program and came across the border illegally. Numbers swelled during the 1950s and following decades. Both Italians and Hispanics were entering a new phase.

After the war, many of the "Little Italies" began to disintegrate. Second and third generations married and left for the suburbs. Now thoroughly Americanized they were indistinguishable from others of European background. They maintained cultural organizations and families gathered for holidays, anniversaries, and birthdays. Few Italians felt compelled to find mates of their ethnicity. They might return to their church for the annual saint's day or to have their children baptized, but that was often the only tie to the "Little Italy" of their parents and grandparents.

After World War II the number of Mexicans entering the U.S. illegally continued to grow, especially single males. They worked in the lowest status jobs, lived clandestinely in cheap, over-crowded housing, and sent as much of their salary home as possible. Some brought their families to the States and over the years they became part of the immigrant community. This constant influx of first generation Mexicans gave rise to bi-lingual programs. Some feared that such heavy concentration of Hispanics in southwestern cities would result in tribalism. In 1960 87 percent of the Mexican population in the United States lived in the Southwest.

A pattern of segregated ethnic enclaves developed in Denver, Los Angeles, Albuquerque, Fresno, and other cities. Most unsettling was the fact that Hispanics ranked near the bottom when looking at the three main indicators of socio-economic status: education, occupation, and income.[22] Equally troubling to some was the fact that their number continued to increase as a result of the family preference system of the 1965 Immigration Act. In the 1970s 60,000 Mexicans entered the U.S. legally every year; one can only guess at the number that entered illegally. But the increasing number, caused largely by the deteriorating economic conditions in Mexico, is a separate issue and not one to linger over in this paper. Suffice it to say that the growing number added to their visibility and lessened their ability to assimilate.

What is of interest is noting what happened when the two cultures — Italian and Mexican — crossed paths. Denver, Colorado offers one example of this. As Denver's Italians moved to the suburbs, the growing Hispanic population began to move into the now available housing. Our Lady of Guadalupe Church, located on the edge of "Little Italy" at 36th Avenue and Kalamath Street, had served the growing Spanish-speaking community since 1936. The Junior High School and

---

[22] Gonzalez, *Mexicanos*, 192–94.

subsequently Middle School, Bryant-Webster, had brought the Italian and Hispanic children together for decades as did North High School. Probably due more to the crusading of Chicano activist Corky Gonzalez, than animosity between ethnics, a nasty incident provoked conflict between the two groups over control of the popular Columbus Park in "Little Italy" in 1969. The park, long the center of recreational activities for Italians, became a sore point between the two groups with Chicanos replacing the "Columbus Park" sign with a sign reading "La Raza." As reported in Gonzalez's newspaper, *El Gallo*, Chicanos became angry at "gringos who sat in the sun all day trying to get brown . . ." so, "200 youths surprised 9 gringos who were lying around, kicked their ass, and told them to get out of our community."[23]

The park continued to be a sore point between the two communities. Italians argued that they had raised $7500 in 1931 to improve the park — ironically they changed the name from Navaho to Columbus at that time. They had fond memories of their park in the 1930s and 1940s — it was a central meeting place, friends watched softball games together; one woman remembered it as the place where she first saw her future husband. But by 1980 the ethnic makeup of the area had changed to 60 percent Hispanic and 6 percent Italian, from 21 percent Hispanic and 12 percent Italian in 1960.[24] In 1988, in an effort to resolve the park issue, the Denver City Council debated a new name, but in a narrow vote upheld the Italian favored "Columbus Park." So hot were tempers after the debate, that Council members left the city hall under police escort.

Today the park stands overgrown with weeds, unkempt, and uninviting. Italians remain bitter over the usurping of

---

[23] Stephen J. Leonard and Thomas J. Noel, *Denver Mining Camp to Metropolis* (Denver: University Press of Colorado, 1990),396.
[24] *The Rocky Mountain News*, May 1, 1988.

their park by Chicanos who put up a "La Raza" sign. Equally upsetting to Italians was their forfeiture of the annual Columbus Day Parade. Objections by Native Americans and Chicanos plus the threat of violence in 1991, should the parade occur, led to its cancellation.[25] While these few incidents have caused Italians to harbor some bitterness, overall the two groups have lived peacefully side by side in the last several decades, at least in Denver. In talking with Italians still in the area, they are quick to say that you could not ask for better neighbors.

This brief overview of the Hispanic and Italian cultures indicates that they had similar experiences in several areas. Their decision to depart from their homeland was mainly economic, and once in the West they found employment in mining and railroad construction — the available jobs. Both groups suffered discriminatory treatment, but for Hispanics it was more threatening to their livelihood. (In this paper, I chose not to introduce the wartime discrimination of Italians, a topic under present congressional discussion and with its own literature.) The critical factor which ended parallel experiences for the two cultures came as Italian immigration tapered off due to the immigration legislation of the 1920s, while Mexicans continued to come in substantial numbers — legally and illegally — with a sojourners mentality. Often males came alone and worked ten months in the United States sending money home to support the family and returning for the Christmas holidays and perhaps on one other occasion. Conflicts with other ethnics arose as Mexicans moved into declining ethnic communities challenging the traditions and cultural symbols of the former dominant ethnic group. This study does not presume to be a generalization for all cities where the two cultures met in the West. Rather, it is meant to raise several points of comparison — further

25 *The Denver Post*, October 9, 1993.

studies of individual cities are necessary to determine how each has responded to the challenge of the interaction of multiple cultures. This is not only relevant for Hispanics and Italians, but given the increasing number and diversity of immigrants in the last several decades, may well be an increasingly common theme for future immigration studies.

# Italian Workers at Theodore Roosevelt Dam: An Intermediate Ethnic Group in a Diverse Work Force

Phylis Cancilla Martinelli
St. Mary's College

Questa ricerca descrive il ruolo degli immigrati italiani nel costruire un grande progetto ingegneristico, la Diga Roosevelt, nell'arido Sudest. Numerosi lavoratori italiani raggiunsero assieme ad altri questa zona remota e la loro visibilità fu tale da far attribuire ad essi la paternità della realizzazione dell'opera, cosa peraltro non vera. Talunti di essi erano lavoratori specializzati, ma la maggioranza erano lavoratori assunti per compiere lavori pesanti assieme ad altri gruppi etnici. Essi furono reclutati nelle città dell'Est e nelle vicine zone minerarie dell'Arizona. Essi pero' non arrivarono direttamente dall'Italia e questo è un altro importante errore compiuto finora nel raccontare la loro storia. In realtà la loro posizione nella forza lavoro utilizzata per quell'opera fu quella di un gruppo intermedio situato al di sotto dei lavoratori anglosassoni o di altre etnie Nordeuropee e al di sopra dei lavoratori neri americani e messicani. Tale loro status fu tipico per gli Italiani in Arizona.

In 1911 President Theodore Roosevelt, with great ceremony dedicated the dam named after him, Arizona's Roosevelt Dam. This colossal project is an important part of 20th-century western history, symbolizing the capstone structure in the Bureau of Reclamation's constellation of projects that brought the semiarid West into the domain of modern industrialism. It was also part of the technological changes that catapulted Arizona into an economically modern state and allowed the development of the Salt River Valley and the Phoenix megalopolis.[1]

Located in a remote and inhospitable region, labor problems assumed paramount importance in bringing this influen-

---

[1] Karen L. Smith, *The Magnificent Experiment, Building the Salt River Reclamation Project, 1890–1917* (Tucson: University of Arizona Press, 1986).

tial project to completion. Over time, two ethnic groups came to be identified with the effort. One is the Apache worker whose teams labored to construct the Apache Trail, a road vital during construction that still links the dam to the Phoenix area. The other group is the Italians who are credited in some sources with building the dam. For example, a 1988 book on the development of dam engineering in the United States noted under a section on special methods that "Many skilled craftsmen came to Arizona from Italy to cut and prepare the huge stone blocks for the dam."[2] That the former group did build the Apache Trail, as well as doing other work is undisputed, however, the credibility of the latter claim is open to debate.

An examination of the role of the Italians is in order since the gradual paradigm shift away from Frederick Jackson Turner work has broadened the interest of researchers to include the history of gender, labor groups and ethnic groups. Despite the growth of new areas of research, it took a while before European immigrants were seen as legitimate to study. In the idealized view of the frontier that developed following Turner, democracy and chances for upward mobility meant that those immigrants who ventured west would be assimilated. Thus, recent research particularly in mining and lumbering industries in western states benefits from new perspectives on the class struggle of workers in the West. As several recent studies illustrate there are many subtle relationships between class and ethnicity that are not limited to the urban areas of the east.[3]

---

[2] Eric Kollgaard, Ed. *Development of Dam Engineering in the United States* (New York: Pergamon, 1988).

[3] See for example: Michael Malone, "Beyond The Last Frontier: Toward A New Approach To Western American History," *The Western Historical Quarterly* XX, No. 4 (November 1989): 408-427. Mary Murphy. *Mining Cultures, Men, Women, & Leisure in Butte, 1919-1941* (Urbana and Chicago: University of Illinois Press, 1997).

Finally, the construction of Roosevelt dam is important to those interested in the role of the federal government's water policy in shaping the industrialization of the West. The assistance of the federal government made large-scale irrigation projects possible. These projects affected the entire ecology of some areas, allowed for a new type of economic development, linked in turn to urbanization and population growth. Theodore Roosevelt encouraged the development in 1902 of the U.S. Reclamation Service, as part of the U.S. Geological Survey. Projects developed quickly with 25 authorized for 17 western states, making dam construction an important area for labor studies. Hundreds of laborers were engaged in these projects, which required diverse groups to live and work together for extended periods of time under often difficult surroundings.[4]

## ROOSEVELT DAM

The Roosevelt project was developed under the shared responsibility of the agency and the Salt River Valley Water Users' Association (today the Salt River Project) in 1903, shortly after Roosevelt signed the National Reclamation Act. The dam was designed to bring irrigation water to some 250,000 acres in central Arizona and involved building a 280-foot-tall cyclopean-masonry, gravity-arch structure, two diversion dams, a power canal, and miles of freight roads to the remote site.[5]

Its total storage capacity was to be 1,340,000 acre feet, testimony to its immense size. Roosevelt was the highest rock-masonry dam in the world, a title still held as later dams

---

[4] Michael Robinson, *Water for the West, the Bureau of Reclamation, 1902-1977* (Chicago: Public Works Historical Society, 1979).
[5] Donald Jackson and Clayton Fraser, *Three Dams in Central Arizona, a Study in Technological Diversity* (Phoenix: U.S. Bureau of Reclamation Arizona Projects Office, June 1992).

used newer technology.[6] The site had several advantages from an engineering standpoint, but also presented several problems. The Salt River and Tonto Creek merged in a steep canyon where sandstone cliffs could be quarried and local clay and limestone deposits allowed cement production at the site. This helped reduce the prohibitive transportation costs to the remote site in the rugged Sierra Ancha and Mazatzal mountains, since it was not accessed by good freight roads. Another problem was extremes in climate with freezing winters, very hot summers and frequent flooding.

LABORERS TO THE DAM SITE

The remoteness of the site, the length of the project, and the discomfort of the working conditions meant that finding and keeping both skilled workers and laborers became a major problem, which added cost and tension to the project. The problem of finding workers for the dam site was also related to national shortages of unskilled laborers in a time of tremendous industrial expansion, a difficulty exacerbated in the West due to a period of rapid growth in construction and railroads. Many different ethnic groups, including Apache Indians, Austrians, African Americans, Irish, Italians, Spanish, German, and Mexican workers, became part of the labor force that built Roosevelt Dam. Part of the reason for such diversity is that new technological advances permitted an increasing use of semi-skilled workers, who were often not Anglos.[7] A component of the labor force still needed to be skilled laborers such as quarry men, blacksmiths, and masons whose work was likened to an artistic

---

[6] Dean Mann, *The Politics of Water in Arizona* (Tucson: University of Arizona Press, 1963).

[7] K. Smith, *The Magnificent Experiment* 84–86, David Introcasso, "Roosevelt Power Canal and Diversion Dam," Unpublished Ms. (Salt River Project Archives, HAER No. AZ-4. 1984); Earl Zarbin, *Roosevelt Dam: a History to 1911* (Phoenix: Salt River Project, 1984).

masterpiece. The new method of construction required less handwork to prepare the vertical joints on the face of the dam. Instead, the masonry could be dumped into place by unskilled laborers.[8]

One ready source in Arizona for laborers needed for industrial expansion was nearby Mexico. Starting in the early 1900s large numbers of Mexicans migrated adding those already there. Apaches, drawn from nearby reservations also became part of the local labor force. African Americans although relatively few in numbers did work at the site but Asians were generally excluded, a pattern not unusual in Arizona labor camps.[9]

Newer arrivals from Southern and Eastern Europe joined these workers. These Europeans were often found in mining towns like Globe and Bisbee where immigrants formed ethnic clusters, diminutive versions of ethnic neighborhoods typical of eastern cities. Older Europeans groups, like the Irish and Welsh, saw them as labor competition and viewed their cultures and racial origins with suspicion, often not accepting them. Additionally, some well-educated Americans were influenced by outspoken eugenicists, who believed culture was linked to biology. Cultural differences translated into a perceived racial inferiority of new immigrant groups and some American social scientists agreed, claiming that Southern and Eastern Europeans' allegedly weaker "race" would contaminate a supposedly purer Anglo racial stock. Those from the

---

[8] Chester Smith, *Construction of Masonry Dams* (New York: Mc Graw-Hill, 1915).

[9] Everett Bassett, "We Took Care of Each Other Like Families Were Meant To. Gender, Social Organization, and Age Labor Among the Apache at Roosevelt," *Those of Little Note, Gender, Race, and Class in Historical Archaeology* Ed. Elizabeth M. Scott. (Tucson: University of Arizona Press, 1994) 55–80; Lawrence Cardoso, *Mexican Emigration to the United States, 1897–1981, Socio-Economic Patterns* (Tucson: University of Arizona Press, 1980); Carlos Velez-Ibanez, *Border Visions, Mexican Cultures of the Southwest United States* (Tucson: University of Arizona Press, 1997).

Mediterranean were particularly stigmatized and seen as physically different.[10] Italians' place in the racial hierarchy of Arizona was intermediate between whites and minorities. Historians have directed attention to this aspect of the U.S. immigrant experience. Barrett and Roediger use the term "inbetween peoples" to describe those European groups who were not considered white when they arrived but who were still above minority groups like African Americans.[11] The term semi-racialized utilized here describes a similar place in the stratification system,[12] to add to the well-known theory of racial formation developed in sociology by Omi and Winant. In looking at the social development of race categories in the United States they examine racialization, the ideological component of this process that results in the subordination of minority groups. They claim that Southern European, Irish and Jewish immigrant groups who were initially considered "non-white" escaped this status while other groups such as African Americans did not. "By stopping short of racializing immigrants from Europe after the Civil War, and by subsequently allowing their assimilation, the American racial order was reconstituted in the wake of tremendous challenge placed before it by the abolition of racial slavery."[13] Evidence

[10] Michel Wieviorka, *The Arena of Racism* (London: Sage, 1995).

[11] James Barrett and David Roediger, "Inbetween Peoples: Race, Nationality, and The 'New Immigrant' Working-Class," *Journal of American Ethnic History* 16, No. 3 (Spring1997): 3–44; Robert Orsi, "The Religious Foundations of an Inbetween People," *American Quarterly* 44, No. 3 (September 1993): 313–347.

[12] Phylis Cancilla Martinelli, "Occupational and Residential Patterns of Mexican and Italian Workers in Bisbee, AZ 1900–1925." Unpublished Ms. (Presented at the 26th Annual Southwest Labor Studies Conference. California State University, Long Beach May 4–6th 2000).

[13] Michael Omi and Howard Winant, *Racial Formation In United States: From The 1960s To The 1980s* (New York: Routledge & Kegan Paul, 1987): 65. They emphasize race as an independent area of social conflict with meaning other than economic in the U.S. Racialization occurs when a social division called race is constructed as people struggle to define what they claim is their own

suggests otherwise. Numerous examples of Southern Europeans and Jews being treated in a category subordinate to "whites" after 1877 and well into the 1900s points to the need for a modification of their view. The term semi-racialized designates those European groups who are not given the full privileges of the white category economically, socially, and politically, sharing some of the lower status of more completely racialized groups. But, they do not consistently receive the full negative impact of this category either and have more opportunities for upward mobility and acceptance.

ITALIAN ROLE IN THE ETHNIC WORK FORCE

Despite an ethnically diverse work force Italians, working as stone cutters and masons, became most closely identified with the dam's construction. What is examined here is why were Italians recruited to work on the dam and whether their numbers overshadowed other groups.[14] Some claimed that Roosevelt dam was built by Italian stonemasons brought directly from Italy by the U.S. government ". . . especially to cut and lay the stones for the dam."[15] However, this is not the case given the passage of the Foran Act in 1885 forbidding contract labor from Europe. This legislation was passed, in part, to keep in check immigrants considered racially inferior to whites. The Chinese topped Foran's list, followed by some newer Europeans. He stipulated that the House vote to keep out the "large numbers of degraded, ignorant, brutal

---

race as inherently superior. Outsiders are labeled with perceived negative and supposedly permanent racial characteristics.

[14] Phylis Cancilla Martinelli, "Italian Workers on the Roosevelt Dam," *Historical Archaeological Investigations at Dam Construction Camps in Central Arizona* Eds. A. E. Rogge and Cindy Meyers Eds. (U.S. Department of the Interior Bureau of Reclamation #DI-BR-APO-CCRS 87, Second Annual Report, 1988): 75-87.

[15] N. Duncan, "Historical Reminiscence of the Construction of Roosevelt Dam." Unpublished Ms. (Arizona Room, Hayden Library, Arizona State University,1955).

Italians and Hungarians who. . . . Being low in the scale of intelligence, . . . are . . . willing slaves."[16]

Furthermore, recruitment of workers from Italy was not
critical since by the time Roosevelt Dam was started many
Italians who specialized in stone-working were already emigrating among the thousands of Italians anxious to escape
the poverty of an economically depressed nation, thus creating a pool of skilled workers in America. In 1900 alone, for
example, there were more than 4000 marble and stonecut-
ters among the new Italian immigrants, three times the number among immigrants in general. In the same year the 5582
Italian brick and stone masons who arrived were double the
number among other immigrants. Because of the level of
their skills these Italian workers were often sought after
for important construction projects.[17]

The explanation of where these workers came from is
complex. Some were recruited, but this was done through
Italian ethnic labor brokers in the United States, called
*padroni*, who supplied laborers throughout the West.[18] Several accounts of Italians arriving in large numbers at the dam
site indicate the involvement of the *padroni*. Chester Smith,
one of the project's chief engineers had Italian stone masons
doing skilled work for him before the contractor O'Rourke
came on the scene. During his work on dams in New York and
Massachusetts he doubtlessly came in contact with skilled

[16] Gwendolyn Mink, *Old Laborer And New Immigrants In American Political
Development, Union, Party, And State, 1875–1920* (Ithaca: New York: Cornell
University Press, 1986): 109.

[17] J.J Casserly, "Barry Goldwater, Arizonan," *Arizona Republic* (January 9,
1981): A 6; Robert Foerster, *The Italian Emigration of Our Times* (New
York: Russell and Russell, [1919] 1968).

[18] Some padroni were solid members of the Italian community and aided immigrants, but most were exploitative. Luciano Iorizzo, "The *Padrone* and
Immigrant Distribution," *The Italian Experience in the United States* Eds.
S.M. Tomasi and M.H. Engel (New York: Center for Migration Studies, 1970):
43–75.

Italian workers, given their large numbers in these areas. He was also aware of labor recruiters or *padroni* since he wrote to Mike Delfino asking him to supply workers for O'Rourke. Recruitment by O'Rourke in 1906 brought some 80 Italian workers, formerly coal miners, from Pittsburgh; in 1907 the contractor used the New York based Labor Information Office for Italians to secure another 45 Italian workers.[19] The arrival of groups of Italians helped create an image of large groups of Italians working on the project. Certainly, there are exaggerations as to their numbers. One source notes that there were "a few hundred" miners brought from Pennsylvania, instead of eighty. The eighty Italian rock men traveled from Pittsburgh, Pennsylvania to Globe on special cars at O'Rourke's expense so the contractor could put them to work quickly.[20] Their arrival made a big impression locally, when photographers made a point of taking their picture for the local papers. Working together on crews, they would have been a sizeable percentage of those working on the dam itself.

Actually, many Italians at the dam were already in Arizona. In 1900 Italians in Arizona constituted three percent of the foreign-born population and were about the same percentage (.57) of the general population as Italians were in Illinois (.49). The 1900 special census of occupations, shows 74 percent of Arizona's Italians in manufacturing, with 58 percent of this category concentrated in mining. Several dam workers came from the Italian community that began forming in the 1890s in nearby Globe, Arizona. Most initially worked

[19] Chester Smith, Diary No. 3 (September 22, 1906); Diary No. 4 (June 14, 1907), *Personal Diaries 1903-1912* (Salt River Project Archives, Phoenix Arizona); D. Lorne McWatters, "The Building of Roosevelt Dam, 1902-1911: Construction Camp or Community?" *Historical Archaeological Investigations at Dam Construction Camps in Central Arizona* Eds. A.E. Rogge and Cindy L. Myers, (Phoenix: U.S. Department of the Interior, Bureau of Reclamation 2nd Annual Report 1988): 4-1 to 4-29.
[20] *Arizona Republican* (June16,1906): 8.

in local mines or ran saloons, boarding houses, or stores that catered to fellow Italians. Recruiters from the dam went to Globe to look for workers, and workers from Globe sought work at the dam. A number of those hired were skilled masons or blacksmiths.[21]

Most of the Italians laborers however, were used for their brawn, not their skills. An account of the arrival of Italian workers from New York in 1907 noted that they were ". . . husky looking fellows. It has been hard to get men at the dam, and the idea of bringing them in wholesale bunches is a good one." Italian *braccianti,* or laborers, along with Mexican, Black, and Apache workers formed the basis of the work force doing the heavy, semi-skilled and unskilled labor that was also required to make Roosevelt Dam a reality.[22] In the early 1900s in the West Italians and other semi-racialized Mediterranean immigrants, like Southern Slavs, Greeks, Portuguese, Spaniards, often worked in "non-white" jobs usually given to low status minorities like Blacks, that needed muscle rather than skill or mental aptitude.

ITALIANS IN THE ROOSEVELT LABOR FORCE

The isolation of the dam site meant developing a community in the Tonto Basin area for all those who worked there. The Reclamation Service engineers set up their headquarters at Government Hill where they constructed an office building, mess hall, hospital, houses for the engineers, and platform tents for other workers. O'Rourke set up workers' quar-

---

[21] U. S. Bureau of the Census, *Twelfth Census of the United States, Special Reports, Occupations* (Washington, D.C.: Government Printing Office, No. 313 1904): 224–227; Ralph Mahoney, "Our Italian American Heritage" *Arizona Days and Ways Magazine* (August 11: 7–10, August 18: 24–29, August 25: 20–24, 1957; Phylis Cancilla Martinelli, "Pioneer Paesani in Globe, Arizona," *Italian Immigrants in Rural and Small Town America* Ed. Rudolph Vecoli (New York: American Italian Historical Assn. 1987): 153–169; C. Smith, *Personal Diaries,* No, 4 (June 25, 1907).

[22] Zarbin, *Roosevelt Dam* 133–4; *Arizona Republican* (September 14, 1907): 8.

ters across the river. A boarding house for the engineers and their families was built, as was a private house for O'Rourke. The foremen had semi-private tents, while many of the general workers, mostly single men, were housed in bunk-houses. As their families joined some workers, they too moved into tents. Italians like the Mexican, Blacks and Apaches had a distinct area at the camp, because housing was to some extent segregated.[23] While the patterns of resi-dence by nationality for Anglo and European workers was less distinct, the Italian section of the camp was described in this way by Mr. Frazier[24]:

> ... The tent houses where the Italian stone cutters lived looked like white rocks shimmering in the bright sunlight against the rocky hillsides. ... They [the Italians] lived with their families in one section of the community. Other laborers and their families lived in frame and tent houses scattered up and down the dusty roadway and in the canyons.

The small town of Roosevelt as the commercial and rec-reational center for the area did not have saloons found in labor camps because the government prohibited alcohol at the work site. However, evidence of wine and others spirits were found near the Italian "tent city." Archaeological analy-sis of the northern hill of the worker's camp found a clus-tering of wine and bitters bottles, like Fratelli-Branca bit-ters, from Italy in two areas which supports Frazier's description of the Italian settlement. The presence of wine bottles raises an interesting set of questions. First, why were such bottles found in quantity at all, given the prohibi-

---

[23] Jeffrey Hantman and Jeanette McKenna, "O'Rourke's Camp: Social Ar-chaeology of an Early 20th Century Construction Town," *Anthropological Field Studies No. 7* (Tempe: Arizona State University 1985): 124–125; Telephone Interview Lucy Hansen by P.M. 1987.
[24] Frazier quoted in Duncan "Historical Reminiscence of the Construction" 39.

tion against liquor on the dam site, a federal project? Second, where did the Italian wine and bitters bottles come from?

Even before O'Rourke's crew began work on the dam the Reclamation officials had problems with alcohol being smuggled onto the work site. There were saloons on the high line road to Globe, and in Mormon Flat and Fish Creek along the Apache Trail to Phoenix, but bids to open saloons closer to the project were firmly rejected since territorial law did not allow saloons within a six-mile radius of a government camp. Hill, the chief engineer in charge of the dam project, took the ban on liquor seriously. He had incoming stages searched for alcoholic contraband, and hired a former Texas Ranger, Jim Holmes, to enforce the regulation against liquor. The archaeological recovery throughout the area of wine, beer, whiskey, and patent medicine bottles containing alcohol suggests difficulty in enforcing the ban on alcohol, especially over the long period of time required to construct the dam.[25] While many smuggled liquor in, Italians were able to have it delivered regularly. Difficulties in keeping workers on the remote dam site probably encouraged the directors ignore the less serious violations of the law after a while. Because Italians were a large segment of the work force their numbers could be used as leverage for special treatment. A tacit agreement was reached with someone, since guards looked the other way when Mr. Rabogliatti, owner of Globe's White House saloon, arrived regularly with a wagonload of liquor. Other entrepreneurs could have supplied alcohol too as a steady supply of imported Italian wine flowed from California to Globe. Globe's Pete Gaudino, for example, advertised that the Eagle saloon carried the "Best Imported Bitters and Liquors." His ad showed a full range of Italian wines including "Italian Vermuth, celebrated Fernet Branca, Ferro-China

[25] Zarbin, *Roosevelt Dam* 108, 115.

Bisleri, Tamarindo Carlo Erba, and Italian grappa."[26] Italian saloonkeepers in Phoenix, a chief supplier of goods, were another likely source for the wine. Wine was confiscated on the stage from Phoenix where many Italians ran saloons. Access to wine shows the link to nearby ethnic communities and raises more questions about the status of Italians among dam workers. Given the scarcity of alcohol did this access give Italians more power and status because of this scarce commodity? Was alcohol sold to others by the Italians, was it used to trade for other goods, or was it given away to gain favor? At this point, these questions must remain unanswered.

Of more concern to workers than alcohol was compensation. In the early decades of the twentieth century Arizona's mining industry had a split labor market. White American workers received higher wages than ethnic workers, and often sided with employers during strikes to protect their own relatively privileged place. Public opinion, fueled by nativist sentiments, frequently supported this system.[27] Ethnic boundaries also played a role in determining job opportunities at Roosevelt. Anglo American and Irish workers were at the pinnacle of the labor force, working as engineers, foremen, and derrick operators. The top wage of $12 per day went to a

---

[26] Taped interview Gene Rabogliatti by P.M. 1981; The Rabogliatti Brothers owned the White House, a rooming house, restaurant and saloon. The saloon carried both domestic and imported liquors. *The Boarder* (Tucson: The Boarder Publishing Co., February, 1909): 19; Ibid 9; Grappa, a highly potent liquor, was probably homemade; Phylis Cancilla Martinelli, "Italy in Phoenix," *Journal of Arizona History* (18 No. 51977): 319-40; *Arizona Gazette* (July 3, 1901): 3.

[27] Andrea Yvette Huginnie, "STRIKITOS: Race, Class, And Work In The Arizona Copper Industry, 1870-1920," Dissertation, Yale University 1991; *Arizona Silver Belt* (August 10, 1905): 4; For a full explanation of the split labor market theory see Edna Bonacich, "A theory of ethnic antagonism: the split labor market," *American Sociological Review* 37 No. 5 (November 1972): 547-59.

few engineers, although others earned between $3.50-4.50 per day.[28]

Italians were not uniform in where they were placed in the wage scale. Roosevelt's skilled workers were paid well. Smith authorized Delfino to hire masons at five dollars per day, minus a dollar a day for board, and laborers three dollars a day. Pay records for the Roosevelt project from 1904 to 1911 shows several Italian sub-foremen who earned between $2.50 to 5.00 per day with the average wage $3.00. These wages were comparable to the wages paid in 1907 at the downstream Granite Reef Diversion Dam site in Arizona.[29] In comparison to miners, dam workers did well. Roosevelt's average wage of $3 for an eight-hour day ranked with the $3–3.50 per eight-hour day paid in 1907 in Bisbee, considered the state's premier copper camp. When compared to wages received in eastern states Roosevelt Dam wages are also competitive. In New York City, Italian laborers were paid $2.00 for a ten-hour day, and skilled rock men received only $2.48 for a 9-hour day in 1907.[30]

Most Italians, however, were unskilled and as a semi-racialized group ranked closer to minority ethnic workers, who as common laborers made $2–2.50 per day, a typical salary in the West. Sometimes they were grouped together with

---

[28] A. E. Rogge, D. Lorne McWatters, Melissa Keane, Richard Emanuel. *Raising Arizona's Dams, Daily Life, Danger, and Discrimination in the Dam Construction Camps of Central Arizona, 1890s–1940s* (Tucson: University of Arizona Press, 1995).

[29] *List of Subforeman, Roosevelt Dam Project,* (Salt River Project Archives, Phoenix, Arizona no date.) Laborers at Granite Reef Dam earned $2.00 per day, drillers made $2.75, carpenters $3.50 to $5.00 per day and sub-foremen made $3.50. Zarbin, *Roosevelt Dam* 146.

[30] At the Roosevelt Dam workers had an eight-hour day, that actually boosted their earnings compared to the longer days in the east. Frank Sheridan, "Italian, Slavic, and Hungarian Immigrants," *Bulletin of the Bureau of Labor* No. 72 (September 1907): 435. Washington D.C.: Government Printing Office; K. Smith, *The Magnificent Experiment* 87; Philip Mellinger, *Race and Labor in Western Copper* (Tuscon: University of Arizona, 1996).

Mexican workers. Chester Smith on his 1907 payroll noted that the "reclamation service had 22 Indians, 80 whites, and 58 Italians and Mexicans."[31] Earlier evidence of Italians working on dam construction in Arizona being among lower paid groups can be found at Camp Dyer when employees with Italian and Spanish surnames earned about 15 percent less than white unskilled workers.[32] This finding also parallels earnings in the state's mining camps, where unskilled Italians received significantly lower wages than other European immigrants. The US Immigration Commission report for 1908–1910 stated that the majority of Mexicans and Italians working in Arizona mining metals earned less than the normal $3.50 paid other miners.[33]

The status of fully racialized workers, such as Black Americans was unambiguous. They were at the bottom of the pyramid where they worked at a variety of labor intensive tasks. O'Rourke recruited Black Americans from Texas primarily to do manual labor such as moving waste material from the quarry site and maintenance roadwork. Mexicans cut wood, worked as teamsters, but generally did heavy labor. Asians were specifically discriminated against by government regulations that did not allow O'Rourke to hire them. However, a few Chinese and Japanese worked as cooks, or farmed truck gardens. Apaches worked doing the heavy labor needed for freight road and on construction projects, for example pouring concrete for the sluicing tunnel floor. Although the engineers made negative comments regarding Italian, Mexican, Chinese, and Japanese labor they generally saw Apaches as good workers.[34]

---

[31] Mc Watters, *Historical Archaeological Investigations* 4–13.

[32] Rogge et al, *Raising Arizona's Dams* 153.

[33] Mark Wyman, *Hard Rock Epic, Western Miners and the Industrial Revolution, 1860–1910* (Berkeley: University of California, 1979).

[34] Mc Waters, *Historical Archaeological Investigations;* Hantman and McKenna, "O'Rourke's Camp" 138; Zarbin, *Roosevelt Dam* 101; *Mesa Tribune*

There is little information available to determine how well Italians worked with the more disadvantaged groups. Most probably they had good relations with Mexicans since Italians and Mexicans cooperated in mining strikes on several occasions in Arizona, for example the 1903 wildcat strike in Morenci.[35] Furthermore, research has found that Italians and Spaniards sometimes lived in mixed ethnic neighborhoods with Mexicans, for example in Globe and Bisbee.[36] While many towns had barrios, segregation was usually not totally enforced.

Hantman and McKenna cite an article stating that ". . . the Negroes do not mix well with the children of Southern Europe [the Italian workers]." There could have been many sources for friction. For example, the work crews rotated being "water boys," and there were arguments if it was felt a crew got more water based on ethnic differences. Yet, Italian and Black workers were known to cooperate, for example going on strike together in 1909 at a California lumber camp, so sustained tension may not have been the case.[37] Local nativists viewed this multiethnic work force with antipathy. An editorial in a newspaper serving the Globe-Miami area suggested that labor problems at the dam site were related to the difficulty of keeping ". . . enough high grade white labor in camp to make a satisfactory leaven for the mass of Indi-

---

(September 21, 1966): 8; Telephone Interview Josefina Estevez by P.M. 1987).

[35] James Byrkit, *Labor in Arizona, 1901–1921: with Particular Reference to the Deportations of 1917* (Tucson: University of Arizona Press. 1972).

[36] Antonio Rios-Bustamante, "As Guilty as Hell, Copper Towns, Mexican Miners & community, 1920–1950: The Spatial & Social Consequences of the Mining Industry in Arizona." Unpublished Ms. (Chicano Collection Hayden Library, Arizona State University, CHSM-336 1003 1993); Martinelli, "Occupational and Residential Patterns."

[37] Hantman and McKenna "O'Rourke's Camp" 27; Paola Sensi Isolani, "La Pelle in California, I Soldi in Italia: The Italian Strike in McCloud, California, 1909," *Studi Emigrazione* 27 No. 97 (Spring 1990): 108–19.

ans, Mexicans, and European foreigners . . . who have congregated in the Salt River Basin." This attitude parallels views expressed in Arizona's self-proclaimed "white man's camps. " Editorials in Bisbee, for example, viewed the presence of South Slavs and Italians with antagonism, fearing that they did not fit as whites, thus confusing the labor hierarchy that favored Anglos and Northern Europeans.[38]

Hostility surfaced at the dam at times. In 1906, an argument between an Anglo supervisor and an Italian worker almost escalated into a strike involving all the Italians on the dam. John Conchion, a foreman, became involved in a dispute with one of his Italian crew members. Name-calling escalated into a fight, with Conchion attacking the worker with a crowbar. The Italian required hospitalization for stitches after the men were separated; the remainder of the Italians refused to return to work until some sanctions were imposed on the foreman. The management, fearing a major strike, had Conchion arrested. He was fined six dollars, and returned to work, while the nameless "Dago," as he was called by the newspaper, had to stay home to recuperate from his injuries.[39] This is another indication of a similar status for Mexicans and Italians since Huginnie cites newspaper articles that omitted the names of Mexican workers injured in mining accidents as a sign of the social distance between the Mexican and Anglo communities. This Roosevelt example and similar incidents were also found for Italians.[40]

There was also conflict between O'Rourke, the contractor, and Italian workers. Four Italian workers, hired from the New York Italian labor agency in 1907, at one point hired

---

[38] Quoted in Rogge *Raising Arizona's Dams* 150–51; Jane Eppinga, "Ethnic Diversity in Arizona's Early Mining Camps." *History of Mining in Arizona, Volume II* Eds. Michael Canty, and Michael Greeley, (Tucson: The Mining Club of the Southwest Foundation, 1991): 49–58.

[39] *Arizona Republican* (May 29, 1906): 3.

[40] Hugginie, "STRIKITOS."

a lawyer and contacted the Italian consulate in Denver, Colorado about being fired without cause after they had been promised two years of work at Roosevelt. Other dissatisfied Italians probably left, rather than trying to rectify the situation.[41] Despite various kinds of tensions, Italian workers continued work at the dam site through the final stages of work. In 1910, as the work on Roosevelt Dam neared completion, census takers enumerated the local population in the Tonto Basin area. Italians and Spaniards were the largest foreign-born groups in O'Rourke's Camp. Italians were the largest foreign-born group at Government Hill, however none were found in Newtown where Mexicans and Native Americans lived. Mc Watters points out that the presence of Italians at Government Hill, where they were half of the small immigrant population, was unexpected since most sources only mention Italians at O'Rourke's. He suggests they represent Italians working for the Reclamation Service. This indicates that, as in the mining towns, Italians clustered where they could find work.[42]

What actually happened to most of the Italians is unknown. Some settled in nearby towns, and others returned to Italy, eastern states, or went on to California. Nativism increased in Arizona during World War I, and legislation directed at limiting foreign-born workers, such as the Alien Labor Law of 1914, put pressure on immigrants. At the same time activism increased, with immigrants taking increasingly important roles in the local mining unions. The combined stigma of being foreign and pro-union forced many newcomers to leave. For example, many Italian workers left Globe after the mining strikes of 1917, when American citizenship became a criterion for employment, and the number of foreign-born workers declined.

[41] K. Smith, *The Magnificent Experiment* 87; McWatters, *Historical Archaeological Investigations* 4–14.

[42] Mc Watters, *Historical Archaeological Investigations*.

CONCLUSION

This research delineated the role of Italians in a construction project that helped shape the growth of the greater Phoenix metropolitan area. Dam construction is an area in which the composition and role of the labor force needs more investigation. Although their numbers were significant, they were only part of a larger multi-ethnic workforce where they fell in an intermediate place between Anglos and minority groups. These multiethnic workers raise questions interesting in light of labor relations in other parts of the West, for example Ludlow, Colorado. To what extent were Italians and others semi-racialized and what advantages did they have? Some claim European immigrants soon learned the racism of the dominant society, and did not cooperate with other ethnic groups of different races.[43] However ethnic groups in Arizona show cases of ethnic solidarity, organization, and commitment to union goals, in efforts aimed at correcting the inequities of the prevailing split labor market. Under what conditions did these Europeans cooperate or have conflict with minority groups lower on the status hierarchy? How did these European groups move from their semi-racialized status, while others like Mexicans did not? Hopefully a deeper interest in such issues will stimulate future research into the broader question of ethnic pluralism in Arizona and other western states.

---

[43] Omi and Winant, *Racial Formation* 65.

# THE ITALIAN WORLD OF WORK

# Italian Entrepreneurs in the Central Valley of California

Adele Maiello
University of Genova

Il contributo riguarda la storia degli italiani che si sistemarono nella Central Valley della California ed in particolare nella San Joaquin Valley, che ha al centro la citta' di Stockton. La presenza degli Italiani e' descritta secondo una sequenza cronologica di tre periodi: 1849 (Gold Rush) 60, 1860–1880, 1880–1921 (primo Quota Act). Lo studio si avvale, fra l'altro, dei censimenti fino al 1920 per la contea di San Joaquin. L'obiettivo della ricerca e' evidenziare la caratteristiche della cultura e del comportamento degli Italiani di origine ligure che si insediarono nella zona. A tal fine, oltre ai censimenti, la ricerca utilizza, come fonte qualitativa, dei City Directory e in particolare delle raccolte di biografie di *prominenti* locali scritte all'inizio del XX secolo. Le minute delle riunioni della societa di mutuo soccorso dei giardinieri (orticultori) italiani della zona hanno offerto poi uno spaccato interessante della cultura di questi uomini che riuscirono a creare una propria ricca ed influente presenza nell'agricoltura della vallata, alla cui affermazione e sviluppo contribuirono silenziosamente, ma consistentemente

This research addresses the interpretive problem that has arisen between scholars who have studied Italian immigration to the West Coast of the United States. While differences between those Italians who settled in the West and other parts of the United States were many, both in the time of arrival, in the protagonists,[1] and in their numbers,[2] most work on Italian immigration to the West Coast has focused on their generally greater economic success. A particular by-product of this perception has rested on the cultural anthropological identities of the two "groups" as Northern and the Southern Italians. This generalization implies a certain superiority of the Northerners, who appar-

---

[1] Mainly Northerners and Tuscans settled in California.
[2] The number who settled in the West were much lower.

ently had been able to overcome differences among themselves and with Americans, making for an easier and more successful assimilation.[3]

I do not intend here to follow this path and to extrapolate patterns of professional and social behavior without first providing a historical context. My aim in this paper is to analyze the contribution of entrepreneurs of Italian origin, and in this case of a particular Italian region, Liguria, to the growth of one Italian community in California. My study attempts to understand how much the characteristics of these immigrants came from their original culture and history, and how much they were the result of the peculiar historic, geografic, economic and social setting they found on the West Coast.

Andrew Rolle, starting from the consideration that Italians were able to make their own fortune in agriculture — uncommon for Italian immigrants in the USA — holds that they had achieved unusual economic success.[4] Paola Sensi Isolani and Phillys Martinelli, instead, suggested that it was necessary to make distinctions within the Italian group as far as their success is concerned.[5] Dino Cinel claimed that Italians in S.F. where really successful when they abandoned their regional identity,[6] while Sebastian Fichera has suggested that the entrepreneurial behavior of those Italians who mi-

---

[3] "*This perception has incorporated also the folk notion that Northern Italians who predominate in California, were racially superior to the Southerners.*"M. Di Leonardo, *The varieties of ethnic experience*, Ithaca and London, Cornell U.P., 1984, pp.22–25.

[4] A. Rolle, *The Immigrant Upraised: Italian Adventurers and Colonists in an Expanding America*, Norman, 1968.

[5] P. Sensi Isolani, P. C. Martinelli, *Struggle and Success: An Anthology of the Italian Immigrant Experience in California*, New York, Center for Migration Studies, 1993.

[6] Dino Cinel. From Italy to San Francisco. Stanford University Press, 1982.

grated to California and were successful, has had a direct impact on the level of life of the entire immigrant colony.[7]

While my research project which focuses on the Central Valley and the Bay Area, in this paper I will limit myself to analyzing the role that the Italian community played in shaping the development of the Central Valley, most particularly of San Jaquin County. My focus will of necessity be on those first arrivals, most of who came from Liguria, a region marked by early emigration, first to Europe, then to South America and California. In California, these Italians arriving at their new destinations became pioneers in some settings and professions, and were not restricted to a simple immigrant identity. The manner chosen by these first Genoese arrivals to improve their position will be examined. My initial analysis suggests that their culture of origin was instrumental to the success of the group, their entrepreneurial attitude following very closely the path chosen by other Italians in San Francisco.

With the help of the U. S. Censuses from 1850 to 1920, city directories, personal stories written on those who were the most successful, the history of Italy, some newspapers and proceedings of their most important mutual benefit society, I have divided the history of this group into three periods. The first, from the Gold Rush (1849) to the beginning of the 1860s, which saw the initial wave of immigration made up mainly of sailors and merchants, many of whom became entrepreneurs. Besides the professions they frequently had, these men were mainly adventurers and therefore open to any change in life and job. The big pull factor for this initial

---

[7] S. Fichera, *Entrepreneurial behaviour in an immigrant colony. The economic experience of San Francisco's Italian-Americans 1850-1940*, in 'Studi Emigrazione/ Etudes Migrations,' XXXII, n. 118, 1995, p.321. The general case of California Italian immigrants has been reproposed in S.L. Baily, *Immigrants in the lands of promise. Italians in Buenos Aires 1870 to 1914*, Ithaca and London, Cornell U.P., 1999, pp., 223-228.

wave was gold. The second period extends from the beginning of the 1860s to the 1880s, a period which saw the establishment of California agriculture in the world market. At this time, a large wave of laborers (mainly farm laborers), gardeners and farmers settled in the county, with former gold miners also becoming farmers. The third period began in the 1880s and ended with the first Quota Act of 1921, which reduced the number of immigrants. This was a period when the mass of laborers coming from all over Italy was accompanied by a new kind of immigrant such as artisans and professionals, needed by the more complex society which was taking shape in the country.

Like Americans coming from all over the United States, also the first Italians to arrive in the area, so near to the Mother Lode's gold mines, were attracted to California by the Gold Rush of 1849. Many of them came from Liguria, one of the poorest regions of the Italian peninsula. These Ligurians, all hard workers, either lived in the countryside and had already been used to temporary migration, usually at the time of harvest, or on the coast, where they had contact with the rest of the world as sailors and merchants.

The first to come were mainly people from the Ligurian coast. Their characteristics, as financiers and merchants, were well known, as was their fame as sailors and mercenaries. These qualities were an asset for the first period of settlement in North Western California, just as the toughness of the Ligurian peasants who arrived later was also of great value in working land of the so called Delta, where the Sacramento, S. Joaquin, Mokalumne, Calaveras and other rivers meet. These rivers created a huge area where land, while potentially rich for the agriculture, still had to be prepared for cultivation and, in a large part, also drained.

For this first period, going trough the censuses of San Joaquin County we find that Italians were among the first to settle in the newly founded city of Stockton (1847). The city was the first destination for immigrants given its proximity to the gold mines and the presence of the large Delta where ships could sail straight from San Francisco and the open sea. The 1850 census for the county, which consisted mainly of the city of Stockton, lists the names of 27 Italians out of the 3.644 residents.[8] Out of these twenty-seven, twenty were merchants and traders, the few left were clerks, musicians, muleteers and trade miners. They were the second largest foreign group in town after the Germans, one of which, Charles Weber had founded the town itself. The page where they were listed in the Census gives us a hint of their identity as "city dwellers."[9]

The personal story of some of these merchant pioneers has been written in those collections of biographies (usually short life stories of less than a page) so popular in the first quarter of the 20th century, when the most recent bourgeoisie had to assess its achievements. These biographers shaped the personalities and acquisitions of those included, emphasizing their great desire for adventure and their capacity to adapt to difficult times, when everything had to be built up in a new land. Some of these pioneers came with money of their own that enabled them to set up enterprises that supplied goods and services that were totally lacking. Others didn't come with the same amount of money but were also successful enough to still have been considered worthy of inclusion in these volumes. While not all Italians have a biography of their own, their presence in the city directories gives us a

---

[8] The total Italian presence in California was 228 people, mostly concentrated in the counties of the gold country.
[9] Holt Atherton Special Collection, USA *Census, 1850*, California, St. Joaquin County, Stockton.
As for their identity I agree with D. S. Walker, *The Italian Presence in the Northern San Joaquin Valley* in 'The Far-Westerner. Quarterly Publication of the Stockton Corral of Westerners,' v. XXXV, n.2, fall 1994.

hint of the services needed at the time and that they supplied.

These were all primary ones: hotels, boarding houses, restaurants, saloons, bars, health care, transportation, merchandising.

So among the first to arrive were a good number of boarding house keepers, whose names we find often only in one Census, and of hotels owners that have left only their name and that of their hotels. These names are also interesting because they can help us identify their place of origin. Louis De Ferrari of 'The Garibaldi House'; Gabrielle Foppiano of the 'Roma Hotel'; V. Pellegrini of the 'Europa Hotel' and P.M. Ricci of the 'Hotel of Italy,' all seem to be from Liguria, only for one of them, Pellegrini, can there can be some doubt.

There were also people who produced food and opened restaurants during this period. Italians who immigrated were mainly young adult men, used to food of their home country, which was generally at the time looked upon with suspicion in the United States. The fortune of these bars and restaurants was often short-lived, like the presence in town of their customers, many of whom were so called "birds of passage," men determined: to earn enough money and then return home. In some cases we find them only in one Stockton directory, while new names replaced them in the next one. These were all Ligurian names, Bonzi, Repetto, De Ferrari. Here we find also the name of Charles Gallo, a wine maker who began the largest fortune in this trade in North America.[10]

---

[10] *Statistical County Directory of San Jaoquin County*, Stockton, D. H. Berdine, 1878; *Stockton City and San Joaquin Directory*, 1887-88, San Francisco (California), Publ.Co., 1888; *The Mail's Stockton City Directory for 1898-99*, Stockton, Colnon & Nunan, 1898.

The extraordinary activity of the group in offering those services during the Gold Rush is also witnessed by the memories of a Piedmontese consul who was there at the times, L. Cipriani, *Avventure della mia vita, diari e memorie*, v. 2, 1849-71, Bologna, 1934, 71.The book has been translated in

But the characteristics of in Stockton's Italians in this first period was not really their short-lived presence, but their ability as business men. As a matter of fact, Italian names of Ligurian origin are present in the list of those paying license fees in 1850 in town and comprise 1/9th of the total.[11] One of the two most important doctors in Stockton in the 1870 and 1880 censuses was an Italian, Nicolas Sposati who was also sponsor and co-owner of Stockton's first horse-drawn street railways. His name is present only in two of the town directories and in the above mentioned censuses, and disappears at the end of the century.

Among the biographies of this period that are not listed in the San Joaquin Valley collections, but are found in the Californian ones, is that of Domenico Ghirardelli, who become the world famous chocolateer. It is interesting to consider his history because he was part of the wave of arrivals from all over the world that rushed to California, in the middle of the 19th century, in search of gold. Ghirardelli went to Peru from the Ligurian town of Genova, where he had learnt his profession in a local shop still in existence to day, the Romanengo pastry shop. Later called by a friend, he sailed from Peru to California in order to find better opportunities. With his wife, Ghirardelli went straight to the gold mines where he soon started to feed the residents. In the newly founded city of Stockton, he opened a chocolate and biscuit shop which was very, but when in 1851, his shop was destroyed by fire he left town to settle in San Francisco, which presented greater prospects for commercial development. There he teamed up with Nicola Larco, another Ligurian entrepreneur, who owned both the most important import-export businesses in San Francisco, and three ships that were going back

English as *California and Overland Diaries of Count Leonetto Cipriani: from 1853 to 1871*, Portland, Champoeg Press.
[11]Holt Atherton Special Collection, MSS 126: San Jaquin County, California: Account Book, 1850–1862.

and forth between California and Italy. Ghirardelli kept the real estate and ranches he had bought in Stockton, and the shop he had founded in its vicinity continuing in this way to be part of the local economy.[12]

A successful and important Italian immigrant in the county was another Genoese, Giuseppe Di Pietri, who Americanized his name to J. D. Peters. A real adventurer, he had already been in the US for at least ten years, when he came to California during the Gold Rush. In 1848 he arrived from Mexico, where during the Mexican war he had served on the US side as an engineer on a steamship. After a start as a miner, he rapidly changed direction, first becoming a teamster, then deciding to offer services to the growing population. Since this population of miners needed food, he leased a small steamer and went around selling flour. The step from this to the opening of a large warehouse on the waterfront wasn't big and in this way he offered the possibility for agricultural products to be stored until he was able to sell them "*at a favorable price for the farmer*," according to his biographer.[13]

J.D. Peters the agriculture of the area in many ways improved. His capacity to understand new needs of the community led him to establish a saving bank, a kind of bank that was meant to be more than others 'on the side of the customer'. Using his professional experience with steamboats, he founded a shipping company, and then created the important California Navigation and Improvement Company. In these new areas of interest, he was able to match his own interest with an eye to the real interests of the people that he had to cope with (customers or debtors). It has been ex-

---

[12] R.Teiser, *An Account of Domingo Ghirardelli and the early years of the Ghirardelli Company*, San Francisco, 1945, 1–25.

[13] J.M. Guinn and George H. Tinkham. *History of the State of California and Biographical Record of San Joaquin County*, California. Losa Anges: Historic Record Co., 1923, #7, pp. 350–351.

pressly written that he "*aimed to pay the highest prices possible*" to the farmers for their crops and "*also gave financial assistance in times of stress caused by crop failures.*"

His popularity didn't push him into politics, though he was asked to run for office many times. This appears to be a typical characteristic of the behavior of Italians of Ligurian origin during this period. They didn't want to be involved in professional politics, even if they could show great concern for the interest of the many. It was the same in the city of San Francisco, according to Cinel,[14] and in Argentina too, according to Nascimbene.[15] In the following years Di Pietri continued to show his social concern and professional interests by the founding a newspaper devoted to agriculture and other minor interests of his, founding a company for the production and trading of an insecticide for flowers,[16] and giving a generous donation for the construction of Saint Joseph's Hospital.

His life story seems very similar to the one of a much more well known Californian banker of Italian descent, Amedeo Giannini, who started his fortune lending money with almost no guarantees, to those Italians who had to rebuild their houses in San Francisco after the earthquake and fire of 1906.[17] What interests us about Peters' life is not only related to the chain of professional changes he went through, from engineer on ships, to miner, merchant, banker, shipbuilder, newspaper's owner, and insecticide trader, all

---

[14] D.Cinel, *Dall'Italia a San Francisco*, pp. 327 e ss.

[15] M. Nascimbene, *Storia della collettività italiana in Argentina (1835–1965)*, in *Euroamericani*, cit., v.2, *La popolazione di origine italiana in Argentina*, pp. 209-219.

[16] This is what tells us his storylife, published in 1923, when he was already dead by 8 years. See G. H. Tinkham, *History of San Joaquin County*, Los Angeles: Historic Record Co.(1923) #6, 350-1: #7, 120.

[17] M. James, B. Rowland James, *Biography of a Bank: The Story of the Bank of America*, New York, Harper &Row, 1954; F. A. BONADIO, *A. P. Giannini, Banker of America*, Berkeley, U. C. P., 1994.

professions devoted to agriculture, with an eye to the social problems involved. His story is also interesting because, just like Giannini, he seems to represent, a kind of capitalism more typical of the European world than of the American one. This was a capitalism with a paternalistic orientation that could be concerned with the social consequences of its deeds, and trying to mitigate them. This happened even in the first period of expansions in California because the Europeans were more preoccupied than Americans about the social unrest produced by too harsh economic pressures on laborers or small entrepreneurs. The history of social movements in Europe is there to remind us of this.

The changing fields of activity of the children of these first arrivals well represent the passage from one period to another. This is the case, for example, of the son of a Joseph A. Gambetta, who arrived in 1855 from Genova, establishing what was probably the first complete Italian family in the S. Joaquin Valley. While Joseph Gambetta was a grocer, his son represented the natural shift from a merchant to a professional, becoming the inventor of a motorboat engine and of a bicycle.

There were even more remarkable professional changes in Ligurian/Italian families' stories that better demonstrate changes that took place with the passing of time. Paul Brichetto, arriving from Genova, went in search of gold in 1859, but he soon understood that people needed to be supplied with fresh fruit and vegetables. He therefore succeeded in saving enough money to buy a ranch on the Stanislaus River (one of the many of the area) near Oakdale. This ranch was considered, in an article published by a local newspaper, among the best in the country and "probably the most attractive combination fruit and truck garden in California." His sons very successfully continued this farming operation. As

Walker reminds us, in the early 1920s they were "the largest taxpayers of the Oakdale Irrigation District."[18]

One more life story can serve to stress the shift the local Italian community underwent when the Gold Rush was over. It is the story of Gaetano Allegretti, son of a "distinguished Ligurian sculptor," according to his biographer (this means that he wasn't poor), who crossed the ocean to find his fortune at the age of 18, in 1859 in California. He immediately arrived in Stockton, where an uncle of his already owned a china shop. He worked there, then purchased the shop, and began investing in real estate, ranches and buildings, ultimately amassing a fortune. He founded with another Ligurian, Davide Raggio, the Commercial and Savings Bank and the Union Safe Deposits Bank, said to be more concerned with the interests of their customers, than only with profit. This suggests a feature of his personality emphasized by his biographer, his concern for the problems of Italian farmers. In fact they considered him a "leader among his countrymen and they sought him for advice because they did not understand the ways in this country, and often became their banker in the earlier days in Stockton."[19]

As I already noted, it is evident from the 1870 and 1880 censuses, that the Stockton area was very promising for farming. Therefore in these censuses — and especially in the 1880s one — we find a large number of laborers and mainly farm laborers, gardeners and farmers, who were already resident in the county. Also the Directory of the city of Stockton in 1871–72 lists about 110 Italian surnames, 39 of these had been identified as laborers, 11 as gardeners and 10 as farmers. It is evident that at this time the Italian community was changing as poor peasants living in the countryside of Liguria arrived in increasing numbers.

---

[18] D.Walker, *op.cit.*, 16
[19] *Illustrated History of San Joaquin Country, California*, Lewis Publishers, 1890, pp. 431, 452.

From the 1870 and 1880 censuses we can determine that the rich potential of agriculture attracted many Italians. In the 1870 census, out of a total of 137 Italians, we find 56 laborers and 14 farm laborers, 12% of who had wives residing with them.[20] By the 1880 census, out of a total of 238 Italians in the country, work relating to agriculture still predominated but had diversified, with 52 gardeners, 15 farmers, 55 farm laborers, and 34 simple laborers, indicating increasing specialization and the birth of large and smaller fortunes. We also notice the beginning of a new economic activity that was to become increasingly popular, the establishment of grocery stores, which in the 1880 census amounted to 12. In these censuses, the presence of approximately 11-12% women/wives with children indicates a tendency toward stability in the community, one that was changing because of the arrival of poor peasants from the inland villages of Liguria.

These more recent arrivals came attracted by the information that was flowing to their villages that, in California, there was a chance for them to earn good wages and also to buy land. Liguria was at the time a region whose agriculture had been damaged by the recent political unification that unified also the national market. The many small farmers there couldn't afford the competition of products arriving from other regions, and as a consequence opted to emigrate. Their expatriation was reported at the time by a Parliamentary Commission (the Jacini Commission) that dates the huge flow of emigrating peasants from the district around the town of Chiavari and other districts to 1879.

After first arriving, life was not easy for these men, and we don't find all of them listed in biographical books. We also find worried reports of the Italian consul in the Western States, Ferdinando Daneo, who writes frightening descriptions of the terrible living conditions of the Italian peasants

[20] *Stockton City—San Joaquin C?ounty Directory, 1871-2*, Stockton, 1872.

in the area — and especially in Stockton — at the beginning of the 20<sup>th</sup> century.[21] While at this time some Italians, mostly Ligurians, also owned a large number of groceries, to own a farm was the goal of many poor farmers or laborers who arrived from Italy. The report of the United States Immigration Commission noted that Italians in the area didn't have to compete with many others as they had to in cities because the price of land was comparably affordable. It noted the success of many, pointing out that "By irrigating and heavily fertilizing their land, the truck gardens have been made very productive and by working long hours and practicing thrift, most of the farmers have been able to live comfortably and accumulate property." This evaluation is particularly noteworthy if we remember that the aim of that commission (the famous Dillingham Commission) was the description of different ethnic communities, in order to decide whether, and if so how, they could shape the further development of American society.[22]

Some of the biographies of the period document how some of these Italian immigrants managed to acquire land. The biographies of Antonio Gotelli and G.B. Leonardini emphasize thrift, hard work and self sacrifice as well as a programission from laborer to leaser of land and finally to landowner. Antonio Gotelli, was described as a man "who had done much to build the horticultural interests in California," arrived in 1888, with a debt of 125 dollars. He worked in a vegetable garden for 33 months at 25 dollars a month and during all this time did not leave the ranch to go to town. He saved his money and paid his honest debt and continuing by industry and frugality he was able at the end of five years to

---

[21] F. Daneo, *Condizione delle Colonie italiane a Stockton, e nelle contee di Sonoma, Jackson e Amador City (California, SUA) e l'Emigrazione Italiana in California*, in 'Bollettino dell'Emigrazione,' 14, 1915; pp.45–58.
[22] U.S. Immigration Commission, XXV, cit., 350, 454; see also 14th Census of the U.S., 1920, v.V, Agriculture, 315–29.

purchase an interest in vegetable gardens. Afterwards increasing his interest he demonstrated his ability as a businessman and in time he become the manager after which the business grew rapidly so that the partners received as dividends 300% more than formerly. John (his son) assisted his father in vineyard enterprise until 1914. . . . Republican in politics and member of the Stockton mason lodge n.218."[23]

G.B. Leonardini, "Native of Varese Ligure in 1884, arrived at the age of 15, joining his brother Domingo. He worked for wages on various farms in the district for 6 years in Stockton; then he leased twenty-six acres of the Solari (another Ligurian name) ranch . . . where he raised fruits for 10 years; he then bought twenty-six acres of bare land on Ashley Road and set in act to peaches, cherries, walnuts, plums and apricots. . . . He married Miss Louise Stagnaro a native daughter of Angelo and Angela (Moresco) Stagnaro, also born in Varese Ligure. . . . Mr. Leonardini belongs to the Giardinieri lodge in Stockton, an Italian American organization. In 1915 a comfortable residence was built on his ranch where family reside."[24]

The beginning of the century was also a period during which this area underwent mass immigration from many other countries. It therefore became important for these Italians to form national associations, in order to maintain their former identity as well as close ties to their ethnic community. Moreover, the Ligurians took with them their own local cultural legacy of mutual aid societies that came from the political republican background of Mazzini's teaching.[25] The

[23] G. H. Tinkham, *op. cit.*, p.1530

[24] *Ibid.*, p.1616

[25] The Compagnia Italiana di Bersaglieri, an association that was initially very popular and affluent, was founded in Stockton and nearby Sacramento in 1887, spreading from San Francisco (1873), as a Mutual benefit society for veterans of the Italian wars of the Risorgimento, in which that corps had been an important protagonist. For a while, their parades and pic nics were very popular in town.

most important of these associations in Stockton proved to be the Società Italiana dei Giardinieri, founded in 1902.

This society presents some important features for our history, most particularly the fact that at its second meeting members decided that they would recruit all the *Italian-speaking* gardeners of the San Joaquin Valley. This decision was remarkable because it meant that the Italian community was ignoring national boundaries in order to include all Italian speakers, regardless of nationality. Therefore in Stockton's Società Italiana dei Giardinieri there were at least three groups of different national origin but which shared the same language: Italians, Swiss Italians, and Dalmatian Italians. This feature is important because it meant that a common culture based on a shared language superseded, in their eyes, all other divisions. This contrasts significantly with mutual aid associations founded in other parts of the United States, which were more commonly based on such restricted identification as the parish, the village or the region.

At this same meeting the Stockton gardeners decided that the aim of the society would be mutual aid and not, as someone had proposed, that of fixing the price of their products on the market.[26] Even if those who advocated for a benefit society prevailed because they lived in a society that provided no public care, the other proposed aim, that of fixing the price of produce they sold, is a sign of these gardeners' important progress and also of their growing economic strength. They in fact appear to have formed a sort of oligopoly of the fruit and vegetable market and, even if their properties were sometimes small, they very productive evidence of their success is the value of the property leased and owned by them. In 1920, this consisted of approximately $7,000,000, while the number of the society's members in-

---

[26] Archives of the Italian Gardeners Society, *Verbali delle riunioni della Societa Italiana dei Giardinieri di Stockton*, 1902-1918 (1st vol), meeting of the 31 August 1902.

creased from 2,417 to 4,453. This meant that they managed 47% of the landholdings in the country, something that was not replicated by Italians in any other part of the United States.[27]

The third period of our history sees the affirmation of two more groups in the Italian community, artisans and professionals. Both these groups came from the second generation of immigrants, whose professional shift we have already singled out. They came also from other regions of the USA, given the great publicity California was starting to have in the press. Another group of Italians that arrived at this time from Italy was that of highly educated people looking for a better life. They were doctors, like the Genoese Leonida Olivieri who invented important medical instruments while in Chicago, and later moved to California for his health. There were also engineers, like the Florentine Louis Barzellotti, who helped the improvement of development and irrigation of cultivated fields, as well as specialized food producers and traders, like James Triolo.

The values stressed by the biographies of these men, written in order to give them a kind of qualification, not only of their success, but also of the cultural qualities that had made them people of that country bears analysis.[28] As usual for all Italians, the value placed on family was emphasized. From reading their stories it is clear that theirs wasn't only an individual story of success, but that whenever possible, the help of some family member or friend made their path easier. It is interesting to see how this functioned among them, enlarging the meaning of the original community that, according to these descriptions, overcame from the very beginning any regional or parochial divisions. Even if they usually didn't intermarry with people from other regions or states,

---

[27] United States Immigration Commission, Immigrants in Industries, XXV, Washington D.C., p.466.

[28] I agree here with D. S. Walker, op. cit., 29–31.

we have the description of many whom encouraged others, hired them, worked with them, and lent them money just because they were Italian. This attitude was present in the Società Italiana dei Giardinieri di Stockton that organized the gardeners no matter what their regional or even national origin. As a matter of fact, this attitude is also found in the many benevolent Italian associations of the area which took care of the general interests of its members, and which did not always prefer to associate with people of the same region, nor keep the regional identity in the name of the association. What appears to have been considerably important was the general sense of human solidarity shown by these Italian newcomers, something that helped them become Americans.

Their religiosity was another feature that these biographies emphasized, and which was considered an important social value in the moralistic America of the period. Therefore generous donations to the Church, or religious initiatives, such as J. D. Peters' donation to St. Joseph's Hospital, were documented. At the same time, one has to keep in mind that there is also in these biographies evidence of a more secular culture, seen in frequent membership in Masonic lodges among many of these Ligurians, most especially those from the coast This anti clerical attitude, a legacy of a strong republican tradition, was deeply rooted in their past as citizens of the very independent, proud and secular pre-1815 Republic of Genova. The figure of Giuseppe Mazzini well represents this legacy. So while many peasants coming from the countryside were very religious, many Ligurians living on the coast tended to be more anti-clerical, e affiliating therefore, with one or more of the many Masonic lodges were flourishing in the San Joaquin Valley.

Another characteristic of the Italians highlighted by these biographies was the right value Italians placed on hard work, money and self esteem. Money had to be seen as a reward for particular skills and hard work, and self-esteem weren't seen as related to the amount of riches really acquired, but only to the amount of hard work necessary to get them, whatever the size of the fortune. There is one last quality that these biographers appear to single out, and that is the Italians' capacity to enjoy life with entertainment, good food, sports and public celebrations, such as the religious feasts other Catholics such as the Irish frowned on. The Società Italiana dei Giardinieri di Stockton, for example, came to hold an important position in the city's social life, with its picnics, musical parties and parades, equaling and quickly overshadowing the successful celebrations of the Società dei Bersaglieri which it was very much tied to, and whose hall it rented for its meetings.

While these collections of biographies are in some ways a manipulated source since in many cases those featured paid for them, they are nevertheless a strong sign of the will of these Italian immigrants to be part of the local community, even without entirely renouncing their own particular characteristics which came from their Italian culture.

# Italian American Food Importers and Ethnic Consumption in 1930s New York

## Simone Cinotto

L'articolo tratta del mercato alimentare di New York negli anni trenta, del comportamento dei consumatori italoamericani e delle diverse strategie degli imprenditori etnici del settore, per sostenere che — anche se non poté essere contrastata politicamente da un conservatorismo di stampo etnico-nazionalista — l'emergere della società di massa negli anni tra le due guerre non necessariamente esercitò un'azione dirompente sull'identità etnica italoamericana. Forme peculiari di consumo etnico non furono né soppresse né rimasero inalterate, ma subirono una ridefinizione. Alcuni imprenditori alimentari continuarono a legare i propri interessi economici alla promozione dell'etnicità utilizzando le nuove forme culturali e influenzando così più sottilmente comportamenti e mentalità dei consumatori.

The impact of consumerism and mass culture on ethnic working class identity is a controversial theme in American history after World War I.[1] A "classical" interpretation argues that consumerism, with its corollary of mass-advertised national brands, was a powerful means of Americanization that crucially contributed to assimilate ethnic working-class values and identities into those of the urban American middle class.[2] Conversely, other scholars stressed that patterns of consumption are a prime example of ethnic cultures' resistance to the homogenizing forces of mass culture.[3] However, the issue has been often approached from the

---

[1] Alice Kessler-Harris, "Social History," Eric Foner (ed.), *The New American History*, Philadelphia, Temple University Press, 1997.

[2] Stuart Ewen, *Captains of Consciousness: Advertising and the Social Roots of the Consumer Culture*, New York, McGraw-Hill, 1976; Richard Wightman Fox and T.J. Jackson Lears (eds.), *The Culture of Consumption*, New York, Pantheon Books, 1983.

[3] Lizabeth Cohen, *Making a New Deal: Industrial Workers in Chicago, 1919–1939*, Cambridge, Cambridge University Press, 1990.

point of view of a conflict between cultures, while less studied have been the dynamics and the dialectics within ethnic
communities and elites. In the Italian American case, the
analysis of the history of the ethnic food market can be particularly illuminating: first, because of the particular symbolic value of food in the formation of an Italian American
collective identity. Second, because of the strong link that
there has always been between economic interests and the
promotion of Italian American ethnicity in the sector of the
food industry. The analysis suggests that some peculiar ethnic forms of consumption were neither suppressed by mass
society's "homogenizing forces," nor remained unaltered;
rather, they were redefined. Such a redefinition was probably the cause of their survival. Crucial to this process was
the presence, in the Italian American business community, of
both "modernizing" and "traditionalist" elements.

The struggle between importers of food from Italy and
local producers of Italian style food for the control of the
Italian American market of New York in the 1930s is a case
that I will use to make my point. Both importers and producers emphasized the national and traditional characteristics
of the products they sold; both appealed to ethnic solidarity,
asking Italian Americans to spend their money within the
community. But, while the former were trying to resist the
forces of change in American society and in the Italian
American community, the latter were managing to master
them. Many Italian American food producers recognized indi-
vidualism and modernity as the basis of their success. They
transposed such values into advertising, appealing to a new
ethnic consumer. Mixing traditional and modern elements,
they dealt with change with the invention of an ethnic version of middle class "Mrs. and Mr. Consumer."

Large-scale imports of Italian foodstuffs began with the
earliest Italian arrivals in New York. Already by 1890 a small
number of Genoese, Neapolitan, and Sicilian wholesale im-

porters controlled most of the city commerce of citrus fruits, pasta, olive oil, and wine. A great amount of power and influence lay in the hands of the richest merchants. Many of them carried out several other services in the Italian community. Leading importers were often the same people who collected immigrants' earnings, made remittances, served as exchange agents, lent them money; who contracted immigrants labor; and who served as agents for shipping lines. Most of the capital was reinvested in food import, a very profitable business thanks to the rapidly growing dimensions of the immigrant community (more than half a million people in 1910).[4] Immigrants supported food imports from Italy with an extraordinary loyalty. Although imported foodstuffs were expensive items for their small food budgets, many immigrants were willing to pay the price to purchase Italian pasta, tomatoes, olive oil, cheese and salamis. In the years of mass immigration (1898–1910) food imports skyrocketed. For example, while in 1898 20.677 hectoliters of wine were imported in 1910 they became 150.689. Pasta moved up from 45.511 quintals in 1898 to 507.151 quintals in 1910; olive oil from 30.159 quintals to 96.040; cheese from 16.185 quintals to 84.101; tomato products from 3.281 to 113.137 quintals.[5]

Wealthy importers were a significant part of that "ethnic bourgeoisie" that had an essential role in the promotion of nationalism among Italian immigrants. The importers' store signs with captions like *"Grande grosseria italiana"* or *"Alimentari italiani"* revealed the attempt to direct the business toward an "Italian community" still divided along regional and local loyalties. Many public activities of leading importers

---

[4] Robert F. Foerster, *The Italian Emigration of Our Times*, New York, Russell and Russell, 1919, p. 339; Mario Maffi, *Nel mosaico della città: differenze etniche e nuove culture in un quartiere di New York*, Milano, Feltrinelli, 1985, p. 108–109.

[5] Camera di commercio italiana in New York, *Nel cinquantenario della Camera di commercio italiana in New York, 1887–1937*, New York, 1937, p. 66.

were also dedicated to stimulate the consciousness of a shared national belonging among immigrants.[6] After the advent of fascism, political alignment became vital for the importers' commercial relations with Italy. Most importers did not fail to show publicly their consent to the regime. They were among the most preferentially treated by Italian authorities in New York and received important offices and honors from the Italian government. In the 1930s the president of the Italian Chamber of Commerce in New York was the Lombard cheese importer, Ercole Locatelli.

World War I had an enormous impact on the importers' fortunes and on the production and commerce of Italian food products as a whole. Total war needs compelled the Italian government to cut down on exports almost completely. The main result in the United States was the rapid growth of local competition, mainly by the agency of ethnic entrepreneurs. In the war years, the Italian American producers of wine grapes and canned tomatoes of California took over large part of the New York ethnic market. Local manufacturing of pasta developed from a household industry to a mass production industry engaging thousands of workers, and drove Italian imports virtually out of business. The latter declined from an annual average of 113 millions pounds in the five-year period 1909–1914 to 2.567.933 pounds in 1927. Taking advantage of fiscal, sanitary, and administrative measures, local companies were soon able to supply products that were similar in quality to the imported ones, at a decidedly lower price.

In the 1920s food importers had to deal with a worsening situation. In addition to the pressing competition by local

[6] John E. Zucchi, "Paesani or Italiani?": Local and National Loyalties in an Italian Immigrant Community," Richard Juliani (ed.), *The Family and Community Life of Italian Americans*, Staten Island, NY, American Italian Historical Association, 1983, George E. Pozzetta, *The Italians of New York, 1890–1914*, Ph.D. Diss., Chapel Hill, University of North Carolina, 1971.

manufacturers, there was the end of the great migratory wave, leaving imports without the crucial factor that stimulated the continuous expansion of earlier decades; the emergence of American born generations, who were less emotionally concerned about the place of origin of food; the reforms of customs duties (mainly the Hawley-Smoot Tariff Act of 1930) which heavily penalized Italian food products. Finally, with the onset of the Great Depression, the price of imported foodstuffs became too high for many families. As a result, food imports from Italy constantly declined from 1925 to 1933 (Table 1).

Table 1. Imports of major Italian food products in the United States, 1925-1933
(values in thousands of gold dollars)

|        | Cheese | Canned Tomatoes | Olive Oil |
|--------|--------|-----------------|-----------|
| 1925   | 8,582  | 5,327           | 6,259     |
| 1926   | 9,321  | 5,503           | 3,780     |
| 1927   | 11,187 | 5,950           | 6,432     |
| 1928   | 12,898 | 4,712           | 1,988     |
| 1929   | 9,745  | 8,960           | 6,158     |
| 1930   | 9,164  | 3,102           | 7,353     |
| 1931   | 7,255  | 3,992           | 5,137     |
| 1932   | 6,666  | 3,572           | 2,875     |
| 1933   | 4,537  | 3,230           | 1,500     |

Source: U.S. Dept. of Commerce, *Commerce Year Book*, V. 2, Special Circular N. 294, Division of Regional Information, Italian Foreign Trade in 1933.

As competition from domestic production became even more problematic, importers realized that if they wanted to hold their ground in an ever growing Italian American market (in 1930 the Italian American population of New York was over one million) they needed to undertake collective action.

In the early 1930s the *Rivista Commerciale Italo-Americana*, organ of the Italian Chamber of Commerce, undertook a campaign to awaken importers to the necessity of opposing local producers' dynamism in the use of the mass media (especially the radio), a field where importers were rather weak. On Italian radio stations, 80 per cent of food advertisements were by "domestic manufacturers."[7] The major pasta producers of New York, for example, in the early 1930s undertook, on ethnic radio stations, a massive advertisement campaign to introduce their new packaged pasta. On the one hand, these brands stressed the advantages offered by mechanized production: the cleanliness, the uniform standard of quality, and the precision of weight of their products. On the other hand, the programs sponsored by Italian American companies emphasized the national and traditional character of foods. They succeeded in making meaningful, brand-named and processed foods toward which Italian American consumers were usually skeptical or hostile, placing them in a reassuring and familiar context. On Sundays, over station WOV, the "Ronzoni Macaroni Co." sponsored the program "A Trip Through Italy," in which an elderly couple described the most famous cities, the beautiful landscapes, and folklore events of the country; while the "La Rosa & Sons" was the advertiser of a high successful daily entertainment program based on Italian songs and opera airs.[8] Company chairman, Stefano La Rosa, had great confidence in progress and strongly believed that Italian American consumers urgently needed to be "modernized." Interviewed about the significance of the introduction of packaged pasta, La Rosa claimed that his firm

---

[7] "Quello che fanno gli altri," *La Rivista Commerciale Italo-Americana*, May 1, 1935, p. 12.

[8] "Ronzoni Using Radio," *The Macaroni Journal*, XIV, October 15, 1932, n. 5, p. 29; Marie Concistrè, *A study of a decade in the life and education of the adult immigrant community in East Harlem*, Ph.D. diss., New York University, 1943, p. 419; "La Rosa" advertisement on *Il Progresso Italo-Americano*, 27 marzo 1937.

always tried to be in step with the times, which are ever changing and ever requiring innovation. Beans and lentils were already sold in package, even oranges and nuts were already sold under a brand; soap, oil, sugar were not sold in bulk anymore, as they used to do in little stores in Italy. Even the poorer housewife learned to demand anything through its brand, when she did the shopping . . . anything but macaroni. No doubt, there should have been a way to teach her to look for her favorite macaroni brand, so she knew what she was carrying home.[9]

Finally, the great importers decided on a planned action in the fall of 1935, and they financed a propaganda campaign on ethnic radio stations and newspapers, under the aegis of the Chamber of Commerce. In order to raise again the fortune of Italian food imports they used appeals to the national feelings of the Italian American community, something in which they were most skilled. The campaign started in the evening. The Italian-Ethiopian War was just under way and the boycott against Italy, voted by the League of Nations, and enforced by England, France and 50 other nations, was pending. The first appeal for the consumption of Italian products was broadcast on WOV on November 10, 1935 and was delivered by the president of the Chamber of Commerce. Locatelli addressed "the great masses of Italians, who more than any other factor, contributed first to create, and then to enlarge the flow of commercial exchanges between the two homelands," demanding them "to defend the Italian products in this country, setting a good example themselves in the first place by consuming them." Then, Locatelli emphasized that "this exhortation is not suggested by a selfish spirit for the benefit of a single class, but rather by the duty which all of us feel bound to help our native land." On November 12, the General Consul of Italy in New York, Gaetano Vecchiotti, appealed to the "Italic feeling of the

---

[9] "Maccheroni in pacchetti," *Il Commerciante Italiano*, 10 ottobre 1936.

immigrant masses" who "represent a rock-like block in defense of the supreme interests of the fatherland," asking them to answer "Present!" to the call for the diffusion and the purchase of Italian products.[10] In the campaign were also Giuseppe Prezzolini, director of Casa Italiana at Columbia University, and Leonard Covello, both of whom stressed that Italian foods and wines were a very important part of Italian culture.[11]

The results of this campaign were absolutely disappointing: in 1936 food imports from Italy sharply declined in comparison with the already bad figures of 1935 (Table 2).

Table 2. Imports of major Italian food products in the United States, 1935 and 1936.

(thousands)

|                 |        | 1935   | 1936   |
|-----------------|--------|--------|--------|
| Cheese          | pounds | 28,173 | 26,400 |
| Olive Oil       | pounds | 28,573 | 22,317 |
| Canned Tomatoes | pounds | 82,602 | 68,000 |

Source: Alberto Cupelli, "Foreign Trade of Italy," May 17, 1937, WPA, *New York City Guide*, Reel #25.

The great importers and their backers blamed disloyal Italian Americans for these negative results. On May 3, 1936, the general manager of Isotta Motors in New York, Elmo De Paoli, burst into an attack against the five million Italian Americans. "Even though these people became American citizens and pitched the tents under the flag of stars, that doesn't absolutely mean that they lost their right and duty to the feelings of friendliness, sympathy, brotherhood, and devotion toward the people of their own race who live in

---

[10] *La Rivista Commerciale Italo-Americana*, November 16, 1935, p. 13–14.
[11] *La Rivista Commerciale Italo-Americana*, December 1, 1935, p. 16; December 16, 1935, p. 13.

Italy. Their imperative, compulsory, peremptory, binding duty is to help Italy, already boycotted by many enemies, by purchasing its products."[12]

Not only did recourse to nationalist propaganda prove to be an inadequate and outdated technique (one that did not lead in itself to a larger consumption of imported food), the communication strategies of Italian American competitors were much more articulated. A recurring cause of frustration for importers was the use of packages with the colors of the Italian flag, or with Italian names, images and characters for products manufactured in the United States. The lack of legislation that clearly guaranteed the origin of foods allowed local producers to freely use Italian names and symbols.[13] Italian-style canned tomatoes made in California could not be named "tomatoes of Italy," but they could be lawfully sold with a label stating "Italian tomatoes." In the mid-1930s, a New York Court decided that the presence of the words "Parmesan style" and "Parmesan type" on labels indicated that the cheeses were of domestic origin, made like the original Italian Parmesan cheese, and it kept those cheeses within the law.[14] "It is very easy, walking in any 'grosseria,' to become acquainted with the names of the most illustrious Italians: kings and queens, princes and generals, poets and artists," wrote in 1934 *Il Commerciante Italiano*.

> Try to ask for an anchovies can and they will offer you the Garibaldi brand; while you turn, you will probably hit your nose against a Dante Alighieri turned into a salami."[15] "A tiny caption 'Packed in California' beneath a huge caption 'Tonno marca Italia' and the shining shield of the royal

---

[12] *La Rivista Commerciale Italo-Americana*, May 16, 1936, p. 10.

[13] Camera di commercio italiana in New York, *Nel cinquantenario*, p. 81–82.

[14] "Frauds and How to Guard Against Them," WPA, Federal Writers' Project, *Let the Buyer Beware*, Reel #123, Municipal Archives of the City of New York.

[15] *Il Commerciante Italiano*, II, 1 agosto 1934.

house it is not enough to make clear to avoid any misunder-
standing between the real Italian product and the Californian one. Do the firm Fontana Hollywood Company of New
York, Inc. believe to achieve its praiseworthy purpose to
avoid any confusion between its product and Italian tuna?[16]

According to Jean Baudrillard, brands and names of
goods are at the core of the social significance of consumption. They are shared signs that form the basis for a dialec-
tical confrontation among consumers.[17] Roland Barthes, who
dealt with the definition of a food consumption semantics,
points out the basic function of brands and advertising in
differentiating products which are otherwise alike; in as-
cribing values to foods, values which are taken from the consumers' cultural world. One of the most effective and recur-
rent themes of food advertising, Barthes points out, is to
reconnect food with a tradition, a national past, and an an-
cient experience.[18] Accordingly, the construction of the
"Italianness" of food aimed at meeting basically symbolic
needs and made up a ground in which the differentiation operated by brands and advertising could be decisive. The use
of names and images representative of a glorious Italian past
in food advertising and presentation could touch the heart
and the psychology of immigrant consumers, whose sense of
national belonging was for the most part acquired in the
United States, as a reaction to the pressures of the American life. "They may not be able to read a word or to speak
anything but a dialect," noted a social worker, "yet they thrill

---

[16] "S'incomincia, Signori!," *Il Commerciante Italiano*, II, 16 settembre 1934.
[17] Jean Baudrillard, "La genesi ideologica dei bisogni," Egeria Di Nallo (ed.), *Il significato sociale del consumo*, Bari, Laterza, 1997.
[18] Roland Barthes, "Pour une psycho-sociologie de l'alimentation contempo-raine," *Annales ESC*, n. 16, 1961.

when they hear the name of Dante, of Michelangelo, of Garibaldi."[19]

More than this, the ethnic producers' advertising was able to combine a representation of "Italian tradition" with a representation of "American modernity," drawing elements from both cultures (or better, from the fictional, but widely shared, perception of those cultures by ethnic consumers). For example, the advertisement of the canned tomato paste manufactured by the "Italian Food Products Co." of Long Beach, California, stated:

> The products that stand high in the favor of the public in the whole North America — Prepared with fresh, rightly ripe tomatoes and the strictest compliance with the most modern sanitary methods of packing under vacuum." While the emphasis was on product conformity to modern, "American," standards of quality, on the other hand the tomato products were branded "Salsa di Pomidoro Campania" and "Tomato Paste Mariuccia." On the labels there were the images of smiling peasant women with handkerchiefs on their heads and a basket in their hands.[20]

While emphasizing their ethnicity and their close inherence to community daily life, Italian American food manufacturers of New York were able to set up strategies in food-processing, advertising, and presentation, capable both to link progress and modernity to "traditional" products, and to reassure the anxieties of ethnic consumers towards processed foods. These "old times," "natural," "Italian" foods stayed clean in spite of the association with aspects — otherwise with negative meaning — of urban American environment (industry, mechanization, uniformity). Thus, the difficulties of importers in holding the ethnic market, by

---

[19] Ida Hull, "Special Problems in Italian Families," *National Conference of Social Work: Adresseses and Proceedings*, New York, 1924.

[20] Advertisement on *Il Progresso Italo-Americano*, 7 settembre 1930.

appealing to the authenticity of food and to immigrants' national solidarity, corresponded to the enthusiasm and ingenuity of many Italian American food entrepreneurs in taking advantage of mass media and mass advertised brands to influence the behavior and mentality of changing ethnic consumers. The success of many of these Italian American-owned companies continued after World War II, when their path-breaking work attracted the interest of big corporations in search of new products and new markets.[21]

What has been said so far suggests, in my opinion, this working hypothesis: the growing consumerism and mass culture of urban American society between the two World Wars did not necessarily bring a disruptive pressure to bear on ethnic working class identity, nor was it necessarily confronted by cultural conservative forms. The new cultural forms pervaded behaviors and mentalities more subtly, they were filtered through ethnicity and ethnic institutions. Peculiar forms of ethnic consumption were neither suppressed nor remained unaltered, but underwent a redefinition. Even the "authenticity" of ethnic cultural products proved to be a mobile and continuously reinterpretable concept.

---

[21] Warren Belasco, "Ethnic Fast Foods: The Corporate Melting Pot," *Food and Foodways*, 2, 1989.

# From Lucca to the 'Bush':
# Lucchesi in Western Australia in the 1920s & 1930

## Adriano Boncompagni
### University of Western Australia

Questo contributo esamina la distribuzione degli emigranti dalla provincia di Lucca in Australia Occidentale, con lo scopo di delineare un modello migratorio, e verificare la loro tendenza a raccogliersi o meno in aree specifiche. Un secondo obiettivo è l'individuazione del ruolo dell'emigrazione toscana nella comunità di destinazione in rapporto all'ambiente anglo-australiano delle aree minerarie dell'Australia Occidentale degli anni Trenta, con lo scopo di accertare se forme di razzismo verso gli italiani fossero causate dai loro modelli occupazionali. I risultati della ricerca confermano che i lucchesi in Australia Occidentale tesero a concentrarsi in specifici quartieri ai margini delle città e nelle aree minerarie. Trovarono da occuparsi all'interno di un numero circoscritto di attività, con il preciso scopo di accumulare velocemente dei risparmi da riportare nelle comunità di provenienza. Questa tendenza influenzò il loro ruolo sociale nella comunità che li ospitava, e spiega altresì la loro limitata interazione con la società anglosassone, talvolta creando frizioni sociali, che si sono rese particolarmente evidenti nell'ambiente minerario degli anni Trenta.

This paper has three aims. The first is to examine the spatial distribution of migrants from the Provinces of Lucca and, to some extent, Massa Carrara to Western Australia during the inter-war period, in order to ascertain their expectations and migratory patterns, and, consequently, to see whether they tended to cluster in a specific number of areas or not. The second objective is to determine whether such migrants followed work patterns related to their original skills or whether they adjusted to the job market in Western Australia regardless of their skills. Thirdly, the paper investigates the place of Tuscan migrants within the host community and their relationship with the Anglo-Australian milieu, in particular with regard to the Western Australian mining areas of the 1930s. The aim is to verify whether forms of racism towards Tuscan and Italian migrants were engendered by their particular work patterns.

The paper will first examine the geographic distribution of migrants from Tuscany within the urban areas of Perth in relation to the skills brought with them from Italy and the activities performed in the host country. Subsequently, it will analyze their presence in rural Western Australia and in the mining areas of the state. In particular, the study will focus upon a number of aspects of the (self) segregation of Tuscan migrants within the mining environment, according to their patterns of 'temporary' migration, which have led to social frictions with the Anglo-Australian community and its labor force.

INTRODUCTION AND METHODOLOGY

Due to the discovery of gold in the Western Australian gold fields around the turn of the century, Western Australia became the main destination for the relatively small Italian migration to Australia. While in 1891 only 36 Italians were officially listed as living in W.A., in 1921 there were still not more than 2,000 (Borrie, 1954). These low figures can be explained by the enormous distance between Italy and Australia, which required twice the amount of time necessary to reach the United States and the Latin American destinations that were more common for the Italian migratory flow. This also explains the pioneering aspect of this early stage of Italian migration in Australia. In 1921, however, the United States immigration policy became stricter, establishing quota systems that limited the total intake of Italian immigrants. As a consequence Australia became a more favorable destination for Italian migrants no longer permitted to enter the United States (MacDonald, 1970: 251).

The period covered by this paper is from 1921 to 1939, from the first restricted immigration entry in the United

States to the outbreak of WWII. It represents the 'intermediate' period of the Italian migratory flow to Australia, between the pioneering stage (1860–1921) and the planned mass migration of Italians to Australia, after WWI to the mid-1960s. This migration was based on informal networks established by the 'pioneers' of the earlier period (Gentilli, 1983), and it is fundamental to an understanding of the mass settlement of Italians in Australia after WWII.

This paper has drawn upon the rich store of information in the Australian Archives of WA, where there is extensive documentation related to migration, such as the naturalization files of foreign residents from 1900 to the mid 1960s. This has made possible the collection of information on approximately 300 people of Lucchese origin who arrived in Western Australia between 1921 and 1939. These records — which provide details such as date and place of birth, occupation in Italy, date of entry into Australia, occupation and place of residence in WA — have been first integrated with additional information provided by interviews with a few first-generation Lucchesi still living in Australia. On a second stage, records have been computer data-based in order to elaborate migratory patterns, occupational status and mobility. For this reason the sources have proved invaluable, and may well also provide the basis for other purposes and in relation to other Italian sub-regional groups.

## FROM LUCCA TO WESTERN AUSTRALIA

The geographic and temporal setting of the migratory flow of this study originated within the most remote Central Italian Apennine communities of northern Tuscany at the beginning of the nineteenth century and continued in Western Australia, bearing testimony to a century-long search for a living. Agricultural resources in the Tuscan communities of the Province of Lucca were never entirely sufficient to support the population. The soil was poor and agricultural holdings were extremely fragmented (Rombai, 1988). The first type of Italian migration flow developed in the mountain communities, both in the valleys and in the northern Apennine ridges, which cross the whole peninsula like a backbone. Some migrated in winter — when agricultural work was low — to France and also to England (Briganti, 1993), and returned to village communities in summer to work their own fields. From the 1860s such migrants began to cross the oceans with South America as their destination, where they worked mainly as farmhands. They also worked in a number of other countries on several continents and made intermittent trips home. This form of temporary migration was seen as a necessary sacrifice to ensure the survival of the family and the continued ownership of the small agricultural properties in the country of origin. These migrants never considered emigration as a separation from the community but rather a means of improving the survival of the community (Dada', 1994).

As stated earlier, the American entry restrictions began to produce effects in the mid-1920s. Until the Australian entry restrictions of 1928, Italians experienced no difficulty entering Australia: there were no visa requirements and, with a sponsor, they could land free of charge (O'Connor, 1996: 3). Between August 1926 and June 1927, 2,356 Italians were registered on arrival in Western Australia (Bosworth, 1993: 72). Many among these were Tuscan. Due to the distance of Australia from Italy, they had to undertake a break with their family and community. Although the reasons for Tuscan migrants to move to Western Australia in the inter-war period were various (Price, 1963: 125), there was one common goal: migrants wanted to achieve the level of well-being that they had perceived as possible from the experience of the first Italian migrants who came as pioneers to Australia at the turn of the century.

Analysis of the data related to the migrants from the Tuscan areas in Western Australia shows that after 1924 there is a steady increase in immigration, which reaches its peak in 1927, then a marked decrease during the period 1930–33, due to economic and international factors, and a rise again between 1937 and 1939. A gender analysis of the figures shows that migrants in the 1920s were mainly men. A confirmation of these figures is reflected also in the total intake of Italian migrants recorded by other Australian scholars (Price, 1963: 111; Macdonald, 1970). In the latter years of the 1930s, on the other hand, women and minors are in the majority (Boncompagni, 1998: 398), due to the tendency of Italian and Tuscan males to bring their wives and partners out several years after their arrival, particularly after the depression years following 1930 (Borrie, 1954: 53). While the settlements and work patterns of Tuscan migrants are variable until the mid-1930s, due to the prevalence of male workers continuously in search for jobs, with the arrival of women and children the community took on more permanent characteristics (Price, 1963: 113). Hence, the increase in the number of naturalizations during the late 1930s can be considered a response to becoming more socially and culturally assimilated, as the arrival of women and children confirm.

Tuscan migrants in this period performed various jobs according to their areas of destination. They were mainly farm hands or laborers, thus following the work pattern of Italians from other areas of origin (Cresciani, 1983: 312 and O'Connor, 1996: 115). In the late 1920s and 1930s, the foci of Tuscan settlements in Western Australia were the urban areas of Perth, the south-western rural corner of the state and the mining towns of the gold fields.

## TUSCANS IN PERTH

Tuscan migrants in the Perth metropolitan area tended to concentrate in the same northern inner-city suburbs to which

Italians from other regions had moved during the same years, as others have previously confirmed (Pascoe & Bertola, 1985: 31), and in the nearby hills of Karragullen (east of the city of Perth). In the late 1920s and 1930s, these were the areas where most of the market gardening for the urban supply of fresh fruit and vegetables was located. If we look at work patterns, we notice that the highest proportion in the range of activities performed by Tuscans is represented, even in the outer metropolitan areas, by market gardening and farming, followed by laboring, the latter category including factory workers and bricklayers (*Table 1*). "When some agricultural blocks, that have been subdivided for the Empire land Settlement Scheme were vacated by their first British migrants occupiers, they were made available to other settlers. This was an exceptional opportunity that several Italian and Yugoslav migrants could not miss" (Gentilli, 1983: 88).

Table 1 — Professional distribution of Migrants from Tuscany to Western Australia (Perth, rural W.A. and mining areas), 1921–1939 (original Source calculated by the Author)

|  | Perth Metro Area | Rural W.A. | Mining Areas |
|---|---|---|---|
| *Farmers (incl. Woodcutters)* | 58 | 29 | 2 |
| *Laborers (incl. Bricklayers)* | 30 | 23 | 1 |
| *Craftsmen* | 4 | 0 | 2 |
| *Other Services (incl. Cooks, Waiters, etc.)* | 6 | 0 | 2 |
| *Miners* | 13 | 8 | 29 |
| *Entrepreneurs* | 14 | 2 | 2 |
| *Traders (incl. Restaurateurs)* | 10 | 1 | 1 |
| *Professionals* | 1 | 0 | 0 |
| *House duties* | 49 | 8 | 9 |
|  | 185 | 71 | 48 |

Besides the presence of a notable number of Lucchesi involved in house duties, there were also a markedly high percentage of entrepreneurs and traders. These occupations were completely absent from the skills that Tuscan migrants had brought with them from their communities (*Table 2*). Many of them relocated to an urban environment and started independent activities, often linked to services for the Italian community, such as running shops, delicatessens, restaurants and boarding houses.

Table 2 — Professional distribution of Migrants from Tuscany to Western Australia, 1921–1939 (original Source calculated by the Author).

|  | in Italy | % | in Australia | % |
|---|---|---|---|---|
| Farmers (incl. Woodcutters) | 187 | 62% | 89 | 29% |
| Laborers (incl. Bricklayers) | 31 | 10% | 54 | 18% |
| Craftsmen | 19 | 6% | 6 | 2% |
| Other Services (incl. Cooks, Waiters, etc.) | 0 | 0% | 8 | 3% |
| Miners | 5 | 2% | 50 | 16% |
| Entrepreneurs | 0 | 0% | 18 | 6% |
| Traders (incl. Restaurateurs) | 3 | 1% | 12 | 4% |
| Clerks | 1 | 0% | 0 | 0% |
| Professionals | 1 | 0% | 1 | 0% |
| House duties/Minors | 57 | 19% | 66 | 22% |
|  | 304 |  | 304 |  |

The reason for the gravitation of migrants from the Tuscan mountain communities into this restricted range of activities in Australia is linked to the traditional peasant desire for independence, since the large majority of them had come from a peasant background. Many could count on a small amount of capital that they had accumulated over a few years from working long hours in heavy manual labor, such as in the woodcutting and mining industries in remote areas of Western Australia. Preference was therefore given to new activities that could be undertaken in urban and suburban areas (Boncompagni, 1998: 401), partly explaining the gradual increase in Perth-bound migrants in the mid-1930s. Market gardening and small family-run businesses were ideally suited to supply this sense of security. Some reasons lay also in the nature of these activities, which made it unnecessary for the migrants to participate in the Australian environment, as they generally avoided competition with organized labor (Price, 1963). This *modus operandi* can also be seen in the mining area and will be examined in detail later in this paper.

Several families of Lucchesi, namely the Bovani from Bagni di Lucca (mid-valley of River Serchio, in the Province of Lucca), the Casotti from Minucciano (from Garfagnana, the upper valley) and the Ghilarducci and Di Marco from Capannori (from the plain of Lucca) had established their residence as market gardeners and orchardists in the outskirts of Perth areas since the mid-late 1920s.[1] In light of what has been stated with respect to patterns of chain migration, it is worth stressing that Ugo Bovani left Italy in 1926 to reach his brother-in-law Dante Di Marco in Western Australia, before he was joined by his family in 1929. The two families decided to buy a small piece of land, which was cleared and adjusted to market garden, orchard and cow grazing.[2] Giovanni Ghilarducci arrived in Western Australia in 1927 with his son Sebastian, leaving his wife and other children in Italy. According to a pattern followed by many other Lucchesi, before coming to Western Australia he had already spent a few years in the United States, while his sister had migrated to Argentina.[3] On his arrival in Australia, he first grew vegetables in a suburb located north of Perth. When his family joined him in 1930, they all moved to the inland rural suburbs of the city and, in 1933, they finally bought land there and developed orchards. In the early 1930s some of those areas were widely forested, and timber was still an important industry of the outer Perth suburbs. As a consequence, Giovanni decided to set up a timber mill, later sold to another Tuscan from Casola Lunigiana, Mr Coli.[4] The mill was so suc-

---

[1] Karragullen Primary School & Pagotto, 1988.
[2] Karragullen Primary School & Pagotto, 1988: 41-41.
[3] Keast, 1987: 74.
[4] Keast, 1987: 34.

cessful that it provided employment for many Italian migrants, mainly from the Lucca area.[5] There are confirmations
that in the late 1930s, especially the Bovani and the Ghilarducci families sponsored many migrants from the Province of
Lucca to Australia.[6] A notable number of them moved to
nearby suburbs, employing themselves in orchards and sawmills at the first stage of their settlement in the country. It
is not surprising that the records indicate that a large proportion of them came from the same communities of origin of
the Bovani (Bagni di Lucca) and Ghilarducci (Capannori), thus
confirming the tightness of Lucchese family and community
links.

The spatial concentration of Lucchesi farmers shows that
they tended to cluster by community of origin. Their settlement in rural areas of Perth confirms that they came from a
very limited range of Tuscan communities. Although there
were about thirty different communes of origin, *Table 3*
shows how in some rural suburban areas of Perth, only three
villages of origin of the farmers (Bagni di Lucca, Capannori
and Casola Lunigiana) are represented.

Table 3 — Spatial concentration of Farmers (>2 per Town per single Community of origin) in rural areas of Perth

|  | Bagni Lucca | Capannori | Casola Lunigiana |
|---|---|---|---|
| Karragullen | 5 | 5 |  |
| Osborne Park/N. Perth |  | 11 |  |
| Upper Swan |  |  | 5 |
| Wanneroo |  | 2 |  |
| Balcatta |  | 2 |  |
| TOT | 5 | 20 | 5 |

For many immigrants the choice of occupational location was
not a matter of great moment: they simply came to join a

[5] Karragullen Primary School & Pagotto, 1988: 72–73.
[6] Interviews with Mr Costantino Giorgi, Highgate WA, 12 May 1998, Mr
Mario Scatena, Tuart Hill WA, 5 July 1997 and Mr Rino Masini, Yokine, 14
August 1997.

friend or a relative in Australia and followed the employment example of those who had preceded them (Price, 1963: 143). One of the records states that one Ernesto Della Santina joined his father (who he had not seen for a few years) in Western Australia in 1927, first working as farm hand in the outskirts of Perth and later in the mid-1920s moving to the remote gold town of Wiluna to work in the mines.

## TUSCANS IN RURAL AREAS OF WESTERN AUSTRALIA

Tuscan migrants in rural districts of Western Australia tended to concentrate in areas where the environment was favorable to their limited range of occupations, such as farming and timber-cutting. The farming belt and the wood-cutting districts are mainly concentrated in the south west of the State. As others have indicated with respect to the settlement of Italians in Western Australia during the inter-war period (Packer, 1947: 72 and Gillgren, 1997: 74), Tuscans moved into the south-west timber industry, where they indubitably played a valuable economic role in providing timber and wood for the mines.

Tuscans classified as farm hands in the rural districts were prevalent, but this category included also woodcutters (*Table 1*). In addition, there was a consistent number of laborers, a category which could have also included general workers employed in the wood-line. The above factor indicates that the figures about activities performed by Tuscans in the rural areas could be slightly doubtful and may possibly hide a relevant number of workers who were employed within the mining industry.

Conversely, the absence of Italian migrants engaged in sheep and cattle grazing requires an explanation. By the time Italians (Lucchesi among them) began to enter Australia in any numbers, most of the good pastoral land was already occupied (Price, 1963: 147). In addition, grazing properties required significant capital to buy and maintain. Italians, including Tuscans — who had been shepherds and grazers in the Apennine communities — realized that they were unlikely to either obtain their own properties or to quickly accumulate the money in this area that they could get otherwise through working long hours in heavy manual activities such as woodcutting and mining. In addition, station life, with its long periods of loneliness, was a far cry from the social conditions of the places of origin of Italians. Market gardening, but also any laboring activity in an urban or semi-rural environment, permitted a way of life akin to the kind of communities in which they had grown up.

It can be inferred that Tuscan and Italian migrants in general liked an active community and social life, similar to the one they had experienced in their area of origin, and, as a consequence, it could be assumed that they preferred to avoid employment in the mining towns of the remote inland of Western Australia. Figures, however, show that the presence of Italian, and in particular Tuscan migrants, was notable in the gold fields in the 1920s and 1930s, and that more than 60 per cent were in fact directly involved in the mining industry (*Table 1*).

As noted above, migrants were keenly motivated towards employment that provided immediate economic reward. It was not the quality (nor, in many cases, the safety) of the activity that was taken into consideration, but rather the potential to make money more quickly in this employment than in any other activity available in Australia during the interwar period. It is vital to understand this concept in order to put into the right context the attitude of 'temporary' migration held by Tuscan workers, and to understand their search for a living abroad as a resource to accumulate, in the shortest possible time, enough money to return home and settle there with more financial comfort they had before their departure.

This fact explains the relatively young age of migrants, the large majority of non-married males, their clustering among friends belonging to the same community of origin, as well as their adaptability in accepting any job regardless of their skills.

## TUSCANS IN THE MINING AREAS OF WESTERN AUSTRALIA

A concentration of Tuscan migrants is recorded in the remote mining towns of Cue, Leonora, Kalgoorlie and Wiluna, all of which had a large percentage of foreign workers who were either single or whose wives and children still lived in the country of origin (Longton, 1997: 128). In fact, if we look at the sex ratio amongst Tuscans in mining areas and we compare it to that of Italian migrants in general in the same areas (as from Pascoe & Bertola, 1985: 30), we can observe a similar ratio for all four towns (*Table 4*).

Table 4 — Sex Ratio amongst Tuscan (calculation by the Author) and Italian Migrants (source: Pascoe & Bertola, 1985) in some mining areas of Western Australia, 1921–1939

|  | Tuscan Men | Tuscan Women | Italian Men | Italian Women |
|---|---|---|---|---|
| Cue | 2 | 1 | 22 | 8 |
| Leonora (incl. Gwalia) | 6 | 3 | 169 | 24 |
| Kalgoorlie | 3 | 1 | 61 | 14 |
| Wiluna | 15 | 3 | 220 | 29 |

The above chart validates the reliability of the records collected on Tuscan migrants and the confirmation of a gold fields' population with a large majority of male workers. Their presence, although prolonged for a few years, was always temporary and aimed at accumulating quick earnings to re-invest in either the community of origin or in other geographical areas of Australia, often urban. As suggested by Gentilli, they undertook the long journey from the mountain communities of Central Italy to the harsh outback of the mining towns because they did not want to expose their wives (if married) and children to the hardship and uncertainties they expected to meet (Gentilli, 1983: 77). In addition, the pattern of 'temporary' migration established in the mountain areas of northern Italy certainly contributed to witness a large number of single male Lucchesi 'wandering' throughout remote Western Australia in search of good earning opportunities to take back to Lucca after a few years spent overseas.

*Table 5* shows how the mining activity performed by Tuscans in the gold fields did not have any similar precedent in Italy. All the migrants employed as miners were farm hands and laborers. Unlike the experience of those who worked in market gardening in Western Australia, whose professional background was, primarily farming, Tuscan miners had a totally different professional background.

The figures confirm both that these migrants chose woodcutting or mining as a way to facilitate the fast accumulation of money and also as a 'temporary' working situation with a view to the investment of small capital in professional areas which were undoubtedly more congenial to them. This choice was also compatible to that of the state government, which was keen to locate Southern Europeans in areas other than urban, in order both to better control them socially and to enhance the economy in areas where the Anglo-Australian community was less than willing to settle. 'The Mines or the Bush' became the catch-cry of immigrant Italians in the inter-war period (Pascoe & Bertola, 1985: 13).

Table 5 — Previous Profession of Migrants from Tuscany to Western Australia, 1921–1939 (original source calculated by the Author)

| Activities in Italy | Activities in Western Australia | | | | | | | |
|---|---|---|---|---|---|---|---|---|
| | Farmers | Laborers | Craftsmen | Miners | Traders. | Housewives | Other Acts. | |
| Farmers | 75 | 33 | 3 | 38 | 13 | 5 | 6 | 173 |
| Laborers | 7 | 8 | | 5 | 3 | 1 | 3 | 27 |
| Craftsmen | 4 | 2 | 3 | 4 | 1 | 2 | 1 | 17 |
| Miners | 1 | 2 | | | 2 | | | 5 |
| Traders/ Entrepr. | | | | | 2 | | 1 | 3 |
| Housewives | 1 | | | | 3 | 33 | | 37 |
| Students/ Minors | 2 | 3 | 1 | 1 | 5 | 13 | 1 | 26 |
| Other Acts. | | 1 | | | | | 1 | 2 |

In the latter years of the 1930s, the major component of arrivals in Australia from Tuscany is represented by women and children (Price, 1963). The change in the migratory pattern was probably due to external factors, such as the growing political instability of the Fascist regime in Italy and the stricter entry conditions adopted by the Australian immigration authorities (Macdonald, 1970: 272). In response to Italian political instability and Australian Federal policy, many Tuscan migrants were induced to sponsor their families to join them in Australia and, if possible, to become naturalized. On the whole, males used to tend to defer naturalization until they had finally established their homes in Australia (Borrie, 1954: 123). With the arrival of their families, the Tuscan group took on more permanent characteristics as did the Italian one in general, becoming the stepping stone of Italian post-war mass migration.

While these latter changes took place only in the late 1930s, this paper aims to focus also on the place of Tuscan miners within the hosting mining community and on their relationship with the wider Anglo-Australian environment.

Italians had begun to arrive in the Western Australian gold fields at the turn of the century, when the gold mining industry was passing into a period of consolidation and rationalization. In order to make new large capital investments, gold companies sought to cut labor costs and to increase productivity. Italian migrants, in particular northern Italians, in desperate search for highly paid labor within their pattern of 'temporary' employment, were perfectly suited to this new labor trend. The main assets that this class of immigrants brought to Western Australia were all labor related: more than specific skills, they were willing to work harder and for lower wages than the local working class, and they exhibited the requisite predisposition of flexibility to accommodate fluctuations in employers' needs (Portes & Boeroecz, 1996: 166).

Italian workers in the mines not only obtained employment — always through intermediaries and third men — at the expense of local labor, but were also used in the process of cutting costs and were employed to break strikes over conditions and piece rates (Bertola, 1993: 7). The Western Australian Labor Party drew attention to this situation on a number of occasions, lodging a petition — which was rejected — to the Federal government in 1906 to extend the Immigration Restriction Act, then applicable to colored workers, also to Italians (Cresciani, 1983: 320–21).

The number of Italians and other Southern Europeans in the mines had increased throughout the 1910s, representing up to 22.65 per cent of the underground workforce by 1913 (Bertola, 1993: 8). Although the recession hit the mining industry in the 1920s and the number of miners fell from a pre-war figure of 13,020 in 1913 to a low of 3,766 in 1928, by

January 1934, on the eve of the riots in Kalgoorlie, Italians and Yugoslavs still made up 18.37 per cent of the underground workforce in Kalgoorlie and 41.33% in the associated mines (figures from Bertola, 1998: 14-15). As a consequence, rising unemployment among Anglo-Australians in the late 1920s drew more attention to the presence of Southern Europeans, inciting the former ones to write to the local press calling for restrictions in Southern European immigration, as happened also in the woodcutting industry (Gillgren, 1997: 75 and 76).

Lucchesi had arrived in the mining towns during the early 1920s in increased numbers, and their presence was reflected in the proliferation of local stores, hotels and boarding houses run by several Tuscans (Pascoe & Bertola, 1985: 22). In 1933, there were 133 Italians in Boulder and 132 in Kalgoorlie (Packer, 1947: 40-41), while in Wiluna there were about 250 (Longton, 1997: 127).

The general aim of Italian miners in the gold fields was, again, to make money as quickly as possible. The higher wages paid in the remote mining areas were perfectly suited to this aim. The relatively small size of Italian settlements worked against the creation of political organizations with a large following. Many migrants, accustomed to staying in any one remote place only for short periods of time, had a 'temporary' attitude to the local working community. This militated against their taking part in social, political and union activities. The effort of keeping themselves above the "bread line" (Cresciani, 1980: 3), deterred many of them from any organized attempt to keep abreast of politics or to become active in political parties and unions.

SEGREGATION

In addition, as is shown by the composition of occupational background in *Table 5*, Lucchesi did not have any articulate middle class, no intellectual elite which could express the range of ideas that might give raise to positive political or union action. On the whole, Lucchesi and other Italian workers preferred to congregate with people of the same community of origin, with whom they shared common heritage and culture. This tendency to form group settlements, within the highly unionized Anglo-Australian mining environment, worked against rapid assimilation.

This devotion of first-generation Italians and Tuscans to the narrow circle of the home and community of origin explains their limited interest in social activities and their apathy towards political affairs. As stated earlier and confirmed by the authoritative work of Borrie (Borrie, 1954), migration chains, which operated after 1921, suggest the movement of groups, including relatives and friends, to be guided by economic and not political reasons. Although there are a few records of Fascist (Fabiano, 1983: 234) and anti-Fascist sympathies (Cresciani, 1979: 151 and Missori, 1982: 319) amongst Italian and Tuscan migrants (O'Connor, 1996: 147 and 153), the large majority of them was driven by economic needs and displayed little interest in politics (Pecout, 1990: 727 and 738), the local Anglo-Australian society or labor organization.

Records collected and set out in *Table 6* show the presence of Tuscan migrants in the mining areas and their composition with reference to five main Apennine communes, even if their areas of origin in the Provinces of Lucca and Massa Carrara cover about thirty different administrative centers. This provides us with context to explain the evident spatial segregation of Tuscan migrants within the host mining community, with particular regard to Wiluna, where the presence of Tuscans was notable.

Table 6 — Spatial concentration of Migrants from Tuscany in mining areas of Western Australia per single Community of origin (>2), 1921-1939 (original data calculated by the Author)

| | Wiluna | Gwalia | Other mining areas | TOT. |
|---|---|---|---|---|
| Piazza Serchio | 5 | | 1 | 6 |
| Giuncugnano | 4 | | | 4 |
| S. Romano Garfagnana | 3 | | 2 | 5 |
| Villa Comandina | 5 | | 1 | 6 |
| Capannori | 3 | 4 | | 7 |
| Other Communities | 8 | 2 | 4 | 14 |
| TOT. | 28 | 6 | 8 | 42 |

The spatial segregation of first-generation Lucchesi was not the result of any conscious withdrawal from the Australian environment, but due rather to the nature of their economic activity. Tuscans and Italians in general, already culturally distinct and isolated, as well as relatively powerless and dependent upon their work, became the object of growing ill-will. It is within this increasingly hostile environment that in January 1934 the Kalgoorlie riots occurred. A Lucchese bartender accidentally killed a local Anglo-Australian sports hero. This accident sparked the resentment of many Anglo-Australian miners against the Italians residing in Kalgoorlie, culminating in two days of riots. A raging crowd of miners devastated and burnt many shops and private dwellings belonging to Italians and other Southern Europeans in Boulder and Kalgoorlie, causing hundreds of them to find shelter in the surrounding countryside (Cresciani, 1983: 339). Notwithstanding the condemnation of this event by the media, the riots did not modify the attitude of public opinion toward Italians in general. In the 1930s the Anglo-Australian community maintained this perception of the cultural inferiority of Italians which owed much to longer-term racial conceptions. These perceptions were prejudices, which, in turn, were reinforced by the lifestyle of the migrants, and "by their apparent willingness to be used in efforts to drive down wages and conditions, and by their inability to transcend the boundaries that separated them from the host culture" (Bertola, 1993: 8–9).

## CONCLUSIONS

Anti-Italian feelings were not merely an aspect of the Western Australian mining environment. This image of Italians comes from a century-long "Italophobia" (Harney, 1985: 9) which encouraged stereotypes about race, culture and level of trustworthiness. Hence, a general antipathy towards Italians may be noted, which was partly based on racial and cultural comparisons inferring inferiority and inextricably bound with questions of Anglo-centrism and with the relations between employers and labor force in the mining community. As a scholar has clearly indicated, "racism was enmeshed with what are termed the social relations of productions" (Bertola, 1998: 21).

As this paper has outlined, Lucchesi in Western Australia tended to concentrate in a few urban outer suburbs and in the mining areas; they found employment within a restricted number of activities with the specific aim of a quick accumulation of capital to take back to their community of origin. This trend has certainly influenced their social and working role within the host community, and explains the limited interaction between them and the Anglo-Celtic community, in such a way as to spark and exacerbate forms of social rejection by the host society, giving rise at times to friction that became particularly evident in the work environment.

### References

Bertola, Patrick, 1993, "Italian Migration to Western Australia before WWI: some observations on ethnicity and conflict", *Italian Historical Society Journal*, I(2), Dec. 1993: 5–10.

Bertola, Patrick, 1998, "Racially Exclusive Provisions in Western Australian Mining Legislation," *Paper presented to the Australian Historical Association Conference, Sydney, July 1998*, 1–27.

Boncompagni, Adriano, 1998, "Migrants from Tuscany in Western Australia," *Studi Emigrazione — Journal of International Migration Studies*, XXXV, No. 131 (September 1998): 390–406.

Borrie, W.D., 1954, *Italians and Germans in Australia*, Melbourne, Australian National University.

Bosworth, Richard & Michal, 1993, *Fremantle's Italy*, Rome, Gruppo Editoriale Internazionale.

Briganti, Lucilla, 1993, "La Lucchesia e il Brasile: storia di emigranti, genti e autorità," *Documenti e Studi*, 14/15, 1993: 161–229.

Burawoy, M., 1976, "The Functions and Reproduction of Migrant Labor: Comparative Material from Southern Africa and the United States," *American Journal of Sociology*, 81: 1051–1087.

Cresciani, Gianfranco, 1979, "Italian Anti-Fascism in Australia 1922–1945" in De Felice, Renzo (Ed), 1979, *Cenni storici sull'emigrazione italiana nelle Americhe e in Australia*, Milano, Angeli, pag. 143–163.

Cresciani, Gianfranco, 1980, *Fascism, Anti-Fascism and Italians in Australia 1922–1945*, Canberra, Australian National University.

Cresciani, Gianfranco, 1983, "L'Intergrazione dell'emigrazione italiana in Australia e la politica delle Trade Unions dagli inizi del secolo al fascismo," in Bezza, B., 1983, *Gli Italiani fuori d'Italia: gli emigrati italiani nei movimenti operai dei paesi d'adozione 1880–1940*, Milano, Franco Angeli.

Cresciani, Gianfranco (Ed.), 1983, *Australia, the Australians and the Italian Migration*, Milano, Angeli.

Dada', Adriana, 1994, "Lavoratori dell'Appennino Toscano in Corsica nel secolo XIX" in *Altre Italie*, n.12: 6–38.

Fabiano, Domenico, 1983, "I Fasci italiani all'estero", in Bezza, B. (Ed.), 1983, *Gli Italiani fuori d'Italia: gli emigrati italiani nei movimenti operai dei paesi d'adozione 1880–1940*, Milano, Franco Angeli.

Gentilli, Joseph, 1983, *Italian Roots in Australian Soil*, Marangaroo, Italo-Australian Welfare and Cultural Centre.

Gillgren, Christina., 1997, "Boundaries of Exclusion: a Study of Italian and Croatian Immigrants in the Western Australian Timber Industry 1920–1940," in *Limina*, 3: 71–82.

Harney, Robert F., 1985, "Italophobia: English speaking malady," in *Studi Emigrazione/Etudes Migrations*, XXII (77), March 1985: 6–43.

Karragullen Primary School & Mary Pagotto, 1988, *Valley of Solitude, Pioneers in Kalamunda District*, Kalamunda, Karragullen Primary School.

Longton, Adelma, 1997, "Wiluna in the Thirties: the Italian presence. A case study," *Studi Emigrazione/Etudes Migrations*, XXXIV (125): 123–137.

Lowry, I.A., 1966, *Migration and Metropolitan Growth: Two Analytical Models*, San Francisco, Chandler.

Macdonald, J.S. and Leatrice, 1970, "Migration from Italy to Australia: Conflict between Manifest Functions of Breaucracy Versus Latent Functions of Informal Networks," in *Journal of Social History*, III (3), Spring 1970.

O'Connor, Desmond, 1996, *No need to be afraid — Italian settlers in South Australia between 1839 and the Second World War*, Kent Town, S.A.

Packer, D.R.G., 1947, *Italian Immigration into Australia*, Melbourne, University of Melbourne, MA Thesis (unpublished).

Pascoe, Robert & Bertola, Patrick, 1985, "Italian Miners and the Second Generation Britishers at Kalgoorlie, Australia," in *Social History*, Vol. 10, 1985: 9–35.

Pecout, Gilles, 1990, "Dalla Toscana alla Provenza: emigrazione e politicizzazione nelle campagne (1880-1910)," *Studi Storici*, Vol. 3 (July-September 1990): 723–738.

Portes, Alejandro & Borocz, Jozsef, "Contemporary Immigration: Theoretical Perspectives on Its Determinants and Models of Incorporation," *International Migration Review*, XXIII (3): 606–630.

Price, Charles A., 1963, *Southern Europeans in Australia*, Melbourne, Oxford University Press.

Shreshtha, N., 1988, "A Structural Perspective on Labor Migration in Underdeveloped Countries," *Progress in Human Geography*, 12: 179–207.

Zelinsky, W., 1971, "The Hypothesis of the Mobility Transition," Geographical Review, 61: 214–249.

# ITALIAN AMERICANS AND
# SOCIAL/CULTURAL TRANSFORMATIONS

# The Women We Are:
# Images of Italian-American Women in the Cinema

Dawn Esposito
St. John's University

L'approccio idologico del cinema produce una definizione sia dell'individuo sia della popolazione di appartenenza. Il cinema americano ha il compito di definire l'identità etnica nell'ambito della categoria generale "l'americano." Questo contributo delinea I parametri della definizione della donna italoamericana. Utilizzando le definizioni delle donne articolate nel "culto della vera femminilità" esso delinea I tratti caratteriali assegnati ai ruoli cinematografici di "mamma," "figlia," "giovane vicina di casa," "donna del mafioso." Si analizza anche l'impatto di queste rappresentazioni ideologiche sulla coscienza della donna italoamericana e lo spettatore è spinto a resistere a tali messaggi negativi e fuorvianti.

The clear separation of lived experience from media imagery, if ever it existed, has been seriously challenged from two fronts that have themselves previously been perceived as distinct: theory and spectators who wholeheartedly embrace images intended to represent who they are to themselves and others. Italian-American spectators individually accept or reject, scrutinize or disregard the images on the silver screen; yet there has been no sustained attempt at delineating what these images are. This paper begins such an attempt. It is a postmodernist project of "asking after the process of the subject's construction' (McRobbie 69). It takes "the deep interrogation of every breathing aspect of lived experience by media imagery as a starting point" (McRobbie 14) and it will consider images as they relate to, against and across from each other. The subject under scrutiny is female; thus this work is part of a feminist, postmodern project. It assumes that individuals become sexed through forms of representation, particularly language and that "this process of being sexed is one of the key modalities of power inscribed in our bodies" (Braidotti 185). While images of men will not be discussed, they inform the discussion of women. They act as one of the unspoken binaries that signify difference; the reader is asked to keep the representations of men in mind.

I have previously argued (1996) that the representation of Italian-Americans in the cinema takes place within a structuring racial binary distinguishing white from nonwhite. The qualities and attributes of the nonwhite other are situated in the hegemonic representation of blacks. I've assumed, as have other film critics (Bogle 1973), that the standard for the representation of race can be traced back to the film *Birth of a Nation* (1915). What is strikingly clear about the representation of blackness in this film is that it falls outside the parameters of hegemonic ideology signified through white men and women. Everything connected to the cinematic beingness of black men and women is rendered undesirable and dangerous to social order; everything connected to whiteness is constitutive of social order and the good. But as Derrida has argued, all binaries are inherently unstable (Norris 1982). The binary of racial representation is imploded creating the space for new associations and resistances (Baudrillard 1981) when the representation of white ethnics is scrutinized. Through a comparison of *Birth of a Nation* (1915) and *The Godfather* trilogy (1972, 74, 90), I have demonstrated that the representation of Italian-Americans falls within the category organized around blackness. This makes it possible to locate white ethnics on what I have called a continuum of otherness. Locating Italian-Americans on this continuum opens a space for the deconstruction of identity as a construct that denies fluidity and contradiction. It leads to the conclusion that the construction of identity in the cinema must be seen as intentionally serving to reproduce hegemonic power by marginalizing all who fall outside the category of whiteness — people of color and white ethnics.

The subject of this paper takes up the location of Italian-American women on the continuum. I assume that the standard for the representation of women is set by the ideology referred to in feminist discourse as the cult of true womanhood (Ryan 1979) which appears in the mid-nineteenth century. "In this period male and female characters became expressed in the familiar antinomies: rational/emotional, aggressive/passive, courageous/timid, strong/delicate, and so forth" (Ryan 153). Love became central to female identity and was best expressed through "intense emotional attractions with sacrificial overtones" culminating "in subordination to a male in the bonds of matrimony" (Ryan 157). A wife's greatest satisfaction was to "provide a maternal bosom for her spouse, to be a nurturing, asexual mother" (Ryan 157). Women were instructed in a childrearing method called gentle nurture "which promised that by exercising control over the child's emotions, the mother could weld her offspring to lifelong compliance with the virtues of propriety, diligence, self-control and conscientiousness" (Ryan 160).

What follows is a typology of characters consistently employed to represent Italian-American women in the American cinema. The specific characteristics of each type will be discussed and contrasted with the hegemonic representation of the type. Changes in the representations will be identified and assessed for the progressive or regressive impact they have in shifting the overall representations on the continuum of otherness. My intention is to stimulate social agency on the part of the spectator-reader. For me, agency sometimes entails delineation of the negative images in order to self-consciously and thoroughly know them and sometimes it means, following Susan Sontag's discussion of camp (1967) taking over forms that can then be used for one's own positive assertions of self and group identity.

## THE MAMMA

There are two versions within this type. The old woman-as-mamma who is first generation and the more Americanized version, second or third generation women who carry on the work of mothering. The old-woman-as-mamma is always dressed in black because she is always widowed and is circumscribed within an obsessive concern for her sons. The mother depicted in *Marty* (1953) is a prototypical example. She is first seen eliciting information from her nephew on places her son can go to meet girls. She wants Marty married and pushes him to go out on a Saturday night. He tells her that he's "gone out every Saturday for his whole life looking for a girl and all he's gotten for his trouble is heartache." He "doesn't want to be hurt anymore." She pushes him anyway completely impervious to the deepness of the pain he has just expressed. He screams at her "I'm ugly ma what do you want from me; I'm miserable enough as it is. I'll go but all I'll get for my trouble is more heartache." This exchange reveals that the mother's motivation is not loving concern for her son's happiness as the hegemonic demands but rather a selfish concern for her own well being. Her dependency is what drives her. Her sister Caterina lives with her son and his family. They want Caterina to move in with Marty and his mother because they have no privacy with her living in their three-room apartment. Caterina's son Tommy wants his own life. The implication is that Caterina also fails in the hegemonic because instead of being lovingly cared for she is being rejected by her son. Caterina tells her sister it's a "sada thing when your son has no place for you in his house;" she warns that the same fate awaits her sister. "What you gonna do when Marty gets married" she asks; the answer she receives is a silent, worried look. Caterina presses the point saying, "Marty will be wanting to marry and sell this house; in a couple of months you'll be sleeping on your daughter-in-law's couch."

Soon after, the prophecy appears to be coming true. Marty meets a girl, a college graduate, the night his mother forces him to go out. They have a good time; he falls in love. Soon after, Marty begins to notice the shabbiness of the house and suggests that they sell and move to a smaller place. His mother calculatedly tries to destroy Marty's newly found happiness. Echoing her sister, she comments that "college graduates are one step from the streets." On the church steps after mass, she tells Marty that "she's not a pretty girl . . . older than she says she is . . . she's not an Italian girl . . . there's something about her I don't like . . . don't bring her up to the house no more . . . she's not an Italian girl, there's plenty of Italian girls around." Marty's mother again reveals her failure in relation to the hegemonic. Because she is tainted, she wants her son to marry a woman like herself in order to prevent him from the possibility of attaining hegemonic legitimacy.

A common message in later movies is that mothering by non Italian women provides the only opportunity for Italian men to achieve inclusion in the hegemonic. Marty appears to give in to his mother's resistance. He doesn't call as he had promised. Instead he sits in the bar with his friend and says "you don't like her, my mother don't like her, she's a dog, well I'm an ugly man. I had a good time with her and if I have more good times then I'm gonna get on my knees and beg her to marry me." Marty doesn't resist the opportunity for happiness. He is able to act in a healthy way because he is not completely damaged from the mothering he's received. This is an important moment in the representation of Italian mothers because as we will see in more recent films, the sons mothered by Italian women are damaged and dysfunctional. These are sons that fall outside the parameters of hegemonic masculinity because Italian women nurture them. The depiction of the mother in *Marty* resists an easy inscription in the category of the other. This mother is named, and her name Teresa is enunciated. She is afforded an embodied space in the film; one missing in later films.

In films such as *Mac* (1993) and *Fatso*, (1980) the Italian-woman-as-mamma never appears on screen. This absence signifies her danger. The opening scene in *Fatso* begins with the son Dom's birth. He sucks vociferously from the breast and we hear his father say about his wife "you such a good mother." We then see a woman's hand sticking cake into little Dom's mouth whenever he cries. The mother's face is never shown. Dom's obesity is the subject of the movie. He wants to lose weight, can't and blames his mother for it. After bingeing on a Chinese take-out dinner for six, Dom crying, yells at his mother's picture ". . . you made me a damn fatso, it's killing me — oh momma." Dom is saved from the damage inflicted by his mother through the intervention of his girlfriend Lydia who identifies as Polish despite the fact that her mother was Italian. The corrective device for mothering by Italian women used in movie after movie is the non Italian wife and mother. Only she can raise children free from damage. Kaye, Michael Corleone's wife is able to rescue their son Anthony from the destructiveness of his father's Italian nature. She supports his desire to sing opera and escape the family business. In the final scene of destruction that closes *The Godfather III* (1990), Anthony is on the steps with his mother far removed from his father. He watches with her as his sister standing beside them is killed.

Vito Corleone's wife perhaps best demonstrates the point that Italian women fall outside the hegemonic as mothers. Mothers, as the arbiters of morality are expected to raise god-fearing, law-abiding children — children, who as adults can assume respectable positions in the legitimate community of their peers. Mrs. Corleone's sons are completely inscribed within the category of the other. They are promiscuous and unfaithful; they beat their women and fail to protect them from other men. They kill women and men without remorse. They kill each other.

While there is some diversity in the representation of the Americanized Italian mother, this is not enough to locate her within the hegemonic. She is depicted as shrewish, a quality associated with the old woman in *Mac* (1993) who is signified through a screeching, disembodied voice that emanates from behind a half-closed door and seen quite clearly in *Household Saints*, (1993), vulgar and violent. Dom's sister Antoinette in *Fatso* (1980) is the quintessential example. She uses the curse 'rat bastard' quite often and is always seen hitting her children. She beats Dom with a stick despite the fact that she cares about his well being. One can only assume that she's emotionally damaged from the mothering she's received. This type makes an early appearance in *Saturday Night Fever* (1977). In this film, the mother is depicted at the dinner table berating and hitting her children; that this is a common trope for the signification of ethnicity is demonstrated in *Last Exit to Brooklyn* (1990). There are only two mothers depicted in this film. One is clearly coded as Italian despite the fact that the family's last name is never revealed. Her first appearance in the film is at the breakfast table. She is screaming and slapping her children. The other mother has a drag queen as a son; her failure is quite obvious. The failure of the Italian mother is demonstrated through her daughter's out of wedlock pregnancy. The father of this baby tells the spectator that the woman was the aggressor. One of the most serious falls from the grace of hegemonic femininity is wanton sexuality. This is a common theme in the representation of Italian daughters.

There are exceptions to what has to be seen as the predominance of negative representations associated with this type. The mother in *Moonstruck* (1987) is one of them. While she sighs deeply throughout the movie and is seen wearing black, her daughter does not want to run from her. This indicates that the mother is capable of fostering a healthy relationship with her child. More importantly, she insists that she is worth something when she tells her husband that he has to stop his affair. But significantly, this mother is not as americanized as others that appear are. It seems that the American cinema uses an Italian/Italian-American as well as an Italian-American/non-Italian-American dichotomy to signify the good/bad mother dichotomy that underpins the ideology of hegemonic femininity. One exception is the mother in *True Love* (1990). She is well tempered and soft spoken, loving and affectionate with her husband and daughters. She is shown engaged in a conversation with her daughter. That the spectator finds this exceptional speaks to the continuing marginalization of Italian-American mothers as the deficient other.

## THE DAUGHTER

There is considerable variation in this type. Yet almost all, if not all of the daughters have loose sexual habits. They fail in the hegemonic compulsion to be virginal and pure. Some are marked by this; others escape. The daughter in *Last Exit to Brooklyn* (1980) is signified through her promiscuity. Her father insists that she be married; her function is seemingly to reproduce one of the most negatively stereotypical cinematic Italian-American families. The daughter in *Jungle Fever* (1991) is regarded, as a slut by her father and brothers, that she wants a black man is only part of it. The daughter in *True Love* (1990) has her fiancée come to her bedroom the night before their wedding. She greets him at the door in a white negligee just given to her by her mother. The couple had been fighting; she offers her body to make everything all right. Women are taught to employ this reasoning through our socialization in the hegemonic, so acting in this way is not inherently wrong. What is wrong is crossing the line between being a slut and being a good woman. This line seems to be drawn around the quality of the relationship to the man. True love demands that the woman offer her body; lust on the part of the woman does not. The primary lesson for women, poignantly presented in *The Summer of Sam* (1999) is that our bodies are in the world for the pleasure of men. This daughter stretches her limits of sexual behavior in an attempt at keeping her husband faithful. That she doesn't succeed is not surprising; what is surprising is the fact that she is rendered with dignity.

*Moonstruck* (1987) offers an interesting depiction of an Italian-American daughter. It differs from what the spectator has come to expect in a number of ways. Loretta is a decade older; her life very much revolves around being in the family. She is not shown to have friends; her job is to do the bookkeeping for neighborhood businesses including her aunt's and uncle's. In the first half of the movie, she somewhat resembles the Italian-woman-as-mamma; superstitious, dowdy clothes, graying, pulled-back hair. She certainly is in competition with one, the dying mother in Sicily, for her intended husband. Fortunately, she is transformed through passion. Loretta is brought into the world on the force that is Ronnie. Yet this force will not take her away from the bosom of her parental home. Together, Loretta and Ronnie signify the continuation of the loving Italian-American family that transcends the crass, working class character associated with immersion in American life. Loretta and Ronnie come from families marked by their closeness to Italian rather than Italian-American ways of being. This is perhaps the reason for the more positive representations of women seen in this movie. The mother asserts her dignity and self-respect; the mother and daughter have an involved, loving relationship; Loretta's sexuality flows from a desire that's not compromised by the urgency of keeping a man.

An unusual disruption of the continuum of otherness occurs in *Moonstruck* (1987). In order for white ethnics to be coded as the nonwhite other, whiteness must be inscribed in the film. This is usually done through one character clearly coded as white; marking this character's superiority is crucial to the dynamics of representation. In *The Godfather* (1972), Kaye serves this function. All the Italian men and women fail to live up to her standard. Her mothering rescues her son Anthony from his Italianness. In *Gloria* (1980) the waitress serves this function; in *Angie* (1994) it is the Irish step-mother Kathy. In *Moonstruck* (1987) whiteness is inscribed through the father Cosmo's mistress Mona. In what is a very interesting inversion of the usual dynamics of representation, she is the woman rendered as cheap and crass, the position the Italian-American woman is usually in. Cosmo ultimately leaves Mona not only because his wife tells him to but because his wife is a woman deserving of his love. The specta-tor is treated to a valorization of the Italian woman intended by the movie; she doesn't need to exert the energy of a re-sisting reading to get there.

The daughter depicted in *Angie* (1994) is damaged. Her damage is expressed through her inability to mother her own son; it is attributed to her mother "an Italian from Texas." We're told that this mother is not talked about; that she was a free spirit who "danced naked in the snow and was taken away." Her mother's schizophrenia is Angie's legacy. Angie tries, without success, to take leave of her background throughout the movie. She refuses to marry her Italian plumber boyfriend Vinnie even though she's carrying his child. She moves in with Noel, a successful English attorney and fantasizes that she and her child will have a life with him. She gives birth to a son with a deformed arm; during his christening party she leaves to go after Noel. It is only his rejection that forces her to return to her father's house and her son.

Angie's unnamed son rejects her from the moment of his birth by refusing to nurse. In a scene that begins Angie's journey back to her mother for purging, the baby begins crying while Angie is in the bathtub. She comes out saying 'this is it; I'm gonna nurse you if it takes all night." She doesn't get the chance; when she enters the nursery, her Irish-American stepmother Kathy has the baby at her breast. She tells Angie, "he just reached for me." Angie runs into her room, packs a bag and runs away. She calls her friend Tina asking her to explain. She tells Tina that she has to "get away . . . long enough to sort things out." Angie tells her, "I guess I'm my mother's daughter; she ran and now I'm running." Angie goes to Texas in search of her mother; all she has of her is her memories and an old photo of the two of them taken when Angie is young. Tina joins Angie on the road; when they seem to reach a dead end she pressures Angie to come home with her. Angie tells her "you don't understand . . . he (her son) don't want me, he knows . . . that everything about me is wrong." Angie articulates a theme that resurfaces in movie after movie. Italian-American women are not capable of competent mothering.

Angie finds her mother and her mother's sister who takes care of her. Her Aunt tells Angie that her mother is schizophrenic, on medication and not really functioning. Yet she tells Angie to talk to her. When Angie responds that she doesn't know what to say, her Aunt says "Angie that's your mama; you just talk with her." The implication is that schizophrenia is not a barrier when it's in the family. Angie shows her mother the picture. When Angie turns her back, her mother takes a lighted cigarette to the picture burning out her image. This sequence can be read in a number of ways. If seen from the hegemonic, it is a complete obliteration of Italian-American mothers by their/our own hand. From a position of resistance, it is a loving attempt at freeing Angie from her mother's corrupting presence. Angie returns home to find her son in a coma. He has been named Sean by her stepmother after the baby she herself had lost. Despite the fact that Angie has consistently rejected this woman as her mother she accepts her now. The viewer cannot help but recognize Angie's acceptance of her mother's self-obliteration. Angie sits at the incubator and tells her son, "Okay, listen Sean. I know what you're thinking. Why should I wake up when she left. You know that since you was born I did everything for the wrong reason. Give me another chance; I'll take care of you." When he wakes up she tells him, "let's make a deal. You gotta eat something; think of me as a human fridge." She doesn't claim status as his mother; on some level she knows, as does the woman spectator, that Kathy is more suited.

The daughter depicted in *Household Saints* (1993) is as unusual as the conditions that brought her birth family into being. Her mother, initially depicted in the story as a daughter herself, is won in a pinochle game. Her mother-in-law never accepts her. Katherine gives birth to her daughter Theresa after the mother-in-law's death. The death becomes an occasion for the family's move into a more modern, American way of life. Katherine is seen transforming the apartment and boxing up the old woman's religious statues. These efforts are in vain; her daughter Therese has no interest in having an American childhood. She becomes obsessed with religious fervor and aspires to be a Carmelite nun. Since her father will not allow her to enter the convent, Theresa is forced to serve god in a different way until her father relents. She engages in the monotonous performance of onerous tasks offered to God. While ironing her boyfriend's shirt, she thinks she has a conversation with Jesus. Therese is sent to the nuns to recover but instead dies. Her father and the neighbors come to think of her as a saint. She's reputed to answer petitions left in her coffin. Only her mother resists. She knows that Therese was connected to her grandmother, a grandmother grounded in superstition and old, black clothes. The daughter as saint has no place in the version of

Italian-American life depicted in the cinema. Her rejection of carnality comes too close to marking her as white thus risking location on the continuum of otherness.

## THE NEIGHBORHOOD GIRL

Adolescent young women who aren't located within families and friends fall within this category. Both character types tend to be rendered in very stereotypical ways. Friends, unlike the leading woman character, are the women who choose to stay in the neighborhood. They are the women who have the biggest hair, the biggest earrings and the tackiest clothes. They also have the biggest hearts. Mostly they function at helping the leading character transcend her condition. The film *Working Girl* (1988) opens with Tess and Cindy riding to work on the Staten Island ferry into Manhattan. Tess plans to work her way out of the secretarial pool; her girlfriend Cindy despite having reservations supports her efforts. At the movie's end, it is Cindy who Tess calls from her new, private office to describe her view. We see Cindy in the middle of a circle of women excitedly telling them the news. This scene reinforces what has transpired in the unfolding of the narrative. Tess has moved up and out of the neighborhood; Cindy has married her long-time boyfriend and is going nowhere fast. The spectator, despite the fact that cross-ethnic friendships are not a usual pattern in films, is not surprised to know that Cindy is Italian and Tess is not. The continuum of otherness as a socializing device has inculcated us into this awareness.

The girlfriends in *Jungle Fever* (1991), *True Love* (1990), and *Angie* (1994) are strong women. Their support is constant even when it means challenging the men they are connected to. In *Jungle Fever* (1991), Angela's friends take her from her father's after sustaining a beating for having a black lover. They use their bodies to enclose her within a circle and walk her away from the house, yelling at the gawking neighbors, "what are you lookin at?" While they are uncomfortable with her choice of a black man, they work at giving up their long-held prejudices because they want their friend to be happy. These women are capable of self-transformation even if they never leave the neighborhood.

The friends in *True Love* (1990) work hard at supporting Donna. It's clear that Michael, her soon-to-be husband, is not ready for their impending wedding. They indicate that it would be all right for Donna to call it off. When she resists saying, "I can't live here if I don't marry him" they support that decision. They stay with her through a long night, do the wedding tasks Michael doesn't get around to, and comfort her when he wants to go drinking with his friends after the wedding reception. They represent the strength that Angela lacks. When they come to comfort her in the bathroom at the wedding reception, they are clear. She has a right to stand up to Michael and tell him that she doesn't want him to leave her on their wedding night. These are not women who will be pushed around by their men.

Unfortunately the same cannot be said for Tina, the friend in *Angie* (1994) who is pushed around by her husband. He calls her "Orca the killer whale" referencing the fact that she's overweight. He shouts that "no one else would have her but a loser like him." This degradation is consistent throughout the movie. Yet, in a display of mutuality in friendship rarely seen, Angie defends Tina at every turn. The female spectator is not surprised. Tina is a wonderful woman deserving of such love. Tina is present for Angie on her journey. She supports her during her pregnancy, is there in the delivery room and makes sure Italian sauce is served at the baby's christening. When Angie leaves in search of her mother, Tina joins her on the road saying "finding your mother is a big deal. I'm not letting you do it alone. I'm going with you." She is large and wonderful in her Italian self on the bus. As they go to their seats Tina says, "it's like a friggin morgue in here." She sits and holds Angie's hand. She is capable as well of being angry with Angie. When it appears that they have reached a dead end, Tina encourages Angie to come home and be with her son. She says in response to Angie's opposition, "I know you can be cold." When Angie argues that her son knows that everything is wrong about her, Tina tells her that she's "pathetic" and wonders "why she is still her friend." Tina leaves Angie saying that even though her husband is abusive towards her "he would never abandon his kid." When Angie comes back to Brooklyn her son is in intensive care. Tina is there with him. Her support transcends her anger.

The neighborhood girls, Annette and Stephanie, featured in *Saturday Night Fever* (1977) perhaps best represent the failure of the Italian-American woman to fulfill the standards of hegemonic femininity. These are the women without families. Similar to the way in which women of color are rendered, they are completely inscribed by their sexualized bodies, though to varying degrees. The woman spectator, recognizing her commonality with the Italian-American characters on the screen has to make identification if she is to find redemption from her own nature. Since the narrative makes clear that Annette is doomed, the spectator understands that it is through identifying with Stephanie and following her example that she can save herself. Annette, Tony's dance partner worships him. She offers her body as a way of getting him to like her. She tells him, "I'm gonna do it with you." His response "you gonna be a nice girl or a cunt" clearly delineates the options for a woman. She chooses the second option. The spectator sees her again waiting for Tony on the street, condoms held out in her hand. He has dismissed her as his dance partner; he now dismisses her again because he's interested in Stephanie.

Tony enters the dance contest with Stephanie as his partner. During their rehearsals, he becomes interested in her sexually but she brushes him off. She makes it clear that she is getting herself out of the neighborhood. She talks of her "interesting job" and the apartment she's moving into in the city. The spectator learns that her transcendence is due to her training by her former boyfriend, someone clearly white who took her under his wing at the office. Stephanie tells Tony that he "gives her advice about books, trains her." She calls him "a friend who she slept with for a while." She justifies that "he helped her" because "a girl can't do it on her own." It's his apartment she's moving into; he's "leaving the furniture" because she "picked most of it out anyway." The message is clear; Italian women need white men to help them. The contrast with Tony is clearly drawn. Tony works as a clerk in a paint store, has no money and no prospects. All he can do is dance.

Annette's path to doom winds itself down to the night of the dance contest. She gets drunk while watching Tony in the club with Stephanie. When the contest is over, Stephanie leaves on her own and Tony goes for a ride with his friends. One of them brings Annette along. Two of the men fuck Annette in the backseat. Despite her crying, Tony attempts no intervention. When the car is brought to a stop on the Verrazano Bridge, Annette jumps out. It appears that she will fling herself off the bridge; instead one of the friends does; all attention turns to him. The spectator is left knowing that as women we can't fully escape our destiny. We are invisible and we are cunts.

## THE MAFIA CHICK

This type is comprised of women who most certainly fall outside the category of hegemonic femininity; they don't serve as mirror images for the personality of men. They scorn dependence and they control their bodies. They plot revenge and are tough enough to kill. The bad girl image is intended to reproduce the hegemonic. The representation of two Corleone women Connie and Mary, Michael's daughter functions in this way. Connie marries a traitor and brings death to her brother Sonny. Unable to realize her culpability, she rants at Michael for the revenge he takes, abandons her children and lives a life filled with sex and booze. She resurfaces in *Part III* (1990) trying to mother Vincent, Sonny's illegitimate son. She takes it upon herself to further Vincent's interest with Michael and is successful; she nurtures a killer. She herself kills without remorse and in the final scene drapes a shawl over her head becoming the old-woman-as-mamma. She's reinscribed back into the fold without ever having really left. Connie acts for the family never herself. Mary is marked as Michael's daughter. Her inherent badness is impenetrable; her white mother can't save her. She actively pursues a sexual relationship with Vincent her first cousin. Since incest is definitely outside the hegemonic, Mary will have to be punished. She is shot pursuing Michael on the opera house steps resisting his decision to send Vincent away. Death is her rightful end.

Fortunately for women spectators there are some bad girls in this category that we can really get behind. Gloria, in the John Cassavettes film of the same name (1980) is a stellar example. She is tough yet tender, in charge of her life. As she tells us early on, ". . . I worked my whole life, got my money, apartment, clothes, perfume, cat, and a gun." We know she's been in jail. She rejects the maternal. When Tony Tanzanni, her former lover and mafia boss, asks her to give over the boy she's protecting, he says to her "I understand you are a woman; he's a little boy. Every woman's a mother; you love him." Gloria responds, " I'm not a mother; I was one of those sensations, always a broad. I never liked the milk. . . . I don't love the kid." And when the little boy Phil asks if she'll be his mother since his own mother, Gloria's friend was killed in a hit ordered by Tanzanni, Gloria responds that she "wants to be family." She will protect him in the true Sicilian meaning of that familiar movie phrase. Gloria's efforts to escape with Phil to Pittsburgh are the subject of the movie. Tanzanni's men pursue them relentlessly with no success. When they come to her apartment door, she tells the boy in a relaxed, nonchalant tone, "Okay here it is . . . don't be scared. I got my gun; it's nothing for me to blow someone's brains out, believe me, I just hope it's someone I know" then she calls out in a sweet, tender voice, "who is it? She's so good at what she does that Tony, in a meeting she's arranged, says to her "you can't keep shooting our people. Every time we send someone to talk you pull a gun." Needless to say Gloria and the kid get to Pittsburgh.

Despite the positive appropriation the film makes possible, there are occasions in the film that lend themselves to reproducing the hegemonic location of Italians along the continuum of otherness. The movie plays with ethnicity. The family that's originally killed has a Jewish father and a Puerto Rican mother. We never know Gloria's real last name. She's rendered through conflicting signifiers. Though Gloria speaks with the crude, working class inflection spectators have come to associate with Italian Americans; her hair is not as big as it could be. She's clothed in pastels rather than bright, primary colors; they match her white skin and very blonde hair. The spectator learns from a news reporter that the woman seen leaving the building after the murders is Gloria Swinson, "modeled after Gloria Swanson," he says. The reference to a goddess recognizable as white makes it clear, Gloria is trying to pass. It's not surprising then that Gloria never quite achieves the respect normally afforded the white woman. Phil who is seven, despite her efforts on his behalf yells at her "he's the man." He asks if she's "ever been in love" and appears to kiss her on the lips. He calls her "Chiquita and little insect." This serves to reinforce Gloria's inferior status. When they are in the restaurant, Gloria can't get the waitress to give them service. The only people she commands respect from are a black cabdriver and Tony Tanzanni.

The message is that she can't escape her nature; Italian women are not quite white.

*Prizzi's Honor* (1985) another positive film for women opens with a wedding scene. May Rose, clad in a sexy, red dress and wearing a big, black hat signifies that 'she's got a reputation to live up to." The spectator is not surprised to hear her say, "I'm the family scandal." Her father tells her she's "dressed like a puttana." The narrative reveals that May Rose has disgraced him, her former boyfriend Charlie Partana, and the entire family. May Rose tells us that 'she can't even go to Brooklyn anymore." She intends to correct that situation. May Rose and Charlie were supposed to be married, but when he flirted, making her jealous she retaliates by running away with another man. Her father had sent his men after her, but as she tells the spectator "the dishonor had been done;" by now we know what that means. The wedding is her first appearance in four years. She hasn't abandoned her desire. When Charlie goes to her apartment the day before his wedding to talk, she greets him at the door in a sexy negligee. Before long, she says, "you wanna do it Charlie, that what you want? Nobody took it slower than me — 4 years. Answer the question . . . do you wanna do it?" Charlie does "wanna do it." She says "let's do it on the Oriental with all the lights on." The unfolding narrative makes clear that this is a trap she's set for her own advantage.

Through her grandfather's intervention, May Rose is restored to her father. She has the privilege of taking care of him. The spectator sees beautiful May Rose appearing downcast, dressed dowdily in black with self-applied, mascared, dark circles under her eyes. Her father says to her at the table. "Gee May you look awful . . . my beautiful daughter is turned to an old woman. Charlie did this to you. He had an opportunity to join the Prizzi family but he had no use for you." The father reveals that his daughter is nothing but a conduit for family business. Connie Corleone may have accepted this use of her but not this girl. May responds, 'oh he had use for me papa. The night before he left to get married he came to my apartment and forced himself on me. He did it to me; he screwed me three or four times I don't remember." Daddy responds "Are you sure?" "The size of him (she demonstrates with her hands); yah I'm sure." He screams "where's your honor?" " I have no honor anymore" is her deep-throated reply. This response is too much for her father; he grabs his heart and May brings him a glass of alcohol instead of water. She smirks as he spits it out; it's clear that patricide is on her mind.

She proceeds with the rest of her plan. She discovers on a trip to Las Vegas that Charlie Partana's new wife has stolen a considerable amount of money from the family. She offers this information as a gift to her grandfather who in appreciation says, "I wish you had been a son, you are a true Prizzi." May going too far, insists Charlie's wife "has dishonored us she must pay." This scene attempts to position May Rose as more debased and diabolical than her grandfather the Don. Her grandfather says to her, "What will this do to Charlie? He's like my son. I pledged to be his second father." May protests demanding that the family honor come first. Her grandfather curtly tells her to "shut up" and then using a sweet tone "have another cookie." The spectator knows that May Rose will resist this containment. She's waited too long to not have things on her terms. She is a true Prizzi. As the plot unfolds, Dominick, May's father is shot on the street. The grandfather says to Charlie, "Dominick got old; maybe it was his daughter, who knows?" That the killer is not searched for indicates how certain the old man is. Charlie is asked to be the head of the family but he has to kill his wife. When he returns he calls May to invite her to dinner. May, bathed in white light answers the phone; it accents the floral-print dress and pearls she's wearing. Her long hair is flowing past her shoulders; she looks young, virginal. She's going to pass as the hegemonic woman with attitude. The movie ends with May Rose saying, "Holy cow, Charlie, tell me where you want to meet."

When positioned in relationship to hegemonic femininity, these mafia chicks are really bad girls but as any frequent movie viewer knows, all Italian-American women fall into that position in one way or other. What characters like Gloria and May Rose do is live life on their own terms, the very thing hegemonic femininity discourages. They serve as models of resistance to marginalization. The Italian-American woman spectator is wise to follow their lead.

### Works Cited

Baudrillard, J. *For a Critique of the Political Economy of the Sign*, trans. C. Levin. St. Louis, MO: Telos Press, 1981.

Braidotti, Rosi (1992). "On the feminist female subject or from she-self to she-other" in G. Bock and S. James (eds.), *Beyond Equality and Difference: Citizenship, Feminist Politics and Female Subjectivity*, New York: Routledge, 176–92.

Esposito, Dawn. "Looking at Myself But Seeing the Other: Images of Italian-Americans in the Cinema." *The Italian-American Review* 5.1 (Spring 96): 126–135.

McRobbie, Angela. *Postmodernism and Popular Culture*. New York: Routledge, 1994.

Norris, Christopher. *Deconstruction. Theory and Practice*. New York: Metheun, 1982.

Ryan, Mary. "Femininity and Capitalism in Antebellum America" in Zillah Eisenstein, ed., *Capitalist Patriarchy and the Case for Socialist Feminism*. New York: Monthly Review Press, 1979.

Sontag, Susan. *Against Interpretation*. London: Eyre and Spottiswode, 1967.

## Movies Cited

| | Year Released | Director |
|---|---|---|
| *Angie* | 1994 | Martha Coolidge |
| *Birth of a Nation* | 1915 | D. W. Griffith |
| *Fatso* | 1980 | Anne Bancroft |
| *Gloria* | 1980 | John Cassavetes |
| *The Godfather I* | 1972 | Francis F. Coppola |
| *The Godfather II* | 1974 | Francis F. Coppola |
| *The Godfather III* | 1990 | Francis F. Coppola |
| *Household Saints* | 1993 | Nancy Savoca |
| *Jungle Fever* | 1991 | Spike Lee |
| *Last Exit to Brooklyn* | 1990 | Ulli Edel |
| *Mac* | 1993 | John Turturro |
| *Marty* | 1955 | Delbert Mann |
| *Moonstruck* | 1987 | Norman Jewison |
| *Prizzi's Honor* | 1985 | John Huston |
| *Saturday Night Fever* | 1977 | John Badham |
| *Summer of Sam* | 1999 | Spike Lee |
| *True Love* | 1990 | Nancy Savoca |
| *Working Girl* | 1987 | Mike Nichols |

# Analyze This Goombah:
# Mafia Comedy as Italian American Cultural Expression

## George Guida
## New York City Technical College (CUNY)

I film sulla mafia hanno sempre suscitato le ire degli intellettuali italoamericani. Col tempo questi film sono diventati sempre più comici. *Goodfellas* e *The Sopranos* ed altre commedie hanno sfruttato l'identificazione degli spettatori con i gangster, rappresentati come personaggi che conducono generi di vita molto più simili a quelle dell'"uomo medio" che non a quelle di eroi mitici. Mentre gli intellettuali possono continuare a discutere circa il valore relativo ed il pericolo di questi nuovi ritratti comici, due cose sono comunque certe. La commedia sulla mafia è diventata un veicolo per la diffusione di una genuina espressione della cultura italoamericana ed inoltre rappresenta uno stadio nel processo di disintegrazione degli stereotipi (specialmente maschili) che riguardano gli italiani nella società americana.

> These positive developments [in Italian American film] are accompanied by what might be called an 'involution,' an adherence to the status quo in that a good part of the production of Italian American filmmakers, minor as well as major, remains fixated on the gangster/crime film, which continues to serve as the primary vehicle with which to represent Italianness in mainstream commercial cinema.
>
> —Pellegrino D'Acierno, "Cinema Paradiso: The Italian American Presence in American Cinema"

FADE INTO POSTMODERN CINEMA

INT. A SOCIAL CLUB—EVENING

The interior of the club in Manhattan's Little Italy is dimly lit. From the shadows emerges the image of a Mafia don seated at his desk, straight from The Godfather. It is Marlon Brando, reading the evening newspaper.

ANGLE ON BRANDO/THE DON

ANGLE ON MATTHEW BRODERICK/CLARK KELLOGG

Broderick is Clark Kellogg, a clean-cut American lad. He approaches The Don's desk, his eyes riveted on Brando. He is led by The Don's nephew, played by Bruno Kirby, who also played the young Clemenza in *The Godfather*, Part II. Kirby/Nephew introduces Broderick/Kellogg to Brando/The Don.

                    BRODERICK/KELLOGG
                    (to Brando/The Don)

         You know, you look just like the God . . .

                    KIRBY/NEPHEW
            (interrupting Broderick/Kellogg)

         Clark, you never told me your last name.

                    BRODERICK/KELLOGG

                        Kellogg.

                    BRANDO/THE DON

      Just like the cereal. Like the breakfast cereal.

Following some polite conversation about espresso and a photograph of Mussolini hanging on his wall, Brando/The Don smiles.

                    BRANDO/THE DON

                  How'd you like a nut?

He offers Broderick/Kellogg a bowl of walnuts. More polite conversation.

                    BRANDO/THE DON

           My nephew tells me you're from Kansas.

                    BRODERICK/KELLOGG

                        Vermont.

KIRBY/NEPHEW

Six of one, half a dozen of the other.

BRANDO/THE DON

Kansas, Vermont . . . you know, the most important thing is that we're all Americans. That's right?

BRODERICK/KELLOGG

That's right.

CUT TO REALITY

Like the 1990 film itself, the above telescoped transcript of Andrew Bergman's *The Freshman* conflates characters with the actors who play them, to prove a point about mainstream (white) United States' collective cultural consciousness: However they interact with Italian Americans in real life, United States' citizens like Clark Kellogg continue to be fascinated by screen images of mafiosi.

The truth is that mafiosi, Italian American criminals and brutes, remain as much a part of United States' culture as cowboys, or, more analogously, Indians; it's just that, over time, these original gangsters have come to appear tame, familiar, domestic, and in some cases rather white, when compared with others: Asian mafias, Jamaican posses, Arab terrorists, Columbian drug lords, and those old stand-by imaginary villains, non-singing African American men. Up to the 1970s, Italian American men often stood front and center in the great United States' rogues' gallery. Since then, however, as an imagined threat to public safety, mafiosi (and the Italian Americans for whom they stand) have gone the way of the Mohicans.

Sometime in the mid-1970s, on an episode of *The Carroll Burnett Show*, Steve Lawrence donned a pinstripe suit, shoved wads of cotton in his cheeks, and played a bumbling, mumbling Mafia don. From roughly that time, *The Godfather* mystique has never been the same. A decade later, the mafioso as stock comic character had ascended to the right hand of mafioso as stock dramatic character. As much as or more than an United States' symbol of alien power, he became an United States' symbol of alien power mocked. Former child actor Dean Stockwell as Tony "The Tiger" Russo in Jonathan Demme's 1988 film *Married to the Mob* took his place next to newly-made mob boss John Gotti. Marlon Brando as Carmine "The Toucan" Sabatini in *The Freshman* sat face to face with his younger self as Don Vito Corleone.

As fear often breeds laughter, and familiarity mockery, so the United States' fascination with the Mafia has bred comedy, a clear sign cultural acceptance (Davies qtd. in Mintz 25), akin to that of the angry Black man or inhumanly stoic Indian. To the United States mind, the mafioso has gone from fearsome criminal to semi-articulate, buffoonish goon, lovable outlaw, fixture of United States' culture.

Since the mid-1980s, comic screen mobsters have ranged from Jack Nicholson's raffish, sympathetic Charlie Partana in *Prizzi's Honor* (1985) to Dom DeLuise's in every sense ridiculous Don Calzone (a.k.a. "The Oddfather") in the straight-to-video flop, *The Godson* (1998). In each case, the mafioso, still the most visible representative of Italian Americans in the media, is a subject of comic derision. The United States public loves to laugh at him for what Aristotle would call his "flaws" or "ugliness," which are funny because they are not "painful or injurious" to the audience (10). These flaws (physical, mental or moral) include an indifference, even enthusiasm for violence, inability to control passions, amoral familism, and contempt for United States society's institutions. Instead of inspiring fear and loathing (and admiration, as in *The Godfather* films and other outlaw flicks), these deficiencies now inspire derisive humor.

Mafiosi have become the subject of derisive humor for several reasons. From World War II until the 1970s, Italian American organized crime families, structured and run more like corporations than actually families, wielded immeasurable power in United States' cities, sometimes through overt intimidation, but more often through the covert corruption of the United States' political institutions (Mobilio 1). Through films such as *The Godfather* and *The Godfather, Part II*, the Mafia came to be both feared for their brutality and admired for their corporate efficiency. In admiring mafiosi, the public (including many Italian Americans) have also come to identify with them (Vecoli 55). Over the past two decades, as the Mafia's power has crumbled, as the federal government has cracked down on Italian American organized crime (Mobilio 2), and as other ethnic organized crime groups have muscled in on their turf, the mafia's public image has become less fearsome and tragic, more sympathetic and comic.

One of the most recent Mafia comedies, *Analyze This*, takes stock of these changes. When a friendly capo remarks to Don Paul Vitti (Robert DeNiro), that "made guys are goin' to the feds," and "then you got the Chinese and the crazy Russians"; that, in short, "things are changin," Vitti sardonically replies, "Whaddya want me to do, open a website?" Ultimately, Vitti finds that his only way to keep up is to get out. Thankfully, the script's semi-sophistication keeps him from parroting Don Michael Corleone's famous line from *The Godfather, Part III*, "Just when I thought I was out, they pull me back in." (Paulie Walnuts, a Mafia henchman in the HBO series, *The Sopranos*, does repeat the line, but only so that the show's creator, David Chase, can make a point about the Mafia's late-stage self-consciousness and their own ironic awareness of the mafioso's place in United States' culture.) It is easy to identify with Vitti's dilemma, but not with the character himself. United States' citizens often experience stress on the job, brought on by competition and the need to update their skill sets, but they rarely face Vitti's specific problems, and are generally not homicidal. Vitti weeps, seeks out an analyst, and reveals secrets of his childhood, but he is never thoughtful or admirable. At one point, after a brief introductory session with Doctor Sobel (Billy Crystal), Vitti warns the analyst, "If I go fag, you die"; and after a subsequent nervous episode, tells him that his advice "didn't take." At no time does Vitti appear to be anything more than a selfish goon with a problem, a subject of parody.

Parody leaves characters flat and makes them appear ridiculous shadows of human beings. Anyone concerned with the public image of Italian Americans may see Vitti's parodic flatness as a blessing or a curse. On one hand, a sympathetic mafioso will only broaden the appeal of the mafioso image, and in the bargain make mafiosi, and by extension Italian Americans, appear less than human beings. On the other hand, a parodic mafioso will disarm and demystify the mafioso (and Italian Americans). To weigh its merits and to understand the significance of Mafia comedy, we have to consider the nature of comedy itself—comedy of derision versus comedy of identification.

While it may involve a degree of audience identification with subject, parody is essentially comedy of derision. It derides its subject, without seeking to reform it, as satire would (Hill 221). For better or worse, it has proven the rule of Mafia comedy, recasting even as it cements (slight pun intended) the screen image of the mafioso. Numerous film and television Mafia parodies have transformed the mafioso, but have also guaranteed that he remain the figure with whom Italian Americans are most often identified (D'Acierno 643). We should ask then, does the development of the parodic mafioso represent progress for the public image of Italian Americans?

If it does, it represents progress like the progress of dirt through the body of a transparent worm. The United

States public now identifies Italian Americans with parodic Mafiosi, as do many Italian Americans themselves, like the fictional Italian American Nick Shay in Don DeLillo's 1997 novel *Underworld*, who performs comic mafioso impersonations for his non-Italian American colleagues. Through Mafia parody, Italian Americans continue to be identified and to identify themselves with cold-blooded criminals, but criminals who are ridiculous — less than human and less powerful than before.

Mafia parody is especially unfortunate, as it parallels the real-life integration of Italian Americans into an ever-widening variety of United States' geographical regions, ethnic groups, social classes, and professions (Monti 24–26). For example, a number of Italian Americans can count themselves among the United States' leading filmmakers. *Per fortuna*, some Italian American filmmakers have recognized the cultural currency of the mafioso figure, and in their films humanize him and use him as a means of Italian American cultural expression.

In spite of a recent spate of parodies — including *The Don's Analyst* (1997), The Godson (1998), Jane Austen's *Mafia* (1999), *Analyze This* (1999), and *Mickey Blue Eyes* (1999) a Mafia comedy of identification has appeared on the scene since 1990; a comedy that presents complex characters in mundane United States' situations, with whom and with which general the United States' audiences can identify. Americans of the United States now can laugh with the Mafia — and Italian Americans — instead of laughing at them. And an audience who laughs with rather than at the comic subject will be more receptive to cultural messages sent through that subject.

The first Mafia comedy of identification was Martin Scorsese's *Goodfellas*. Its characters demonstrate a wit and emotional complexity (if not always an intelligence) previously foreign to the Mafia genre. These Italian and Irish American gangsters not only have two families, but they interact with the members of their families in ways that make them appear at times glamorous, at times ridiculous, and at times ordinary. Yes, Jimmy Conway (DeNiro) and Tommy DeSimone (Joe Pesci) indulge in hyper-violent murder, and, yes, they commandeer shipments like Old West stagecoach robbers — during one such robbery, Tommy points his gun in a victimized truck driver's face and yells, "Where's the strongbox, you fuckin' varmint?" — but these same dashing gangsters also sell cigarettes from the trunks of cars, vacation on the Jersey shore, dine in tacky restaurants, live in still tackier houses, and with the exception of weekly trysts with girlfriends, enjoy mundane domestic lives. Their lives are familiar not only to Italian Americans, but also to those in the United States in general.

These outlaw citizens are living symbols of Italian American cultural traits with which Italian Americans and non-Italian Americans alike can identify; they are symbols of Italian American assimilation. When Tommy and the boys stop by his mother's house at 2 a. m. for a shovel which they need to bury a body stowed in the trunk of their car, Tommy's mother, all'italo-americana, is there waiting with a full meal. She urges Tommy to "get a nice girl, so you can settle down," and then tells a funny story that "in Italian . . . sounds much nicer." Her story itself is a symbol: a story of the old Italian comic figure, the cuckold (D'Acierno 612). The Italian American signs in this scene may only be intelligible to an Italian American audience in touch with its heritage, but the mild mother-son antagonism is recognizable to any audience from the United States; it is a scene of family — like a number of scenes from *The Godfather* movies and others — with which they can identify.

Those who claim that films like *Goodfellas* do more harm than good for the public image of Italian Americans may have a point. The Italian American man as mobster remains an anti-social American of the United States (Talese, qtd. in Haberman B1); however, his tendency toward sociopathy makes sense (in lesser degrees) to anyone from the United States who has never wanted to play that other stock comic type, the little soul, the fool, to an overbearing government or to the kind of mind-numbing existence to which Henry Hill (Ray Liotta), the most Americanized of the Goodfellas, is doomed.

Tony Soprano, of David Chase (nee DeCesare)'s HBO series, *The Sopranos*, epitomizes this sort of Italian American sociopath. Tony is as far from Don Corleone as he can be. His underworld "empire" in Northern New Jersey is crumbling. The series opens with a shot of Tony lying flat on his back, speaking in voice-over to his therapist, Doctor Melfi, remarking, "It's good to be in something from the ground floor. I came too late for that, I know. But lately I'm getting the feeling that I came in at the end. The best is over." In both his personal and professional lives, Tony suffers various symbolic forms of castration, hence his last name. As Mafia don, he contends with his resentful uncle (archly named "Junior") who puts a contract out on him, and a gang of incompetent or subversive subordinates. His nephew Christopher, one of his soldiers, dreams of selling his screenplay about Mafia life; one of his most trusted paesans, Big Pussy Bonpensero, is a government informant; and the brother of the former family boss, the ruthless Richie Aprile, openly defies his authority.

As son, husband, father, and brother, Tony's power is even more dubious. His mother strongly suggests to Uncle Junior that he be killed and continually undercuts his attempts to discipline his children and run his business. At the dinner table, as the family debates how Anthony, Junior ought to be disciplined for misbehaving in church and school, Livia, Tony's mother, blurts out, "His father was the same way. I practically lived in the principal's office." Other women too challenge Tony's traditional position as patriarch of the

Italian American family. When he tries to teach his children a lesson about Italian tradition, the historical contributions of Italians, his daughter asks smartly, "Who invented the Mafia?" And when his sister Janice returns to New Jersey from Seattle, she forces Tony to lift a retaliatory ban on discussion of Livia in the Soprano household, and interferes in the punishment of his daughter. Later, this same sister pre-empts his strike on her boyfriend, the insubordinate soldier Aprile.

Whenever Tony argues with his wife, she stops him dead with complaints about his extra-marital affairs and failure to show her affection. On the latter count, Tony, like his Uncle Junior, is not completely guilty. He often hugs Carmella and kisses her affectionately, but he only rarely makes love to her and rarely shows affection in public. Uncle Junior, meanwhile, is madly in love with his long-time girlfriend, until word reaches him that she has been talking publicly of his prowess at cunnilingus, at which point Junior smashes a pie in her face and walks out on her forever. Their behavior with their women indicates that both Tony and Junior wrestle with the traditional Italian American male code of romantic conduct. According to that code, to be overly sentimental, sensitive, affectionate, or, *Dio!*, submissive, with a woman shows intolerable weakness (Gambino 145). When a symbolic intra-family Mafia war breaks out, Tony remarks to Doctor Melfi, "Cunnilingus and psychotherapy brought us to this." Departure from the traditional codes threatens Italian American unity and (male) identity. Still, the family conflict does not deter Tony from analysis; and we may safely assume that it will not deter Uncle Junior from oral sex. Both men represent contemporary versions of Italian American male identity, versions that challenge received macho screen images of Italian American men. This more accurate representation is made possible by this particular therapeutic brand of Mafia comedy.

Like millions of other Americans in the United States, Tony is undergoing psychotherapy. As an "old school" Italian American man, Tony should keep his mouth shut to EVERY-ONE about family business, but he breaks the code of silence, *omertà*, when he visits Doctor Melfi. Through Junior's and Livia's disgust with Tony's therapy, his "weakness," the Y2K audience of the United States comes to understand the rules of this code and the consequences (expulsion from the family, death) of violating those rules. The audience can also sympathize with Tony's plight as surburbanite on the couch. Therapist/patient exchanges strike a familiar, often-comic chord with the audience. These exchanges are, therefore, ideal media for the comic expression and translation of Italian American ideas and values in Italian American language, and for an airing of the internecine Italian American debate over the identity and public image of Italian Americans at the end of the twentieth century (Alaya). In one of his early sessions with Doctor Jennifer Melfi, Tony voices a skepticism of psychotherapy and its jargon, a skepticism common among Italian Americans, when he yells, "Dysfunction, *va fa'n'cul'* [up your ass]." The language and the sentiment are specifically Italian American, but the frustration with therapy-speak and the audacious expression of that frustration is universal.

Caught between his mother, wife, children, and crime family, Tony admits to Doctor Melfi, "No matter what I do, I feel guilty." The Italian American doctor's response cuts to the heart of many issues for (Italian American) men and their identity: "You accord this little old lady [your mother] an almost mystical ability to wreak havoc." Doctor Melfi's diagnosis emerges from the combination of training and intimate cultural knowledge. She is a psychoanalyst trained in the United States and dressed in business attire; she uses the methods of her United States' profession to approach problems. She is also, however, an Italian American woman familiar with the power structure of the Italian American family; she recognizes the typical Italian American mother-son relationship, one familiar to many non-Italian Americans: the domineering mother, the resentful but devoted son. With a pained expression on his face, Tony comes to Livia's defense. "She's a good woman. She put food on that table every night." What we see of Livia Soprano as a potentially lethal younger mother — at one point, brandishing a kitchen knife, she tells young Tony that she should stab him in the heart — belies Tony's defense. From her children she exacts the high price of security and self-esteem. Her behavior as a young mother, like her later suggestion that Tony be clipped, demonstrates that the Italian American model of woman's self-sacrifice for the men of the family (Bona 207, 210–13) camouflages the true order of Italian American society, which is, to borrow Luigi Barzini's term for Italy, a "crypto-matriarchy" (202). In the series' second season, this matriarchy emerges from the shadows in the form of an Italian woman don, Donna Annalisa, and, more powerfully, in the form of a steeled Carmella and a killer Janice.

Only in his leisure time does Tony appear completely in control. He lives the life of the immature, irresponsible bachelor, pampered only son (though we learn that as a child he was not this), and wayward husband, a stock type of Italian and Italian American culture, and increasingly, of United States' culture. He spends much of his spare time at a strip club called Bada Bing!, some time with his impudent Russian American mistress, and some time on his boat named "*Stugots*," a phonetic rendition of the Southern Italian dialect "*stu'cazz'*," or "*test'u'cazz*" equivalent of the Standard Italian, "*testa di cazzo*'," in English, "dickhead." In other words, Tony revels in the role of (Italian) American playboy, despite having a wife, two children, and a house in the suburbs. He is the casual patriarch both of an Italian American family secretly run by women and of a post-War United

States' "dream" that squelched women's subtle power only by force of unreal prosperity, and then only for a brief historical moment. His real power lies only in escape from these institutions.

*The Sopranos*, of course, does not have a monopoly on the comic combination of Mafia don and psychoanalyst. In his comedy of Mafia psychotherapy, *Analyze This*, director Ivan Reitman uses therapy to perpetuate the mafioso character type and so perpetuate Italian American stereotypes. Reitman's don emerges from analysis as a selfish, good-hearted (Shepard 27), but unremorseful brute, who is simply worn out from having to contend with "cunning" "animals" (rival mafiosi) and bumbling cafoni (his henchmen). Through therapy and other forms of able assistance from his establishment Jewish American psychiatrist, Doctor Sobel, Don Vitti escapes his criminal world, to live happily ever after in the civilian United States, without having to live as a schlemiel. At a climactic meeting of the dons, Sobel avoids a rebellion against Don Vitti, by putting his rival, Primo (Chazz Palmintieri), on the couch. When Primo begins to yell about Vitti's absence, Sobel asks him, "Do you feel you have to get angry to be heard, so people will listen to you?" When Vitti finally arrives, he informs the other mafiosi that he is "in a good place right now" and wants to retire, and instead of killing a turncoat underling, advises him, to "Look inside the inner self and find out who you are." Don Vitti, the Italian American killer has suddenly taken on an air of rectitude, and in his place has arisen Paul Vitti, assimilated disciple of psychotherapy of the United States — though Paul Vitti neither repents nor pays for Don Vitti's crimes.

By freeing the don from his Italian American family, *Analyze This* imposes the values of psychiatry in the United States on the least respectable of all Italian Americans. Despite Vitti's protests ("Freud was a sick fuck, and you are too!"), and Doctor Sobel's temporary need to resort to violence, in the end analysis triumphs over *onore*; the paternalistic white rationality of the United States overcomes childlike Italian American irrationality. We are left with a miraculously converted, unredeemed, flat Italian American hero, and with an outcome as derisive as comedy will bear.

In 1997, two years before the release of *Analyze This*, and nearly thirty years after the publication of Philip Roth's *Portnoy's Complaint*, Anthony Valerio published *Conversation with Johnny*, a comic novel in which Johnny, a Mafia don, analyzes and advises Nicholas, a culturally wayward Italian American writer. Whether or not it inspired 1999's *Analyze This* or *The Sopranos*, Valerio's novel does presage Chase's and Reitman's use of analysis as a comic means of Italian American cultural expression, and presents an alternative to negative exploitation of the mafioso type. *Conversation with Johnny* places the Italian American character, Italian American power embodied by the don, in the analyst's chair, and thus imposes Italian American values and ideas on the assimilated Nicholas, on its narrative, and on its audience. Johnny demands of Nicholas, the writer, "the whys and wherefores of your fuckin' tears" (62), and thus sets him on the path to understanding that his Italian American identity begins and ends with the women in his life, especially the Italian American women of his childhood; and that his future, the future of Italian American identity, lies in intermarriage and the selective reclamation of ethnic heritage.

More episodic than *Analyze This*, more like a novel, *The Sopranos*, like *Conversation with Johnny*, allows Italian American culture to answer the charges that the United States' culture brings against it. Tony Soprano often has an Italian American answer to his more assimilated analyst's therapy-speak of the United States. Tony, one Italian American, continually reminds Doctor Melfi, another Italian American, of her *italianità*. In an early episode, glimpsing the name on her diploma, he asks her, "What part of the boot you from, Hon?" As it happens, she is not from the same part (Avellino) as he, but in the United States, he implies, to resist discrimination, and cultural loss, Italians must stick together and remind each other of who they are. Tony consistently stresses the importance of this cultural identification, as does the entire series. This attitude is a valuable alternative to Don Vitti's empty valediction.

In two of its many dinner scenes, *The Sopranos* presents Tony's family discussing the historical contributions of Italians and Italian Americans, and Doctor Melfi's family debating the humanity of mobsters and the deleterious effect their presence has on the public image of Italian Americans. Following a FBI search of the family house, Tony complains about a certain Agent Grasso. "What's he think, he's gonna make it to the top by arresting his own people?" "He'll learn. He'll see." When Tony mentions the vowel at the end of Grasso's name, Anthony, Junior says, "We have a vowel," to which Tony replies, "F'in right, and you be proud of it. Jesus Christ, you'd think there never was a Michelangelo, the way they treat people." By "they," Tony means the "'*Merigan*'," mainstream Americans from the United States. His use of "they" indicates that this discussion of them is meant for Italian Americans only. Thus, Chase candidly shows Italian American points-of-view on United States' prejudice. The conversation that follows reflects these points-of-view. Carmella asks, "Did you know that an Italian invented the telephone." Anthony, Junior, in his cultural ignorance, responds, "Alexander Graham Bell was Italian?" And Tony, the mafioso as cultural conduit, retorts, "You see what I'm talking about? . . . Antonio Meucci invented the telephone, and he was robbed! Everybody knows that!"

Around the Melfi family table, discussion centers on Tony, who, as a patient (and symbolic mafioso), must remain anonymous in conversation. When Doctor Melfi hints she may have a mafioso patient, her mother worries, "I just hope he's not one of those crumbs they're talking about on the news." Her ex-husband Richard interjects, "He's scum, and you shouldn't help him with his bed-wetting." The doctor, who has dealt with Tony as one Italian American to another, defends him. But Richard, an Italian American cultural activist, gives her no quarter. "People like him are the reason Italian Americans have such a bad image," he declares. "Ask any American to describe an Italian American in this country, and invariably he's gonna reference *The Godfather*, *Goodfellas* . . . and the rest of them are gonna mention pizza." Doctor Melfi's college-age son Jason then quips, "Good movies to eat pizza by," but Richard continues his protest. "Why do you think we're never going to see an Italian President." Doctor Melfi again defends Tony as a mere individual, replying, "I realize that you're involved in the anti-defamation lobby, so go after Hollywood if you feel you absolutely have to. Leave my patient alone." Still, Richard, the Italian American intellectual, attacks. "It's a synergy," he claims. "News items and the constant portrayal of Italian Americans as gangsters." The debate grows more complex (as it generally has among Italian American intellectuals), when Jason remarks, "Wasn't the Italian anti-def deal started by Joe Colombo, a mobster." Ignoring this subtlety, Richard, the crusader, laments that the infinitesimal "fraction" of the Italian American population who have been mafiosi (5,000) have cast "a dark shadow over twenty million hard-working Americans." Although he recognizes discrimination, Richard also trumpets the Americanness of Italian Americans, as most Italian Americans would. Unimpressed, and perhaps more secure in that United States' identity, Jason answers, "Dad, at this point in our cultural history, mob movies are classic American cinema, like Westerns." Representing the dismissal of ethnic activism, Doctor Melfi's father chimes in, "I have to agree there, Rich. You never saw the Scotch-Irish pissin' and moanin' about being portrayed as rustlers and gunslingers," to which her mother responds, "That's absurd."

These serio-comic discussions are unique in film and television from the United States. They expose a vast United States' audience to two of the *discorsi* that for the past several decades have occupied producers and scholars of Italian American culture. In the process, they reflect a variety of Italian American views on the place and image of Italian Americans. They also reveal Chase and his writers as Italian American artists who question their own use of the mafioso image to create Italian American popular culture, a phenomenon until recently limited, as Richard suggests, to Italian food, vicious criminals, and chaotic families. These discussions can exist on television, because *The Sopranos* enjoys not only critical acclaim (sixteen 1999 Emmy nominations), but also and especially because it enjoys wild popularity (Mifflin E27), a popularity that derives probably from its superb writing (the popularity of less well-written shows may prove otherwise) and certainly from its subject matter, the Italian American Mafia, sadly but still the most recognizable and widely appealing symbol of Italian American culture.

Should we then try to transform this negative symbol into a positive one, as Chase, Valerio, and to some degree Scorsese, have done? Should we ignore it? Should we protest it? Certainly, protests such as Bill Dal Cerro's impassioned article "Hollywood vs. Italians" have a place, but to change America's collective consciousness mind by mind, we need to control our own myths (Valerio, Interview with Lopate) — in this case, by "we" I mean producers of Italian American culture. United States' history indicates that although protest may win civil rights, it will not necessarily convince white United States that its stereotypes of the people it fears do not exist. It may even cause those in the United States to react by, metaphorically speaking, brandishing malapropisms, pinstriped suits, and heaping bowls of spaghetti and meatballs in Italian American faces. (Watermelon-wielding Italian Americans themselves reacted in a similar way to African Americans during Al Sharpton's 1989 protest of the killing of Yusuf Hawkins). Anti-Italian American sentiment will be given voice and form, then simply go underground. History also indicates that overcoming stereotypes often requires the preliminary steps of comedicizing stereotypes—transforming monstrous images to human images. Italian Americans artists must, however, dictate the terms of that comedicization, as they have begun to do. I'm suggesting that the new Mafia comedy may represent the final phase of comedicization, and an artistic appropriation of the mafioso myth. If Italian American writers and filmmakers leave this myth to mainstream United States, we will get comedy of derision: Dom DeLuise as a moronic Don Calzone hitting his son for no reason and telling him, "It's the Italian way. I'm expressing love." But if mafiosi are portrayed as ordinary schlemiels, and if they convey real Italian American values and ideas to a national audience, values and ideas with which most poeple from the United States can identify, then as media figures they will cease to fascinate the public of the United States for the wrong reasons, cease to inspire public ridicule of Italian Americans, and in the process will do us a valuable service. They will clear the screen for a spectrum of rounded, human Italian American *personaggi*, and for varied, realistic projections of Italian American experience.

## Works Cited

Alaya, Flavia. "Re: Mafia Comedy Paper." E-mail to the author. 5 Dec. 1999.

*Analyze This*. Dir. Ivan Reitman. Perf. Robert DeNiro, Billy Crystal. Warner Brothers, 1999.

Aristotle. *On Poetry and Style*. Trans. G. M. A. Grube. Indiana: Bobbs-Merrill Educational Publishing, 1958.

Barzini, Luigi. *The Italians*. New York: Atheneum, 1964.

Bona, Mary Jo. "On Being an Italian American Woman." *The Italian American Heritage*. Ed. Pellegrino D'Acierno. New York: Garland Publishing, 1999.

D'Acierno, Pellegrino. "Cinema Paradiso: The Italian American Presence in American Cinema." *The Italian American Heritage*. Ed. Pellegrino D'Acierno. New York: Garland Publishing, 1999.

Dal Cerro, Bill. "Hollywood vs. Italians." *Fra Noi*. Jan. 1999: 54-56.

DeLillo, Don. *Underworld*. New York: Scribner, 1997.

*The Freshman*. Dir. Andrew Bergman. Perf. Marlon Brando, Matthew Broderick, and Bruno Kirby. Tri-Star, 1990.

Gambino, Richard. *Blood of My Blood: The Dilemma of the Italian Americans*. Garden City: Anchor Books, 1975.

*The Godfather*. Dir. Francis Ford Coppola. Perf. Marlon Brando, James Caan, and Al Pacino. Paramount, 1972.

*The Godfather, Part II*. Dir. Francis Ford Coppola. Perf. Al Pacino, Robert DeNiro, and Diane Keaton.

*The Godfather, Part III*. Dir. Francis Ford Coppola. Perf. Al Pacino, Diane Keaton.

*The Godson*. Perf. Don DeLuise, 1998.

*Goodfellas*. Dir. Martin Scorsese. Perf. Robert DeNiro, Joe Pesci. Warner Brothers, 1990.

Haberman, Clyde. "A Stereotype Hollywood Can't Refuse." *New York Times*. 30 July 1999, early ed.: B1.

Hill, Hamlin. "The Future of American Humor: Through a Glass Eye Darkly." *Critical Essays on American Humor*. Ed. William Bedford Clark. Boston, G.K. Hall & Co., 1984. 219-226.

Lawrence, Steve, perf. *The Carroll Burnett Show*. Perf. Carroll Burnett, Harvey Korman, and Tim Conway. CBS. WCBS, New York, 1973.

*Married to the Mob*. Dir Jonathan Demme. Perf. Dean Stockwell, Michelle Pfeiffer. Orion, 1988.

Mifflin, Lawrie. "In a Coup for Cable, HBO's *Sopranos* Receives 16 Emmy Nominations." *New York Times*. 23 July 1999, early ed.: E27.

Mintz, Lawrence E. "Humor and Ethnic Stereotypes in Vaudeville and Burlesque." *MELUS*. 21.4 (1996): 19-28.

Mobilio, Albert. "Why Organized Crime Isn't What it Used to Be." *The Village Voice Online* 29 (Sept.-5 Oct. 1999). 25 Jan. 2000 <http://www.villagevoice.com/issues/9939/mobilio.shtml>.

Monti, Daniel J., Jr. "The Working and Reworking of Italian-American Ethnicity in the United States." *Italian Americans in a Multicultural Society*. Ed. Jerome Krase and Judith N. DeSena. Stony Brook, NY: Forum Italicum, 1994. 19–34.

Shepherd, Jim. "A Wry Look at the Days When a Don was a Don." *New York Times*. 4 April 1999, early ed.: 27.

*The Sopranos*. Creat., David Chase. Perf. James Gandolfini, Nancy Marchand, Lorraine Bracco,Edie Falco. Various episodes. HBO. 1999–2000.

Valerio, Anthony. *Conversation with Johnny*. Toronto: Guernica Editions, 1997.

_____. Interview with Leonard Lopate. New York and Company. Natl. Public Radio. WNYC, New York. 7 August 1997.

Vecoli, Rudolph J. "The Search for an Italian American Identity." *Rivista di studi anglo-americani* 3 (1984): 29–65.

# A Brief History of Italian/American Literary Criticism: Sixty Years of Breaking Silences

Steven J. Belluscio
Purdue University

Questo saggio traccia lo sviluppo della critica letteraria italoamericana dalla prospettiva di tre periodi diversi: inizio, transizione,
maturazione. Lo stadio di partenza, degli anni Trenta e Quaranta, è
segnato dagli inizi sporadici di una critica indigena di specificità
culturale. In seguito, il periodo transizionale degli anni Sessanta e
Settanta è caratterizzato dalla proliferazione di organizzazioni
dedicate allo studio della cultura italoamericana e dal primo tentativo di codificare la prosa italoamericana. Il periodo della maturazione a sua volta è cominciato negli anni Ottanta e continua tuttora.
Quest'ultimo momento si distingue inoltre per i più frequenti ten-
tativi di teorizzare la critica letteraria italoamericana. Infine,
questo periodo segna anche l'inizio di una essenziale dialettica
critica fra gli studiosi della letteratura italoamericana.

Italian culture survived a hard trip across the Atlantic
Ocean. In the late-nineteenth and early-twentieth centuries, when the overtaxed, disease-stricken, politically oppressed, and hungry southern-Italian poor became the over-
worked, underpaid, and poorly housed Italian/American poor,
Italian culture was brought into direct conflict with the potentially deracinating forces of American nativism, progres-
sivism, and prejudice.[1] Still, Italian culture survived in the

---

[1] Between 1880 and 1914, some four million Italians arrived on the shores of
the United States. Andrew Rolle, *The American Italians: Their History and
Culture* (Belmont, CA: Wadsworth Publishing, 1972) 47. For a more detailed
survey of the Italian/American experience, consult any of the following
works: Patrick Gallo, *Ethnic Alientaion: The Italian-Americans* (Cranbury,
NJ: Farleigh Dickinson University Press, 1974); Richard Gambino, *Blood of
my Blood: The Dilemma of the Italian-Americans* (Toronto: Guernica, 1996);
Luciano Iorizzo and Salvatore Mondello, *The Italian Americans* (New York:
Twayne Publishers, 1971); Joseph Lopreato, *The Italian Americans* (New
York: Random House, 1970); Jerre Mangione and Ben Morreale, *La Storia*:

New World, from the outright discrimination of the early Italian/American experience, through the homogenizing "consensus" of the 1950s, to its contemporary state of advanced assimilation — a state that has provoked some sociologists to wonder if Italian Americans could exist indefinitely as a distinct ethnic group.[2] Regardless of one's position on assimilation, there is little doubt that Americans of Italian descent do share a history of allegiance to Italian social and religious traditions, a reverence for *la famiglia*, and, at the very least, a common sense of *italianitá*. Intuitively, so long as there has been a distinct Italian/American history, there has been a distinct possibility for an Italian/American literature, informed by the dual traditions of American literature and *italianitá*.[3] For the purposes of this essay, I will define Italian/American literature as including any work, written by an American of Italian descent, which serves as a creative representation of the multifarious aspects of Italian/American history, ethnicity, and experience.

Anthony J. Tamburri defines *italianitá* and associates it with the Italian/American literary tradition in the following way:

*Five Centuries of the Italian American Experience* (New York: Harper Collins, 1992).

[2]Herbert J. Gans and Richard Alba both argue for a "straight-line assimilation," in which European/American ethnicity steadily disappears as ethnic groups intermarry and socially, politically, and economically integrate themselves into the mainstream of American life. See Herbert J. Gans, *The Urban Villagers* (New York: The Free Press, 1962); and Richard Alba, *Italian-Americans: Into the Twilight of Ethnicity* (Englewood, NJ: Prentice-Hall, 1985).

[3]Later in this essay, I will more fully explain the ideology behind using a slash in place of the hyphen in the adjective "Italian/American." See Anthony J. Tamburri, *To Hyphenate or not to Hyphenate: The Italian/American Writer: An Other American* (Montreal: Guernica, 1991). Also note that for the purposes of this essay, "Italian Americans" will refer to those Americans of Italian descent in the mainland United States.

*Italianitá* is indeed a term expressive of many notions, ideas, feelings, and sentiments. To be sure, it is any and all of these things which lead young Italian Americans back to their real and mythical images of the land, the way of life, the values and the cultural trappings of their ancestors. It could be language, food, a way of determining life values, a familial structure, a sense of religion; it can be all of these, as it can certainly be much more. . . . [S]uch a cultural concept is possible to perceive and ultimately interpret through the evidence found in the large body of Italian/American creative literature.[4]

Early Italian/American literary works, such as Jerre Mangione's *Mount Allegro* (1942), Pietro di Donato's *Christ in Concrete* (1939), and Mari Tomasi's *Like Lesser Gods* (1949), are written directly from experience by second-generation Italian Americans. Each novel depicts the joys, trials, work, and play of immigrant families in Italian districts of Rochester, NY; Hoboken, NJ; and Barre, VT, respectively. Contemporary Italian/American writers, such as novelist Tina de Rosa, fiction writer Tony Ardizzone, and poets Rachel Guido de Vries and Maria Mazziotti Gillan engage in acts of *recovery* in order to intelligently seek out and creatively represent the cultural sources of their *italianitá*.[5] Nevertheless, in or-

---

[4]Tamburri, *Hyphenate*, 21–22. This quote originally appeared, in a slightly different form, in Anthony J. Tamburri, Paolo A. Giordano, and Fred L. Gardaphè, "Introduction," in *From the Margin: Writings in Italian Americana*, eds. Anthony Julian Tamburri, Paolo A. Giordano, and Fred L. Gardaphè (West Lafayette, IN: Purdue University Press, 1991) 6. With regard to the "large body of Italian/American creative literature," Fred L. Gardaphè's *The Italian-American Writer* (1995) lists 346 major works of Italian/American fiction and poetry. Fred L. Gardaphè, *The Italian-American Writer: An Essay and Annotated Checklist* (Spencertown, NY: Forkroads, 1995) 25–50.

[5]See Tina de Rosa, *Paper Fish* (New York: The Feminist Press, 1996); Tony Ardizzone, *Taking it Home: Stories from the Neighborhood* (Urbana, IL: University of Illinois Press, 1996); Rachel Guido de Vries, *How to Sing to a Dago* (Toronto: Guernica, 1996); Maria Mazziotti Gillan, *Where I Come From* (Toronto: Guernica, 1995). Each of these works, in its own way, deals with

der for Italian/American literature to be considered a legitimate concept, it needs an intelligent, ongoing, culture-specific criticism to note and codify the many continuities and discontinuities of the genre. According to Fred L. Gardaphè, "The culture-specific approach examines the multicultural contexts out of which emerges the 'other' American text and relates texts to indigenous cultural histories and philosophies."[6]

Italian/American literary criticism begins in the 1930s with the first attempts at such an "indigenous" criticism.[7] From this breaking of critical silence, Italian/American literary criticism can be traced through three broad phases of departure, transition, and maturation. The departure is represented by isolated attempts of Italian/American critics to read works of Italian/American literature and assess their ethnic verisimilitude or to draw attention to their contributions to American literature. In the transitional stage of the late 1960s and early 1970s, critics and scholars of Italian Americana, inspired by the contemporary "ethnic revival," founded important organizations and periodicals that worked to unify the Italian/American critical voice. It is in this stage that the first attempt at proffering a unifying theory of Italian/American literature occurs. The 1980s and 1990s witnessed a period of maturation, in which critics sought to tie together the many strands of Italian/American criticism and delineate a culture-specific approach to Italian/American literature. At the very same time, the future of Italian/American literary criticism has been secured by a willingness on the part of Italian/American critics to engage in a self-perpetuating dialogue fueled not only by a reconsideration of

---

the issue of reclaiming and reconstructing an Italian/American past and identity.

[6] Fred L. Gardaphè, *Italian Signs, American Streets: The Evolution of Italian American Narrative* (Durham, NC: Duke University Press, 1996) 9.

[7] Ibid., 7.

critical themes, but also by the creative and critical articulation of traditionally marginal(ized) areas of Italian Americana — for example, those occupied by women, lesbians, and gays. With this essay, I shall trace the development of Italian/American literary criticism and its sixty years of breaking silences.

In its early days, criticism of early Italian/American literature was most frequently left to non-Italian/American reviewers who were erratic in their recognition of and sensitivity to literary ethnicity. In his review of *Christ in Concrete*, Fred T. Marsh speaks glowingly of Pietro di Donato's debut as "a fine and unusual first novel." Still, while the reviewer displays a good understanding the novel's central conflict between the immigrant and "Job," he cannot resist essentialistically referring to the "Latin sense of dearness and innocent sexuality," "Latin graceful amorousness," and "Italian gregariousness."[8]

Another reviewer, Louis Adamic, himself an immigrant, criticizes the structure and fluidity of *Christ in Concrete*, yet still lauds it for its allusions to Italian poetry and its translation of "Italian lyric conversation and colloquialisms into American speech."[9] Meanwhile, Jerre Mangione's *New Republic* reviews of *Christ in Concrete* and *The Grand Gennaro* (1935), by Garibaldi La Polla, are quite possibly the first attempts by an Italian/American critic at Italian/American literary criticism. In Mangione's review of the former work di Donato praises the author for his "genuine feeling about Italians . . . working and living together," noting that di Donato's life as a second-generation Italian American has made him a writer with "the obvious advantage of being close to his materials." Like Adamic, Mangione is critical of di Donato's

[8]Fred T. Marsh, "A Fine and Unusual First Novel," *The New York Times*, 20 August 1939, 6.
[9]Louis Adamic, "Muscular Novel of Immigrant Life," *The Saturday Review*, 26 August 1939, 5.

style, yet still appreciative of his literal translation of Italian speech into English, thereby giving the dialogue the "often rich and poetical" "flavor of the foreign language spoken by the characters."[10] Some four years prior to this review, Mangione praises La Polla's *The Grand Gennaro* for his "Italo-Americans who are vivid and alive" and unlike the one-dimensional stereotypes provided by the "gangster movies" of the time. Mangione reads La Polla's novel in relation to the Italian/American experience of earning a living and attempting to assimilate in America.[11] Such critical culture-specificity, while important, was nevertheless sporadic.

By 1949, Olga Peragallo's *Italian-American Authors and Their Contribution to American Literature* had been posthumously compiled and published. The book consists of a series of short summaries of Italian/American writers' origins, educations, personal biographies, and literary accomplishments. As useful as the book has been to critics of Italian/American literature, it does little, if anything, to theorize about what, beyond a surname, makes a writer Italian/American. Included are renowned Twain scholar Bernard De Voto, anarchists Nicola Sacco and Bartolomeo Vanzetti, and assimilationist attorney and historian Gino Speranza. Nevertheless, the book is among the beginnings of a much-needed "common voice" for Italian Americans, who, as of the late forties, had no "large-scale social organization, . . . effective historical society [,] or . . . magazine" to serve this very purpose.[12] Some seventeen years would pass before this would happen.

---

[10]Jerre Mangione, "Little Italy," *New Republic*, 30 August 1939.

[11]Jerre Mangione, review of *The Grand Gennaro*, by Garibaldi M. La Polla, In *New Republic*, 23 October 1935. *The Grand Gennaro* tells the story of Gennaro Accuci, a rapidly acculturating junkman who uses questionable business practices to "make America" and develop a lucrative business for himself.

[12]Giuseppe Prezzolini. "Preface," in *Italian-American Authors and Their Contributions to American Literature*, Olga Peragallo, ed. Anita Peragallo (New York: S. F. Vanni, 1949) ix.

In the wake of the "ethnic revival" of the 1960s and 1970s, Italian/American criticism would enter a transitional stage in which scholars would not only address the need for national organizations and journals devoted to the study of Italian/American cultural output, but would also make an initial attempt at a theory of Italian/American fiction. In 1966, the American Italian Historical Association (AIHA) was formed. Centered in Staten Island, New York, AIHA's constitution defined the association as:

> a non-profit organization devoted to the promotion of Italian-American studies. Its objectives shall be the collection, preservation, development, and popularization of material having reference to the Italian-American experience in the United States and Canada.[13]

AIHA's first officers were President Rudolph Vecoli, Vice President Francesco Cordasco, Secretary-Treasurer Silvano Tomasi, Recording Secretary Albert Nofi, and Curator Leonard Covello.[14] In a brief history of the organization's first twenty years, Frank J. Cavaioli stresses the importance of AIHA's annual conferences, which began in 1968 and have included papers from a variety of disciplines, including history, sociology, creative writing, literary criticism, and popular culture.[15]

In 1974, editors Ernest Falbo and Richard Gambino expressed a similar concern for the preservation of Italian/American cultural history when they founded *Italian Americana*, a journal devoted to the study of the Italian/American contribution to American history and culture. The first issue

---

[13]Frank J. Cavaioli, "The American Italian Historical Association: Twenty Years Later, 1966–1986," in *Italian Americans: The Search for a Usable Past*, eds. Richard N. Juliani and Philip V. Cannistraro (Staten Island, NY: American Italian Historical Association, 1989) 282.

[14]Ibid., 284.

[15]Ibid., 286.

contained essays of sociohistory, immigrant history, literary criticism, book reviews, memoirs, and creative works by the likes of fiction writer Joseph Papaleo and poet Felix Stefanile.[16] The journal went defunct in the early 1980s only to be resurrected in 1990.

Also in 1974, Rose Basile Green published her seminal *The Italian-American Novel: A Document of the Interaction of Two Cultures*, which was the first attempt at a codification of Italian/American prose. Green views Italian/American prose as the creative representation of the interaction between American and Italian(/American) cultures, a conflict which, over time, has provoked writers to varying degrees of ethnic allegiance and/or suppression. Green's work is chronologically based, which, though a helpful critical approach, generates occasional peculiarities. For instance, Green categorically limits Italian/American writers to those of the first, second, and third generations only.[17] Still, her work is comprehensive and important. In *The Italian-American Novel*, Green partitions the Italian/American literary tradition into a series of stages that coincide with similar stages of Italian/American sociohistory: "autobiography," "early impact" (of Americans upon Italians and vice versa), "the need for assimlation," "revulsion" (against the Italian cultural heritage), "counter-revulsion," "the branching of an Italian culture rooted in American soil," and "contemporary" Italian/American literature, which includes works "from the second half of the 1960s through 1970."[18] Unfortunately, Green's book did not create the "stir" needed to give "Italian/American literature" conceptual and critical legitimacy: this would require yet another wait.

[16] *Italian Americana* 1:1 (1974)
[17] Rose Basile Green, *The Italian-American Novel: A Document of the Interaction of Two Cultures* (Cranbury, NJ: Farleigh Dickinson University Press, 1974) 21.
[18] Ibid., 23–24.

The postmodern scholastic climate of the 1980s and
1990s gave legitimacy to ethnic readings of American literature, and while straight-line assimilationists were pronounc-
ing the imminent death of Italian/American ethnicity, numerous Italian/American writers were looking to their Italian
ancestors for inspiration. Helen Barolini's *Umbertina* (1979),
Tina de Rosa's *Paper Fish* (1980), and Rachel Guido DeVries's
*Tender Warriors* (1986) each contain strong maternal figures
who inspire younger characters to return to certain fundamental values of their ancestral culture.[19] Analogously, critics
of Italian/American literature have been inspired by a need
to connect the literature to the roots of Italian(/American)
culture in order to more accurately delineate an Italian/
American literary tradition. While critics such as Houston
Baker, Jr., and Henry Louis Gates, Jr., were attaching great
sociocultural and folkloric significance to works of African/
American literature in order to discover what makes a text
black, critics such as Robert Viscusi were searching for what
makes an Italian/American text Italian/American.[20] In "*De
Vulgari Eloquentia*: An Approach to the Language of Italian
American Fiction," Robert Viscusi demonstrates the continu-
ity between the "confusing array of dialects and grammars"
in the poetry of Dante Alighieri and the language of Italian/
American writers.[21] Viscusi views the language of Italian/

[19]Helen Barolini, *Umbertina* (New York: Seaview, 1979[Feminist Press,
1999]); Tina De Rosa *Paper Fish* (Chicago: Wine Press, 1980 [Feminist Press,
1996]); Rachel Guido deVries, *Tender Warriors* (Ithica, NY: Firebrand
Books, 1986).
[20]See Houston A. Baker, Jr., *Blues, Ideology, and Afro-American Literature:
A Vernacular Theory* (Chicago: University of Chicago Press, 1984); and Henry
Louis Gates, Jr., *The Signifying Monkey: A Theory of African-American Literary Criticism* (New York: Oxford University Press, 1988).
[21]Robert Viscusi, "*De Vulgari Eloquentia*: An Approach to the Language of
Italian American Fiction," *Yale Italian Studies* 1:3 (1981): 21. For other general theoretical treatments of Italian/American literature, see also Robert
Viscusi, "Narrative and Nothing: The Enterprise of Italian American Writing," *Differentia* 6:7 (1994): 77-99; and Robert Viscusi, "A Literature Con-

American fiction as an authorial negotiation between American English, Italian, and an amalgam of the two languages, which Michael La Sorte would call "Italglish."[22] Thematically, Italian/American fiction, whether rendered in English, Italian, or "Italglish," contains liturgical, patriarchal, heroic, and diplomatic tropes that can be related to aspects of both Italian culture and Dante's work.[23]

In "Breaking the Silence: Strategic Imperatives for Italian American Culture," Viscusi looks again to the roots of Italian culture as a means to keep Italian/American culture alive and perpetuated by a healthy "tradition of self-critical discourse."[24] In order to do this, Italian Americans need to recover their language, reclaim their history, and engage in a vigorous critical dialectic — something Peragallo and Green generally lacked — to ensure the progression of Italian/American cultural criticism.[25]

Fortunately, while Peragallo's and Green's books became library curiosities, Viscusi's urgent call was *heard*. Viscusi's "Breaking the Silence" appeared in the first volume of *VIA: Voices in Italian Americana*, one of the best journals of Italian/American creative writing and literary and film criticism to date. In 1990, *Italian Americana* was resumed, and the late 80s and early 90s also witnessed the brief appearance of *la bella figura*, a literary journal founded by Rose Romano that was devoted mostly to the writings of Italian/American

sidering Itself: The Allegory of Italian America," in *From the Margin: Writings in Italian Americana*, eds. Anthony Julian Tamburri, Paolo A. Giordano, and Fred L. Gardaphè (West Lafayette, IN: Purdue University Press, 1991) 265–81.

[22]For a general definition of "Italglish," see Michael La Sorte, *La Merica: Images of Italian Greenhorn Experience* (Philadelphia: Temple University, 1985) 159–60.

[23]Viscusi, "*De Vulgari Eloquentia*," 24–38.

[24]Viscusi, "Breaking the Silence: Strategic Imperatives for Italian American Culture," *VIA* 1:1 (1990): 2.

[25]It would not be farfetched to state that a sizable majority of Italian Americans cannot speak Italian.

women. In 1991, Fred L. Gardaphè, Anthony J. Tamburri, and Paolo Giordano published *From the Margin: Writings in Italian Americana*, a collection of Italian/American fiction, poetry, and criticism. Its purpose was to bring to light contemporary Italian/American writers at the same time that it updated Italian/American criticism. The selective criterion was simple: "excellent representatives of works of American writers whose work is informed by *italianitá.*"[26] Again, we see the contemporary impulse to trace Italian/American art back to its Italian roots, for it is these signs of Italian influence that make a work Italian/American far more than an Italian/American surname (something critics of the first two phases of Italian/American criticism had difficulty recognizing). Included among the essays are Gardaphè's "From Oral Tradition to Written Word: Toward an Ethnographically Based Literary Criticism" and Franco Mulas's "The Ethnic Language of Pietro di Donato's *Christ in Concrete,*" a sophisticated expansion upon Mangione's early reading of the *italianitá* of di Donato's language.[27]

In 1991, Anthony J. Tamburri added his voice to the increasing critical noise Italian Americans were making. *To Hy-*

---

[26] Anthony J. Tamburri, Paolo A. Giordano, and Fred L. Gardaphè, "Introduction," in *From the Margin*, 2.

[27] Gardaphè, "From Oral Tradition to Written Word: Toward an Ethnographically Based Literary Criticism," in *From the Margin*, 294–306; Franco Mulas, "The Ethnic Language of Pietro Di Donato's *Christ in Concrete,*" in *From the Margin*, 307–315. Mulas's essay is now included in his book *Studies on Italian-American Literature*, a collection of essays he delivered at various conferences during the decade prior to the book's publication. I do not deal with Mulas's book in the main body of the text because I am here primarily interested in the critical voice of Italian/American critics within the United States. Otherwise, I would also include a discussion of William Boelhower's *Immigrant Autobiography in the United States: Four Versions of the Italian American Self.* Franco Mulas, *Studies on Italian-American Literature* (Staten Island, NY: Center for Migration Studies, 1995); and William Boelhower, *Immigrant Autobiography in the United States: Four Versions of the Italian American Self* (Verona: Essedue, 1982).

*phenate or not to Hyphenate: The Italian/American Writer: An Other Writer* is a position paper designed to draw attention to Italian/American literature as a legitimate category of (ethnic/)American literature that had yet to be recognized. In this little book, Tamburri sets out to change traditional conceptions of the hyphenate American writer, with a particular focus upon the Italian/American writer. Drawing on Daniel Aaron's theory of the "hyphenate writer," Tamburri views the hyphen in "Italian-American" as a means to create "distance" between the ethnic writer and the American literary dominant culture.[28] Therefore, Tamburri proposes the slash in order to reduce the ideological distance between "Italian" and "American" and to underscore the Italian/American writer's status as "an/other" American writer — all with the hope that some day Italian/American writers will have their place within the Bahktinian heteroglossia that is American literature.[29]

Continuing in the fruitful vein of culture-specific Italian/American literary criticism, *Italian Signs, American Streets: The Evolution of Italian American Narrative* (1996) is nothing short of a landmark in American literary studies. *Italian Signs* is the first major work since Green's *The Italian-American Novel* to posit a theory for reading Italian/American literary works and organizing them within their own ethnic/American canon. Gardaphè bases his categories of the Italian/American narrative — the poetic, mythic, and philosophic modes — upon Enlightenment philosopher Giambattista Vico's three stages of culture: the Age of Gods, the Age of Heroes, and the Age of Man. Gardaphè writes that "the Age of Gods [is] the early period of social development in which men create gods in their own image and set up the socioeconomic rules for survival, resulting in what Vico calls divine

[28]Tamburri, *Hyphenate*, 10–11. See Daniel Aaron, "The Hyphenate Writer and American Letters," *Smith Alumnae Quarterly* (July 1964): 213–17.
[29]Tamburri, *Hyphenate*, 35–36.

societies."[30] Gardaphè finds that this stage of early civilization is analogous with a "poetic mode" of the Italian/American narrative in which the early exposure of Italians to American society produced writers who were inclined to write in a pre-modern, realist vein — the *vero narratio*.[31] Further linking the poetic mode with Vico's Age of Gods are the recurring literary themes of destiny and the power of the divine. In this stage of Italian/American writing, there is also a preponderance of strong Italian signs and a conspicuous need to explain Italian culture to a hopefully sympathetic American readership.[32] Gardaphè chooses, among other writers, Constantine Panunzio as a representative of the poetic mode. Panunzio, an Italian immigrant who achieved remarkable academic and professional success, wrote the autobiographical *The Soul of an Immigrant* (1921) to tell of the plight of the Italian immigrant in America.[33] Thinly autobiographical, ideologically assimilationist, and apologetic in tone, *The Soul of an Immigrant* is essentially "an argument that pleads for understanding and acceptance of [Panunzio's] people by the Anglo-American culture."[34] According to Gardaphè, Panunzio's straightforward, *vero narratio* approach places it within the seminal "poetic mode" of Italian/American literature.

Vico's second stage of culture is the Age of Heroes, "in which aristocratic rule is developed."[35] For the Italian/American narrative, this necessitates the emergence of literary and authorial "heroes" who combat the forces of destiny and divinity that influenced writers and characters of the poetic mode, hence bringing Italian/American literature

---

[30]Gardaphè, *Italian Signs*, 15.
[31]Ibid.
[32]Ibid., 16.
[33]See Constantine Panunzio, *The Soul of an Immigrant* (New York: the MacMillan Company, 1921).
[34]Gardaphè, *Italian Signs*, 49.
[35]Ibid., 15.

into a "mythic mode." Authors of the mythic mode tend to write in a modernist style, are more critical of the American dominant culture, and, though visibly Italian/American, are less likely to feel the need to apologize for their ancestral heritage than writers like Panunzio. By far the largest and most diverse category of Italian/American literature, Gardaphè's mythic mode features such writers as Pietro di Donato, Helen Barolini, and Tina De Rosa. In Helen Barolini's *Umbertina* and Tina de Rosa's *Paper Fish*, the divine is supplanted by a powerful grandmother figure who serves as the source of ethnic inspiration for female protagonists who seek to attain empowering self-identities in spite of the male supremacist traditions of Italy, Italian America, and America.[36]

Gardaphè describes Vico's third stage of culture, the Age of Man, as the time "in which rebellion of the servile class creates a democratic society."[37] Gardaphè's analogous "philosophic mode" of Italian/American literature "challenges and destroys belief in previous models."[38] Consequently, Italian/American writers of the philosophic mode either marginalize their ethnicity, like Don DeLillo, or deconstruct it and represent it parodically, like Gilbert Sorrentino and Giose Rimanelli.[39] Each of these writers is evidence of a postmodern Italian/American literature that exhibits a distrust of all master narratives, be they epistemological, literary, or ethnic. Although the Italian/American signs of authorial ethnicity are difficult to detect, and frequently more implicit than explicit, they can exist in thematic tropes such as a tendency toward working-class perspective or a valorization of marginal cultures and subject positions. Gardaphè writes that

[36]Ibid., 123–41.
[37]Ibid., 15.
[38]Ibid., 16.
[39]Ibid., 155–72, 173–92. For good examples of such postmodern "play" with ethnicity, see Don DeLillo, *Americana* (New York: Penguin Books, 1989 [1971]); and Giose Rimanelli, *Benedetta in Guysterland* (Montreal: Guernica, 1993).

"[t]hese authors may have avoided or suppressed dominant ethnic traits in their attempts to transcend ethnicity, but . . . their work contains of *Italianitá* that can be connected to an underlying philosophy which is informed by their ethnicity."[40] To be sure, Gardaphè's critical approach is forward-looking. With a close critical eye, Gardaphè insists upon the ability to read Italian/American writers as such, no matter how far they appear to stray literarily from their ancestral culture.

The importance of Gardaphè's work is evidenced by the fact that critics have already begun to engage critically with his theory. In a 1994 article entitled "In (Re)cognition of the Italian/American Writer: Definitions and Categories," Anthony J. Tamburri essentially agrees with Gardaphè's categories, but suggests another nomenclature. Tamburri notes that Gardaphè's poetic, mythic, and philosophic modes are somewhat parallel to Daniel Aaron's generationally defined three stages of the "hyphenate writer," which include the unassuming pioneer spokesman, the protester and demystifier of ethnic stereotypes, and the mainstream writer of ethnic descent.[41] However, Gardaphè's association of the three modes with American realism, modernism, and postmodernism could cause the critic to place undue emphasis on chronology. Thus, Tamburri uses Peircean semiotics to define three categories — based on cognitive "firstness," "secondness," and "thirdness" — that are clearly reminiscent of Gardaphè's three modes, but less reliant upon the author's

---

[40]Gardaphè, *Italian Signs*, 155.

[41]Tamburri, "In (Re)cognition of the Italian/American Writer: Definitions and Categories," *Differentia* 6:7 (1994): 15-16. For more by Tamburri on Italian/American literary criticism in general, see also Tamburri, "Rethinking Italian/American Studies: From the Hyphen to the Slash and Beyond," in *Beyond the Margin: Readings in Italian Americana*, eds. Paolo A. Giordano and Anthony Julian Tamburri (Madison, NJ: Farleigh Dickinson University Press, 1998); and Tamburri, *A Semiotic of Ethnicity: In (Re)cognition of the Italian/American Writer* (Albany, NY: State University of New York Press, 1998)

birthdate or generation. Under this schema, Italian/American writers create work that may be "expressive," "comparative," or "synthetic."[42] In *A Semiotic of Ethnicity: In (Re)cognition of the Italian/American Writer* (1998), Tamburri elaborates upon this theory as he guides the reader through close semiotic readings of the work of Tony Ardizzone, Helen Barolini, Grose Rimanelli, Gianna Patriarca, and Luigi Fontanella. To date, Tamburri's critical dialogue with Gardaphè marks the most radical move to establish a chronologically independent theory of Italian/American literature, underscoring at the same time the importance of Gardaphè's study and its immediate influence upon the critical world of Italian Americana. Also, the dialogue of Gardaphè and Tamburri is precisely the sort of critical dialectic for which Robert Viscusi calls in "Breaking the Silence," for without this ongoing discussion, Italian/American criticism would merely revert to silence sporadically interrupted by an occasional Peragallo, Green, or Gardaphè. Essential to the preservation of a dynamic, multivalent dialectic is the continual readiness to hear the voices of traditionally marginalized aspects of Italian/American culture. For, just as Italian/American literature strives to add its voice to the heteroglossia that is American literature, so must the voices of women, gays, and lesbians be included in the hetereglossia that is Italian/American literature.

Helen Barolini had this in mind when she compiled *The Dream Book: An Anthology of Writings by Italian-American Women* (1985), the only anthology of its kind until Mary Jo Bona's *The Voices We Carry: Recent Italian-American Women's Fiction* (1994).[43] In an excellent, thought-provoking

---

[42]Ibid., 19. Furthermore, Tamburri sees no reason why one writer may not, depending on the particular work one examines, fall under more than one of these categories.

[43]Ed. Mary Jo Bona, *The Voices We Carry: Recent Italian-American Women's Fiction* (Montreal: Guernica, 1994).

introduction, Barolini asks a burning question she elegantly proceeds to answer: "Why have I never heard of [the work of Italian/American women writers]?"[44] Like other critics of Italian/American literature, Barolini connects the writings of Italian/American women with a sense of *italianitá*.

Barolini, in addition, was one of the first to hyphothesize why Italian/American women writers have been overlooked or forgotten. She attributes this literary silence to a number of "internal" and "external" factors. Internally, Italian/American women, though possessing a rich double identity that "should make [them] into artists," are hindered by the Italian traditions of *omertá* and devotion to *la famiglia*, in addition to the doubly oppressive patriarchal traditions of Americana and Italian Americana.[45] Externally, Italian/American women have lacked the "supportive circle" of fellow Italian/American female artists that women of other ethnic groups have enjoyed. Furthermore, the academic powerbrokers, male and female alike, have traditionally shown little interest in the experiences of women of non-Anglo/Saxon origin.[46] To be sure, Italian/American women have often lacked the literary "connections" necessary to get their works published and to keep them in print.[47] Hence, Italian/American women either are not represented or are misrepresented in American literary history.

To remedy this problem, critics of Italian/American women's writings have not only drawn attention to the works themselves, but have demonstrated how the writings represent a distinct and significant Italian/American women's experience. While *The Voices We Carry* draws attention to the continuing tradition of Italian/American women's writings,

[44]Helen Barolini, *The Dream Book: An Anthology of Writings by Italian American Women* (New York: Schocken Books, 1985) x.
[45]Ibid., 18-25.
[46]Ibid., 30.
[47]Ibid., 39.

Bona's "Broken Images, Broken Lives: Carmolina's Journey in Tina De Rosa's *Paper Fish*" and Edvige Giunta's "Afterword: 'A Song From the Ghetto'" both explore, among other things, the creative negotiation of ethnicity *and* gender in Tina De Rosa's *Paper Fish*.[48]

Meanwhile, in an essay reminiscent of Barolini's introduction to *The Dream Book*, Rose Romano, in "Coming Out Olive in the Lesbian Community: *Big Sister Is Watching You*" (1996), tells of the difficulty she experienced legitimizing Italian/American lesbian writings in a feminist intellectual climate that was often slow to acknowledge certain unexplored avenues of literary ethnic difference.[49] Once again, there was a silence that needed to be broken; and, once again critics of Italian/American were ready to draw attention to the existence of an overlooked aspect of Italian/American ethnicity — this time, the experience of Italian/American gays and lesbians.

---

[48]Mary Jo Bona, "Broken Images, Broken Lives: Carmolina's Journey in Tina De Rosa's *Paper Fish*," *MELUS* 14:3-4 (1987): 87-106; Edvige Giunta, "Afterword," in *Paper Fish*, Tina De Rosa, 123-57. Bona's article appears in an issue of *MELUS: Multi-Ethnic Literature of the United States* devoted entirely to Italian/American Writers. Some other important articles by Bona and Giunta dealing generally with the topic of Italian/American Women Writers are as follows: Bona, "Italian-American Women Writers," in *Italian-American History and Culture: An Encyclopedia*, eds. Salvatore LaGumina, *et al.* (New York: Garland, forthcoming); Bona, "Family Shapes Community: Italian/American Women Writers," in *Taking Parts: Ingredients for Leadership, Participation, and Empowerment*, eds. Eloise A. Buker *et al.* (Lanham, MD: University Press of America, 1994) 135-49; Bona, "Introduction," in *The Voices We Carry* (Montreal: Guernica, 1994) 11-29; Giunta, "Speaking Through Silences: Ethnicity in the Writings of Italian/American Women," in *Race and Ethnic Discrimination in American Literature*, ed. Michael Meyer (Atlanta: Rodopi Press, forthcoming); Giunta, "Crossing Critical Borders in Italian/American Women's Studies," *The Italian American Review* 5:2 (1996): 79-94.

[49]"Coming Out Olive in the Lesbian Community: *Big Sister is Watching You*," in *Social Pluralism and Literary History: The Literature of Italian Emigration*, ed. Francesco Loriggio (Toronto: Guernica, 1996) 161-75.

*Fuori: Essays By Italian/American Lesbians and Gays* features numerous writers who must continually work a compromise between their *italianitá* and their lives "outside" Italian(/American) tradition, between their Italian/American families and their gay/lesbian families. Nevertheless, amidst the continual conflicts the Italian/American gay or lesbian confronts:

> it is the idea of reshaping myths that the Italian/American writers in *Fuori* most fully join in the language of cultural identity. . . . [T]he writers not only commemorate their Italian/American pasts, but they reinvent viable relationships to their families. . . . In this way, they discover something "new" about their ethnic identities as Italian Americans.[50]

Hence, just as the inclusion of the "non-traditional" provokes the cultural critic to reconsider Italian/American culture, so does the inclusion of the "non-traditional" narratives and creative works of Tommi Avicolli Mecca, Philip Gambone, Rachel Guido DeVries, and Mary Cappello provoke the literary critic to reconsider Italian/American literature.

A final book in this pilgrimage through Italian/American literary criticism that I can discuss herein belongs to Mary Jo Bona, *Claiming a Tradition: Italian American Women Writers* (Carbondale, IL: Southern Illinois UP, 1999).[51] In this

---

[50]Bona, "Gorgeous Identites: Gay and Lesbian Italian/American Writers," in *Fuori: Essays by Italian/American Lesbians and Gays*, ed. Anthony J. Tamburri (West Lafayette, IN: Bordighera, 1996), 7, 4.

[51] Two other books dedicated to women's literature that were recently published, but not available at the time of this writing, are: Mary Ann Mannino, *Revisionary Identities: Strategies of Empowerment in the Writing of Italian/American Women* (New York: Peter Lang, 2000) and Mary Francis Pipino, *"I have found my voice": The Italian-American Woman Writer* (New York: Peter Lang, 2000).

groundbreaking work, Bona builds upon the efforts of Helen Barolini to establish the existence of a distinct Italian/American women's literary tradition in American letters. Bona writes that the mid-seventies resurrection of Zora Neale Hurston's *Their Eyes Were Watching God* (1937), which happened in an academic context that was friendly to the idea of exploring the black woman's contribution to African/American literature, is akin to the task facing scholars of Italian/American women's writing today: "claiming a tradition" of Italian/American women's literature that they then must set out to describe. The ethnic and gender differences which both complicate and enrich the lives of Italian/American women lead to narratives containing literary differences that, counterintuitively, move "Italian American woman writers ... toward the heart of American literature" (4), as the quintessential American literary hero has traditionally dwelt in a world of otherness and alienation.

Bona views Italian/American women's literature as a distinctly female representation of the "negotiation between the Italian familial culture and the American milieu" (6). Throughout the course of the study, Bona identifies a number of recurring themes in the Italian/American women's literary tradition, including immigration, the conflict between *la via vecchia* and New World ideals, second-generation assimilation, the Italian/American family, and illnesses that can become symbolic representations of the pressures of ethnic experience in America for both men and women.

After a thought-provoking introduction, the first chapter features critical examinations of two novels dealing with

---

Also published after this writing were two edited volumes: Pellegrino D'Acierno, ed. *The Italian American Heritage. A Companion to Literature and Arts* (New York: Garland Publishing, Inc., 1999); and Salvatore LaGumina, Frank J. Cavaioli, Salvatore Primeggia, and Joseph A. Varacalli, eds. *The Italian American Experience: An Encyclopedia* (New York: Garland Publishing, Inc., 2000).

familial adjustment to American life, Mari Tomasi's *Like Lesser Gods* and Marion Benasutti's *No Steady Job for Papa* (1966). Chapter two explores the darker side of Italian/American family life for women in Octavia Waldo's *A Cup of the Sun* (1961) and Josephine Gattuso Hendin's *The Right Thing to Do* (1988). In chapters three and four, Bona demonstrates how Diana Cavallo's *A Bridge of Leaves* (1961), Dorothy Bryant's *Miss Giardino* (1978), Helen Barolini's *Umbertina*, and Tina De Rosa's *Paper Fish* provide an ethnic female version of the traditional American bildungsroman at the same time that they show evidence of each author's individual perspective. For while Cavallo's and Bryant's novels place great emphasis on the importance of the Italian/American family in shaping character development, Barolini's and De Rosa's works are informed greatly by feminism in the former case and literary modernism in the latter. Finally, chapter five concerns itself with "recent developments" in Italian/American women's literature, which, for example, has now begun to consider the effects of lesbianism on Italian/American family life. Bona has also identified a trend in contemporary Italian/American women's writing that Fred L. Gardaphè also noted in *Italian Signs, American Streets* — Italian/American literary ethnicity as only one of many equally weighted features of the literature. In this chapter, Bona examines the work of Rachel Guido de Vries, Carole Maso, and Agnes Rossi, among others. With this *first-ever* major work on Italian/American women's literature, Bona has made a very valuable contribution to American literary studies.

Italian/American literary criticism has been a history of breaking silences and engaging in the dialogues necessary to ensure that the silences do not resurface. From humble and sporadic beginnings, Italian/American literary criticism (and Italian/American studies in general) has evolved into a serious academic endeavor bolstered by solid organizations, increased scholarly attention, and general interest. In 1997, a

new collection of essays, creative writings, and memoirs entitled *Beyond* The Godfather: *Italian American Writers on the
Real Italian American Experience* was published. It features
both new scholars and "seasoned veterans" of Italian/Ameri-
can studies, such as Richard Gambino, Fred L. Gardaphè, Edvige Giunta, Frank Lentricchia, Gay Talese, and Anthony J.
Tamburri.[52] *Beyond the Godfather* was followed shortly
thereafter by *Beyond the Margin: Readings in Italian Americana* (1998), a collection of critical essays that serves as a
sequel to *From the Margin.* In the introduction, Paolo A.
Giordano and Anthony J. Tamburri write that the purpose of
the new anthology is to assess critically "where Italian/
American literary and cultural studies are today."[53] Giordano
and Tamburri are encouraged by the increased popularity of
Italian/American literature and literary criticism and look
forward to the work of those "numerous young, talented sec-
ond- and third-generation Italian Americans [who] are writing and publishing poems, short stories, and novels on the
Italian/American experience, thus continuing the tradition of
Pietro di Donato, Mari Tomasi, John Fante, and Mario Puzo."[54]
In "Rethinking Italian/American Studies: From the Hyphen to
the Slash and Beyond," Tamburri reiterates and expands
upon his modification of Gardaphè's theory of Italian/
American literature, and attempts a "prediction" of the future of Italian/American literary criticism. He insists that in
order for Italian/American literary criticism to evolve, the
critic must be open to "new and more recent methodologies
and reading strategies [that] can prove helpful in broadening
our various perceptions of Italian/American art forms in

---

[52]A. Kenneth Ciongioli and Jay Parini, eds., *Beyond* The Godfather: *Italian
American Writers on the Real Italian American Experience* (Hanover, NH:
University Presses of New England, 1997).

[53]Paolo A. Giordano and Anthony J. Tamburri, "Introduction," in *Beyond the
Margin: Readings in Italian Americana* (Cranbury, NJ: Farleigh Dickinson
University Press, 1998) 13.

[54]Ibid., 12.

general."[55] I would concur, for Italian/American literary criticism is about more than simply breaking silences, as Viscusi himself had already underscored in his seminal essay: it is about keeping them broken and taking our critical voices to places we had never before considered.

## Works Cited

Aaron, Daniel. "The Hyphenate Writer and American Letters." *Smith Alumnae Quarterly* (July 1964): 213-17.

Adamic, Louis. "Muscular Novel of Immigrant Life." *The Saturday Review* 26 August 1939: 5.

Alba, Richard. *Italian-Americans: Into the Twilight of Ethnicity.* Englewood, NJ: Prentice-Hall, 1985.

Ardizzone, Tony. *Taking it Home: Stories from the Neighborhood.* Urbana, IL: U of Illinois P, 1996.

Baker, Houston, Jr. *Blues, Ideology, and Afro-American Literature: A Vernacular Theory.* Chicago: U of Chicago P, 1984.

Barolini, Helen. Preface. *The Dream Book: An Anthology of Writings by Italian American Women,* ed. Helen Barolini, ix-xiv. New York: Schocken Books, 1985.

_____. Introduction. *The Dream Book: An Anthology of Writings by Italian American Women,* ed. Helen Barolini, 3-56. New York: Schocken Books, 1985.

_____, ed. *The Dream Book: An Anthology of Writings by Italian American Women.* New York: Schocken Books, 1985.

_____. *Umbertina.* New York: Seaview Press, 1979; reprint, The Feminist Press, 1999.

Bona, Mary Jo. *Claiming a Tradition: Italian American Women Writers.* Carbondale, IL: Southern Illinois UP, 1999.

[55]Tamburri, "Rethinking Italian/American Studies: From the Hyphen to the Slash and Beyond," in *Beyond the Margin,* 271. For an expansion upon this very theme of finding new reading strategies for ethnic/American literature, see the previously cited Tamburri, *A Semiotic of Ethnicity.*

_____. "Gorgeous Identities: Gay and Lesbian Italian/American Writers." *Fuori: Essays by Italian/American Lesbians and Gays*, ed. Anthony J. Tamburri, 1-12. West Lafayette, IN: Bordighera, 1996.

_____. "Introduction." *The Voices We Carry*, ed. Mary Jo Bona, 11-29. Montreal: Guernica, 1994.

_____. "Broken Images, Broken Lives: Carmolina's Journey in Tina De Rosa's *Paper Fish*." *MELUS* 14:3-4 (1987): 87-106.

Bona, Mary Jo, ed. *The Voices We Carry*. Montreal: Guernica, 1994.

Cavaioli, Frank J. "The American Italian Historical Association: Twenty Years Later, 1966-1986." *Italian Americans: The Search for a Usable Past*, eds. Richard N. Juliani and Philip V. Cannistraro, 282-93. Staten Island, NY: AIHA, 1989.

Ciongoli, A. Kenneth and Jay Parini, eds. *Beyond The Godfather: Italian American Writers on the Real Italian American Experience*. Hanover, NH: UP of New England, 1997.

D'Acierno, Pellegrino, ed. *The Italian American Heritage. A Companion to Literature and Arts*. New York: Garland, 1999.

DeLillo, Don. *Americana*. New York: Penguin Books, 1989 (1971).

De Rosa, Tina. *Paper Fish*. Chicago: Wine press, 1980; reprint The Feminist Press, 1996.

De Vries, Rachel Guido. *How to Sing to a Dago*. Toronto: Guernica, 1996.

_____. *Tender Warriors*. Ithaca, NY: Firebrand Books, 1986.

Di Donato, Pietro. *Christ in Concrete*. Indianapolis: Bobbs-Merrill, 1939.

Gallo, Patrick. *Ethnic Alienation: The Italian-Americans*. Cranbury, NJ: Farleigh Dickinson UP, 1974.

Gambino, Richard. *Blood of My Blood: The Dilemma of the Italian-Americans*. New York: Doubleday, 1974; reprint, Toronto: Guernica, 1996.

Gans, Herbert J. *The Urban Villagers*. New York: The Free Press, 1962.

Gardaphè, Fred L. "From Oral Tradition to Written Word: Toward an Ethnographically Based Literary Criticism." *From the Margin:*

*Writing in Italian Americana*, eds. Anthony J. Tamburri, Paolo A. Giordano, and Fred L. Gardaphè, 294–306. West Lafayette, IN: Purdue UP, 1991.

_____. *Italian Signs, American Streets: The Evolution of Italian American Narrative*. Durham, NC: Duke UP, 1996.

_____. *The Italian-American Writer*. Spencertown, NY: Forkroads, 1995.

Gates, Henry Louis, Jr. *The Signifying Monkey: A Theory of African-American Literary Criticism*. New York: Oxford UP, 1988.

Gillan, Maria Mazziotti. *Where I Come From*. Toronto: Guernica, 1995.

Giunta, Edvige. "Afterword." *Paper Fish*, Tina De Rosa, 123–57. New York: Feminist Press, 1996.

_____. "Crossing Critical Borders in Italian/American Women's Studies." *The Italian American Review* 5.2 (1996): 79-94.

Giordano, Paolo A., and Anthony J. Tamburri, eds. *Beyond the Margin: Readings in Italian Americana*. Cranbury, NJ: Farleigh Dickinson UP, 1998.

Giordano, Paolo A., and Anthony J. Tamburri. "Introduction." *Beyond the Margin: Readings in Italian Americana*, eds. Paolo A. Giordano and Anthony J. Tamburri, 9–17. Cranbury, NJ: Farleigh Dickinson UP, 1998.

Green, Rose Basile. *The Italian-American Novel: A Document of the Interaction of Two Cultures*. Cranbury, NJ: Farleigh Dickinson UP, 1974.

Iorizzo, Luciano, and Salvatore Mondello. *The Italian Americans*. New York: Twayne, 1971.

Juliani, Richard N., and Philip V. Cannistraro, eds. *Italian Americans: The Search for a Usable Past*. Staten Island, NY: AIHA, 1989.

LaGumina, Salvatore, Frank J. Cavaioli, Salvatore Primeggia, and Joseph A. Varacalli, eds. *The Italian American Experience: An Encyclopedia*. New York: Garland, 2000.

La Sorte, Michael. *La Merica: Images of Italian Greenhorn Experience*. Philadelphia: Temple UP, 1985.

Lopreato, Joseph. *Italian Americans*. New York: Random House, 1970.

Loriggio, Francesco, ed. *Social Pluralism and Literary History: The Literature of Italian Emigration*. Toronto: Guernica, 1996.

Mangione, Jerre. "Little Italy." *New Republic* 30 August 1939: 111-12.

_____. *Mount Allegro: A Memoir of Italian American Life*. New York: Harper & Row, 1989.

_____. Rev. of *The Grand Gennaro*, by Garibaldi M. LaPolla. *New Republic* 23 October 1935.

Mangione, Jerre, and Ben Morreale. *La Storia: Five Centuries of the Italian American Experience*. New York: HarperCollins, 1992.

Mannino, Mary Ann. *Revisoinary Identities: Strategies of Empowerment in the Writing of Italian/American Women*. New York: Peter Lang, 2000.

Marsh, Fred T. "A Fine and Unusual First Novel." *The New York Times* 20 August 1939: 6.

Mulas, Franco. "The Ethnic Language of Pietro Di Donato's *Christ in Concrete*." *From the Margin: Writings in Italian Americana*, eds. Anthony J. Tamburri, Paolo A. Giordano, and Fred L. Gardaphè, 307-15. West Lafayette, IN: Purdue UP, 1991.

Panunzio, Constantine. *The Soul of an Immigrant*. New York: The MacMillan, 1921.

Peragallo, Olga. *Italian-American Authors and Their Contributions to American Literature*. New York: Vanni, 1949.

Pipino, Mary Francis. *"I have found my voice": The Italian-American Woman Writer*. New York: Peter Lang, 2000.

Prezzolini, Giuseppe. "Preface." *Italian-American Authors and Their Contributions to American Literature*, ix-xii. New York: Vanni, 1949.

Rimanelli, Giose. *Benedetta in Guysterland: A Liquid Novel*. Montreal: Guernica, 1993.

Romano, Rose. "Coming Out Olive in the Lesbian Community: *Big Sister Is Watching You*." *Social Pluralism and Literary History:*

*The Literature of Italian Emigration,* ed. Francesco Loriggio, 161–75. Toronto: Guernica, 1996.

Rolle, Andrew. *The American Italians: Their History and Culture.* Belmont, CA: Wadsworth, 1972.

Tamburri, Anthony Julian, ed. *Fuori: Essays by Italian/American Lesbians and Gays.* West Lafayette, IN: Bordighera, 1996.

_____, Paolo A. Giordano, and Fred Gardaphè, eds. *From the Margin: Writings in Italian Americana.* West Lafayette, IN: Purdue UP, 1991/2000.

_____. "In (Re)cognition of the Italian/American Writer: Definitions and Categories." *Differentia* 6/7 (1994): 9–32.

_____. "Rethinking Italian/American Studies: From the Hyphen to the Slash and Beyond." *Beyond the Margin: Readings in Italian Americana,* eds. Paolo Giordano and Anthony Julian Tamburri, 243–83. Cranbury, NJ: Farleigh Dickinson UP, 1998.

_____. *A Semiotic of Ethnicity: In (Re)cognition of the Italian/American Writer.* Albany, NY: SUNY P, 1998.

_____. *To Hyphenate or Not to Hyphenate: The Italian/American Writer: An Other American.* Montreal: Guernica, 1991.

Tomasi, Mari. *Like Lesser Gods.* Milwaukee: Bruce, 1949; reprint, Shelburne, VT: The New England Press, 1988.

Viscusi, Robert. "Breaking the Silence: Strategic Imperatives for Italian American Culture." *VIA* 1.1 (1990): 1–13.

_____. "*De Vulgari Eloquentia:* An Approach to the Language of Italian American Culture." *Yale Italian Studies* 1.3 (1981): 21–38.

_____. "A Literature Considering Itself: The Allegory of Italian America." *From the Margin: Writings in Italian Americana,* eds. Anthony J. Tamburri, Paolo A. Giordano, and Fred Gardaphè, 265–81. West Lafayette, IN: Purdue UP, 1991.

_____. "Narrative and Nothing: The Enterprise of Italian American Writing." *Differentia* 6/7 (1994): 77–99.

*Founded in 1966, the American Italian Historical Association is an interdisciplinary group of scholars and lay people who share an interest in investigating relationships among Italian Americans, Italy, and the Americas. Its members encourage the collection, preservation, study, and popularization of materials that illuminate the Italian-American experience. The Association promotes research through regional and national activities, including the annual conference and publication of its proceedings.*

To order
AIHA volumes of selected essays
or for more information, write to:

DOMINIC CANDELORO, Executive Director
AIHA
169 Country Club Road
Chicago Heights, IL  60411
D-Candeloro@govst.edu
http://www.mobilito.com/aiha

*This book was produced by Bordighera Press and
set in Microsoft Word and QuarkXpress
by Deborah Starewich of Lafayette IN.
It was printed by Printing Services
of Purdue University,
West Lafayette
IN, U.S.A.*